PRAISE FO

STEEL SUN

An amazing adventure - a real page turner

Josephine Quintero, travel writer, Lonely Planet

No money, no back up, but lots of
determination - I take my hat (or helmet) off to
him

Pete Townsend

A wonderful achievement and a bloody good
read.

John Knight, motor cycle writer

Humour, trauma, excitement - this adventure
has it all.

Sentinella Magazine

Java - Bali - Java - Sumatra - Malaysia - Thailand

STEEL SUNSHINE

A ride on a Harley to Bangkok from Bali
in 1994

Michael Lindsay Orr

Good Morning...
It´s just another shitty day in Paradise

Dave Jackman
Sunday 12 June 1994

After a lifetime of creating, inventing, and wandering,
Michael Lindsay Orr has finally put pen to paper. A
retired Chartered Designer, he now resides in rural
Andalucía, where he shares a sun-soaked life with his
Spanish wife and two bossy Yorkshire terriers.

His career has been an eclectic mix of engineering,
design, and globe-trotting—a man equally at home
designing the million-selling HAWS watering can way
back in 1987, inventing The Incredible Lightweight Artic
for Volkswagen, creating the first bilingual audio visual
board game in Irish gaelic and English and somehow
bagging a Gold Disc for Rick Astley's album "FREE." One
can only assume he's never going to give up... making
cool things.

Educated in the glorious pre-university era of
polytechnics, he studied engineering, plastics technology,
and design, back when such things were hands-on
and wonderfully unpredictable. Now, in a well-earned
retirement, he spends his time writing about adventures,
reliving past journeys, and possibly designing something
new just for the fun of it.

Contents

MONDAY 20 JUNE

TUESDAY 21 JUNE   144

WEDNESDAY 22 JUNE   16

THURSDAY 23 JUNE

FRIDAY 24 JUNE

SATURDAY 25 JUNE

SUNDAY 26 JUNE

The Cavalry Charge; The Crown Prince is Disappointed; Bad News from London; Politics and Permits; A Tense Night Ahead

MONDAY 27 JUNE

Jo-Jo's Castle; Breakfast and Business; A Surprising First Impression; The Harley Collection; Meeting The Crown Prince; Mega-Decibels; I Am On The Run Now

TUESDAY 28 JUNE

No Papers to enter Thailand; The Border

WEDNESDAY 29 JUNE

Riders In The Storm; Krabi; Holiday Inn

THURSDAY 30 JUNE

Big Bike; My First Bungee Jump; Dead bike again

FRIDAY 1 JULY

Fat Boy in Paradise Bar

SATURDAY 2 JULY

Burma on the left

SUNDAY 3 JULY

E D Says that "It is Special..."; Bangkok

MONDAY 4 JULY

Mr. T and Five Tons of Solid Gold; River Trip; The Long-Tailed Boat

TUESDAY 5 JULY

Traffic Hell; Sticky Rice in Bamboo; Royal Garden Resort; Search for the Harley Bar; Meeting Frank; Ride my Harley up the Escalator; Show-Stopping Dinner; Mission Caligula; Cruising

WEDNESDAY 6 JULY

A Very Dangerous Day; The Temple Challange; The Crash; Six Sexy Girls, please

THURSDAY 7 JULY

Caligula Go-Go Girls; Waiting for the Girls; In Jeep Shit; The Promontory; The Shootj; Escape from the Beach; Philippe's Party; Where's Sean?; Fracas; Top Gun Ron; I eat a Big Brown Bug.

SYNOPSIS

Steel Sunshine is a raw, adrenaline-fuelled memoir that chronicles one man's audacious journey through Southeast Asia in 1994—long before the days of YouTube, GoPros, and budget travel. Armed with nothing but grit and a Harley-Davidson Fat Boy, he rides over 5,000 kilometres through lands where carrying a camera meant navigating a quagmire of bureaucracy, corruption, suspicion, and real danger.

From the lush jungles of Sumatra to the neon-lit chaos of Bangkok, he faces mechanical breakdowns, corrupt officials, and unforgiving elements. Yet amid the madness, he discovers unexpected camaraderie in the global brotherhood of motorcycle riders—kindred spirits whose generosity and sense of adventure light the way through even the darkest moments.

This isn't just a story about the ride. It's about the untamed beauty of diverse cultures; the wild highs of rock 'n' roll parties, the sting of betrayal, and the soul-deep revelations that come from diving headfirst into the unknown.

For anyone who's ever dreamed of adventure in its rawest, most unfiltered form, Steel Sunshine will ignite your wanderlust and prove why the road less travelled is always the most rewarding.

Steel Sunshine is the story of one man's dream—to ride his Harley-Davidson Fat Boy on an epic journey from Bali to Bangkok.

After following a colourful and varied career path, Mike Orr found himself at a crossroads. One day, he arrived at his office to discover that his business partner had disappeared, taking all the company assets with him. Determined not to give up, Mike enlisted the help and support of his staff, friends, clients, and suppliers. After more than a year of relentless struggle, he managed to restore the business to stability. But the stress had taken its toll. Mike knew he needed an escape.

That escape took the form of a bold and unprecedented adventure: a 5,000-kilometer motorcycle journey through Indonesia, Malaysia, and Thailand, all captured on film. Raising (most of) the funds to finance his own film crew, Mike's epic trip became an exciting and vibrant rock-and-roll documentary—ahead of its time, years before motorcycle journeys were popularized by figures like Ewan McGregor and Billy Connolly.

This was long before the convenience of social media, GoPros, or smart phones made documenting such adventures easy. Every mile and moment had to be captured the hard way, with bulky, professional-grade equipment and an unknown crew—adding another layer of challenge to an already ambitious journey.

As a pioneer in this genre, Mike encountered real dangers and unexpected challenges along the way. Travelling through regions marked by political unrest and cultural complexities, he had no blueprint to follow and no safety net.

This book chronicles the making of the film and the incredible journey behind it—a story of resilience, adventure, and the pursuit of freedom on two wheels.

All together for the first time - the Bangkok Immortals, Farang Angels and Siam Knights...and me!

THE TRAVEL CREW

Michael	*Rider, Writer and Producer*
Steve	*Location Director / initial co-organiser*
Paul	*Camera*
Chris	*Assistant Camera / photographer*
Sean	*Sound*

 SATURDAY 4 JUNE

WE LEAVE FROM GATWICK

There we were—five pale, pink, and typically British individuals surrounded by a mountain of carrier bags stuffed with the gear too delicate or precious to entrust to baggage handlers. The concrete-and-Formica expanse of Gatwick's South Terminal hardly felt like the launch pad for the adventure of a lifetime, but here we were, waiting for the final call to board flight GA 977 to Jakarta, Indonesia.

I wanted to do something no one else had done—ride a Harley-Davidson across the equator. It was a feat possible in only a handful of places, as most of the equator lies across vast stretches of sea or tiny, inaccessible islands. Sumatra became the obvious choice, and with that, the route was set. But as I sat sipping lukewarm Ashbourne water, feigning calm for the sake of my crew, my mind churned with uncertainties.

Three of my four companions I'd only just met, and I couldn't help but wonder how they'd fare under the inevitable pressures of the journey. Would they rise to the challenge or crumble when things got tough? Every mile of our 5,000-kilometer trek through Indonesia, Malaysia, and Thailand would test not just our skills, but our patience, endurance, and trust in one another.

Steve, our team leader, exuded a scruffy confidence that belied his sharp eye for detail as a seasoned pop video producer. Sean, with his rugby-player build and clean-cut charm, seemed easygoing enough, but could he handle the relentless grind of sound recording in unpredictable conditions? Paul, our quiet Italian cameraman, had a steady presence, but I wondered how he'd cope when silence was no longer an option. And then there was Chris, our gofer, with his khaki-clad optimism that felt both reassuring and naive.

The sights and smells of the departure lounge—a faint scent of industrial cleaning products mixed with greasy fast food—were a far cry from the tropical humidity that would soon engulf us. I imagined the thick, sticky air of Jakarta, laced with diesel fumes and the tang of street food sizzling over open flames. The unknown loomed large. What would I find when we landed? How would the crew handle the heat, the chaos, and the inevitable challenges?

THE COSTS AND THE CHALLENGES

The past month had been a whirlwind of frustration, with bureaucratic roadblocks threatening to derail everything. Indonesia's government was notoriously unsympathetic to its own filmmakers, let alone foreign crews lugging in piles of expensive camera equipment. Steve had spent months battling embassy staff, whose smiles masked their inability—or unwillingness—to give clear instructions. Every form, every signature, every stamp came at a cost—not just financial, but emotional.

The costs were spiralling. The budget, always precarious, stretched thinner by the day. Then there was the mental toll of uncertainty. What if the equipment was seized at customs? What if the crew we'd hired in Jakarta turned out to be unreliable? What if the roads were impassable or political unrest blocked our path?

I had no blueprint, no guide to follow. This wasn't a well-trodden adventure popularized by social media influencers or glossy travel documentaries. This was uncharted territory, raw and unpredictable. And yet, that was exactly the appeal. The thought of blazing a trail, of doing something no one else had dared to attempt, was irresistible.

Still, doubt gnawed at me. Could I trust the fixers we'd hired? E.D., the Thai fixer with a volcanic temper, had come highly recommended but at an exorbitant cost. Ron Green, the Australian contact in Jakarta, promised smooth sailing through customs, interpreters, and logistical support. I wanted to believe him, but the stakes were too high to place blind faith in strangers.

As I sat in that departure lounge, surrounded by my team and a mountain of gear, the weight of what lay ahead pressed down on me. The smells of Jakarta, the sights of Sumatra, and the endless unknowns waited on the other side of the world. All I could do was take a deep breath and hope that the adventure would be worth the cost.

THE VISA DEBACLE

Despite the weight of unease pressing heavily on my chest, the flights were finally booked and paid for. Come hell or high water, we were leaving Saturday, 4th June. But there was one glaring problem: it was Thursday, and we still didn't have our visas.

Jakarta, where Ron lived, was six hours ahead of British time. That time difference only added to the tension, forcing us to stay awake until the early hours of the morning to make frantic phone calls. Not that sleep was an option anyway. My mind buzzed with scenarios of what could go wrong, the domino effect of delays threatening to derail everything.

At 3:30 p.m. on Friday, just half an hour before the Embassy slammed its doors for the weekend, we got word from the courier: the visas were ready. Relief hit like a tidal wave. Around 8 p.m., the precious documents finally arrived in a humble jiffy bag, their very presence an answer to our prayers. Steve and I collapsed onto the sofa, clutching the bag as if it were a golden ticket to salvation. There were kisses, hugs, and more than a few muttered expletives of gratitude.

A bottle of whisky—saved for either celebration or commiseration—was cracked open. We poured stiff shots and toasted our miraculous escape from catastrophe. But as the high of relief settled, a creeping sense of doubt gnawed at me. Opening the passports, I carefully examined the details.

And then I saw it.

The wrong type of visa! Instead of business, they were for pleasure—and not for three weeks, but two. My stomach dropped. All that effort, the endless calls, the meticulous forms... and they still got it wrong. To make matters worse, we could've gotten these pleasure visas on arrival without even visiting the embassy.

The rest of the whisky didn't last long. Steve and I sat in stunned silence, the enormity of the situation sinking in. We were now more restricted than the average tourist. Had this been a deliberate stitch-up? I didn't know, but I did know one thing: Ron better be ready to play the superhero because we'd been dropped into a vat of kryptonite, and it was going to take some serious powers to climb out.

MONEY AND THE DREAM

This trip wasn't just about crossing geographical borders; it was about chasing a dream - a seemingly impossible one - To ride a Harley from Bali to Bangkok.

It had started as a seed of an idea on a dreary December day, the kind where the drizzle never stops and the gray sky feels like it's pressing down on your soul. I'd been leafing through my well-worn atlas, the massive tome that always had a place of honour on my coffee table. Its pages were a portal to far-off lands, and that day, I found myself lingering over Southeast Asia.

A friend had just returned from Bali, brimming with tales of paradise. "You'd love it there," he said, showing me photo after photo of sun-drenched beaches and lush, green landscapes. His words struck a chord. "Bali...on a Harley".

But why stop there? My mind raced ahead, mapping out a route that would take me through Java, Sumatra, Malaysia, and Thailand—a journey through some of the most exotic and untouched landscapes on Earth. I could see it: the jungles, the mountains, the open roads. And the Harley—my Fat Boy—would be the ultimate companion, its rumbling engine a soundtrack to the adventure.

The idea consumed me. I wanted not just to ride but to document it, to turn it into a story worth sharing. A book, a film, a calendar... the possibilities seemed endless. "Fat Boy in Paradise" would be more than a title; it would be a brand, a phenomenon.

MAKING IT HAPPEN

Turning the dream into reality, however, was a different beast. There were permits to obtain, routes to plan, and, above all, money to find. Lots of it!

For months, I threw myself into research. I combed through maps, ferry schedules, and political reports to piece together a feasible route. Could we travel safely through these regions? Would we even be allowed? Every question seemed to lead to another, and the answers were rarely straightforward.

Meanwhile, Tony, my friend and rock-and-roll impresario, was tapping into his vast network to assemble a team. His introduction to Steve Graham, a talented pop promo director, was a game-changer. With a portfolio boasting names like Paul McCartney and Eurythmics, Steve brought credibility to the project. His enthusiasm mirrored my own, and soon we were working side by side: Steve focusing on the filmmaking logistics while I tackled the biking elements.

The Harley-Davidson community proved invaluable. Through their network, I made connections in Indonesia, Malaysia, and Thailand—fellow riders who could help us navigate unfamiliar terrain. Harley-Davidson UK even featured our project in their magazine, reaching thousands of enthusiasts across Europe.

Still, the financial hurdles loomed large. Traditional funding avenues—TV networks, production companies—were hesitant to commit. So, I turned to the people who shared my passion: individual Harley owners. I sold shares in the project, offering supporters the chance to be credited in the film and part of something truly unique.

Sadly, I only have an old newspaper photo with Bill Davidson

THE LAUNCH

By March, the dream was taking shape. At the Harley festival in Southport, I unveiled the project. My bike stood as a centrepiece, surrounded by colourful panels explaining our plans. Enthusiasts flocked to learn more, their excitement mirroring my own. Even Bill Davidson, the great-grandson of Harley's founder, offered to help (never did though!).

It was happening. The dream was no longer just mine; it belonged to everyone who believed in the power of adventure.

But as the departure date loomed, so did the challenges. The visa debacle was only the beginning. The road ahead promised obstacles, both seen and unforeseen. Yet, the thought of giving up never crossed my mind.

This was the journey of a lifetime, and I was ready to ride.

THE FINAL PUSH

Slowly but surely, the funds began to trickle in. It wasn't a deluge, but enough to keep the dream alive. Armed with the project report I had painstakingly crafted, I managed to secure some incredible support. The Holiday Inn hotel chain generously agreed to provide free accommodation for the crew in Bali, Phuket, Kuala Lumpur, and Bangkok. Jim Beam Whiskey came through with a few thousand pounds and promised significant marketing support if I and the bike could be part of their promotional campaigns. Avon Tyres chipped in with spare parts, while people from all over Southeast Asia and beyond offered logistical assistance.

The major motorcycling magazines threw their weight behind us, pledging to publicize our journey. Even The Observer ran a feature on me, bringing much-needed exposure. Each piece of the puzzle felt like a small victory, but the pressure was relentless.

I had given myself an impossible timeline: everything had to be in place by the 1st of June. Most projects of this scale take two years to organize. I had six months. It wasn't just ambition driving the deadline; it was necessity.

A major Harley festival was scheduled in Bali for the 11th and 12th of June, bringing together 300 bikes in one spectacular gathering. It felt like fate, a sign that I couldn't ignore. This was the perfect launch pad for the film—an opportunity I could never hope to recreate. We had to be there.

Then there was the weather. Sumatra's rainforests are breathtakingly beautiful but notoriously unforgiving. The roads, primitive in many areas, become treacherous - if not entirely impassable - during the rainy season. June offered the driest conditions of the year, our best and only chance for a successful crossing.

So, it was June or never.

A WING AND A PRAYER

As the departure date loomed, the pressure became

unbearable. The budget was falling short—disastrously short. I had approached every potential sponsor, every possible source of funding. It wasn't enough.

Panic set in. We had come too far to turn back, with so much already committed. The money spent couldn't be unspent, and the promises made couldn't be broken. The only option left was to take a leap of faith, to go on a flier and hope for the best.

I drained every last resource: emptied savings, maxed out credit cards, applied for more credit cards, borrowed from friends, scrimped and saved in every way imaginable. It was all or nothing.

And so, on that fateful day in early June, we found ourselves standing at Gatwick Airport. Everything was on the line— our finances, our reputations, our dreams. We were holding on to sheer determination and an unshakable belief that this journey had to be a success.

As we waited to board, I couldn't shake the weight of it all. This wasn't just an adventure anymore. It was a gamble—a high-stakes, no-safety-net plunge into the unknown. But I knew one thing for sure: the dream was worth it.

With a deep breath and a racing heart, we stepped forward. The journey of a lifetime was about to begin.

SUNDAY 5 JUNE

ARRIVING IN JAKARTA WITH THE WRONG VISA

The flight was interminable—a 22-hour, butt-numbing odyssey of boredom punctuated by grey food on grey trays, all served with a side of stopovers in Zurich, Abu Dhabi, and Singapore. Think of it as a test flight for purgatory. My seat was designed to accommodate precisely no human spine, and the entertainment system seemed to be one long, passive-aggressive suggestion that I should've flown first class.

To be fair, even if they'd handed out champagne and foot rubs, I wouldn't have enjoyed it. My brain was too busy bubbling with stress. Would we even be allowed into Indonesia with our dodgy visas? Would customs hold the motorcycle hostage? What if Ron—the "fixer" I'd never met—turned out to be less fixer and more... fictional? His assurances, relayed via Steve in midnight phone calls, had all the credibility of a late-night infomercial. "Trust me, mate. Everything's sorted!" Yeah, right.

As we shuffled through immigration, I spotted someone waving at us from beyond passport control. "That must be Ron," I thought. He'd managed to talk his way past customs officers, which was either a very good sign or the opening act of a disaster.

Ron turned out to be Australian, with the vibe of a scruffy, slightly sunburned Humphrey Bogart. Picture The African Queen, but swap the gin for Bintang. In his fifties, with a beard that suggested he hadn't met a razor he liked, Ron claimed to have lived in Jakarta for five years, spending that time cultivating relationships with all the right (and possibly wrong) people. Who he really was or how he paid his bills? That remained a mystery. He carried himself with the confidence of someone who could smuggle a grand piano through customs if he wanted to.

We got through immigration with two-week tourist visas. Not great, but better than being detained. Still, two weeks wasn't enough time to ride the archipelago, meet all the Harley contacts, and film the journey. That would be another problem for Ron to sort.

"How are we doing?" I asked, my stomach somewhere near my knees.

"OK, mate," Ron said with a casual shrug. "I've arranged for the bike to go to the 'Rush-In' shed. We bung 'em seven hundred bucks, and we're good to go."

The camera equipment breezed through customs without a hitch, which felt suspiciously like winning a raffle you didn't know you entered. Meanwhile, our five luggage-laden trolleys sat outside an office where Ron was "negotiating." Five minutes later, he strolled out, grinning. No bag checks, no questions, not even a raised eyebrow. Behind us, though, a BBC film crew wasn't so lucky. Their corduroy-clad team looked professional, but they didn't have Ron. Customs officers took everything short of dental impressions. For all I know, they're still filling out forms.

Once past the chaos, we met Dave Jackman, my Harley contact for the Jakarta-to-Bali leg. A Kiwi oil man with a cowboy's swagger, Dave had spent fourteen years in Jakarta, though you'd swear he hailed from a spaghetti Western. He had neat, mousy hair styled like a fifties Tony Curtis, a bushy moustache, and a wardrobe straight out of the Harley-Davidson catalogue: black T-shirt, blue jeans, and cowboy boots. Even his slightly bow-legged walk screamed "trail boss."

Dave spoke with a drawl more Dallas than Auckland and had a penchant for pessimism that could make Eeyore look upbeat. But he was friendly, accommodating, and ready to get us rolling. Just the kind of guy we needed to kick-start this madcap adventure.

TRAUMA AT THE CUSTOMS

There were nine of us now—five in our team, plus Ron, his pretty assistant Eka, Dave, and Ron's local driver. We crammed ourselves into two tiny white knockoff minibuses that could barely contain our hopes, fears, and luggage, and headed to the fabled 'Rush-In' shed. After Ron's Houdini-level customs magic with the camera equipment earlier, we fully expected to find the bike waiting for us, maybe even with a bow on it.

The shed turned out to be a cavernous, corrugated steel monstrosity the size of a football pitch. It was so empty you could practically hear the echo of a cockroach sneezing. To the left of the entrance was a shoebox-sized office where a few men were smoking, chatting, and generally avoiding anything resembling work. By the wide open main doors, three more men in scruffy customs uniforms lounged on a pile of wooden pallets. Their job seemed to involve perfecting the art of looking busy while doing nothing.

Ron, ever the man of action, sauntered off to "handle things." The rest of us stood around, trying to look like we belonged, which was difficult given the fact that none of us really had a clue what was happening. Half an hour later, Ron emerged, looking less like a fixer and more like a man who'd been handed a parking ticket for a car he didn't own. He was trailed by a group of officials armed with clipboards, stern faces, and an excessive amount of head-shaking.

One of the officials announced that the bike, by some cosmic accident—or more likely by design—had been sent to the airport cargo shed instead of the Rush-In shed. And because it was in the wrong place, it couldn't be released. A rookie mistake, apparently.

"Bollocks!" Ron declared, with all the diplomacy of a pub bouncer ejecting someone for spilling a pint. He was convinced this was nothing more than a bureaucratic shakedown—a theatrical performance designed to loosen our wallets.

Off he went again, this time disappearing into a gated, bonded zone that I can only describe as looking like the customs version of Mordor. Thirty minutes later, he reappeared, no bike in tow, but with even more shaking heads in his wake. This was followed by Eka heading off with two customs men, presumably to charm someone with a bigger clipboard at the import shed.

By now, we were all growing increasingly anxious. What had begun as a mildly annoying mix-up was evolving into a Kafkaesque nightmare. Another half an hour passed. No bike, no solution, but plenty of shaking heads—seriously, these guys could've powered a wind farm.

It was now 10:30 a.m., and things weren't looking good: The latest demand? - A letter from the President of the Harley-Davidson Club of Indonesia, inviting us to the Bali rally. Oh, and not just any letter. It also needed to be endorsed by I.M.I. (Ikatan Motor Indonesia), the all-powerful governing body of Indonesian motoring activities. According to Ron, once we had the I.M.I. director's signature, we'd be free to ride the bike anywhere in Indonesia. In theory, it sounded simple. In practice, it felt like being asked to retrieve the One Ring from Mount Doom, except with more paperwork.

Defeated, we did what any self-respecting group of bikers would do in a crisis: we shrugged, grumbled, and trudged off to the nearest bar to drown our sorrows. The beers were cold, the disappointment warm, and the bike? That remained firmly in the clutches of Indonesian bureaucracy.

THE TEXAS BAR

Our first night in Jakarta found us in a peculiar yet oddly comforting spot: the Texas Bar. This wasn't just any bar; it was a painstaking replica of a small-town watering hole straight out of the Lone Star State. Picture dusty cowboy boots, vintage license plates, and enough American flags to outfit a Fourth of July parade. It was a magnet for Harley enthusiasts and English-speaking expats who, by the looks of it, had all been marinated in equal parts nostalgia and beer for decades.

Enter Bob. A tall, fifty-seven-year-old British expat with the sort of slightly frayed elegance that made him look like he belonged more at a village cricket match than a rowdy bar in Jakarta. Bob was a character straight out of a Graham Greene novel. He claimed to have arrived in Java in 1968 to manage a chocolate factory, but somewhere along the line, chocolate gave way to "agriculture." What kind of agriculture? Well, that remained one of life's great mysteries.

"Just agriculture, you know," Bob would say with a vague wave of his hand. "All over Indonesia..."

For all his evasiveness, Bob was a treasure trove of political insight, educating me over beers and chips about the turbulent history of Indonesia. Despite his refined demeanour, years of dedication to the local beer scene had left him with an impressively sizable fold over his belt—a sort of living testament to the expat lifestyle.

Around ten, the conversation with Bob meandered off (as did Bob himself, possibly to do something agricultural), and I found myself chatting with Phil. Phil was an oil company technical advisor, a tall, athletic-looking guy who somehow straddled the line between accountant and action hero. He was polite, well-groomed, and just wild enough to make you think he'd pull an all-nighter without breaking a sweat.

As luck would have it, Phil hailed from Rochdale, a town I knew well, having lived there for a spell in the early '80s. It was a surprising commonality that quickly bridged the gap between two strangers. Phil had also organized the staff house where we were supposed to stay, and generously offered me a lift whenever I was ready to crash.

Spoiler alert: that didn't happen anytime soon. By the time I was a few cans deep into Bintang—the local beer that bore an uncanny resemblance to Becks, my drink of choice back then—our conversation had covered everything from geopolitics to, probably, why toasters always burn the last slice of bread. Not that I could recall any of it. Late-night beer-fuelled conversations have a knack for dissolving into the ether by morning.

Just as Phil and I were gearing up for a Nobel Peace Prize-worthy solution to the world's problems, Steve stumbled over to join us. Equally inebriated and brimming with the kind of camaraderie that only shared drunkenness can bring, he agreed it was time to head for the staff house—our supposed base in Jakarta, about twenty minutes away.

But as the saying goes, "Plans are optional; beer is mandatory."

Phil, with the casual air of a man who knew his priorities, suggested a detour. "My wife and kid are back in the UK," he said, his voice tinged with opportunity. "I've got a big empty house. Why not have drinks there instead?"

And just like that, the staff house was forgotten, and the adventure was to be continued elsewhere!

 # MONDAY 6 JUNE

BACK TO RON'S

After our marathon drinking session the night before, I woke up around eleven to a house so silent it could've been hosting a yoga retreat for mimes. Staggering out of bed, still feeling like I'd been hit by a small truck, I began to explore.

Phil's house was one of those spacious, corporate-rented places designed for function over personality. Everything was magnolia, as if the decorator's motto had been, "Let's not excite anyone." The living room featured two enormous black leather sofas that looked like they had been stolen from a Bond villain's lair, a glass-topped coffee table, and a TV big enough to double as a drive-in cinema.

Downstairs, the kitchen was gleaming and well-equipped but very much a bachelor's domain. His fridge contained the essentials of the single man's diet: beer, margarine, bread, and a Tupperware container of something so unidentifiable it could have been a biology experiment. I managed to scrape together some toast and a cup of Nescafé, but it wasn't the hearty breakfast I'd been dreaming of.

The estate outside was eerily pristine, like Milton Keynes had been transplanted to the tropics and decorated with palm trees. The sun was shining, but the dark wood and marble floors inside kept the house cool—perfect for the climate, but my England-acclimatized self was yearning to feel the full heat of Jakarta.

Finding myself alone in a stranger's house in a foreign city, with no idea where I was or how to find anyone was an experience somewhere between thrilling and terrifying. Fortunately, Phil had left his business card on the coffee table, so I called his office. The response was as casual as could be: "Oh, they left around eight. Said you looked like you needed the sleep. Good luck!"

Luck?! I didn't need luck. I needed aspirin, directions, and a new liver.

I called Ron, who promised to send his driver. "It's not far," he said, "but Jakarta traffic is, well, Jakarta traffic." Which is to say, a swirling, honking, snarling chaos that made London rush hour look like a gentle Sunday drive.

By one o'clock, a white Kejang—a cross between a van and a car that seemed to have inherited the worst traits of both—pulled up outside. The ride to Ron's was my first proper daylight look at Jakarta. What a city! It was a magnificent jumble of "nearly falling apart" and "hanging on by a thread."

The skyline was dominated by a tangle of wires that seemed to exist for no other purpose than to perplex electricians. Thick black cables sagged between wooden poles like hammocks for particularly lazy birds, while others dangled ominously close to the ground. During the rainy season, I imagined, walking the streets would be like playing Russian roulette with a live wire.

The streets themselves were a patchwork of potholes and

graffiti. The graffiti wasn't exactly Banksy-level artistry, more like "Kilroy was here" scrawled in a rush. Yet there was a charm to it all—a vibrant, messy, thriving energy that made the place feel alive.

As we approached Ron's neighbourhood, things began to look a bit more "Westernized." Banks became bigger, proper pavements appeared, and I even spotted a few pedestrians who looked like they knew what a Pret a Manger was. But then, we turned into Ron's street, and it was like stepping off a cliff.

Imagine a road so potholed it made the lunar surface seem smooth by comparison. Each bump felt like a personal insult to my digestive system. By the time we stopped outside Ron's house, I was ready to kiss solid ground.

The house itself was a large white building that looked like it had seen better decades. Its iron railings were flaking, and the roof was undergoing repairs at a pace that suggested it might be finished by the next century. Two workers sat on the roof, moving so slowly they could've been posing for a still-life painting.

Inside, the décor was similarly minimalist: white walls, a couple of desks, and an old-school typewriter clacking away in the corner. Eka and another young woman were working quietly but greeted me with warm smiles as I arrived.

Through the door to the main room, I saw Ron and the boys, already halfway through a beer. And just like that, the chaotic morning melted away. I was back with the gang.

RAIN AND RON'S REALITY CHECK

"Morning, everyone," I called out as I entered Ron's office.

They glanced up, waved, and Ron greeted me with the standard antipodean salutation: "G'day, mate."

"Any luck?" I asked, trying to sound optimistic.

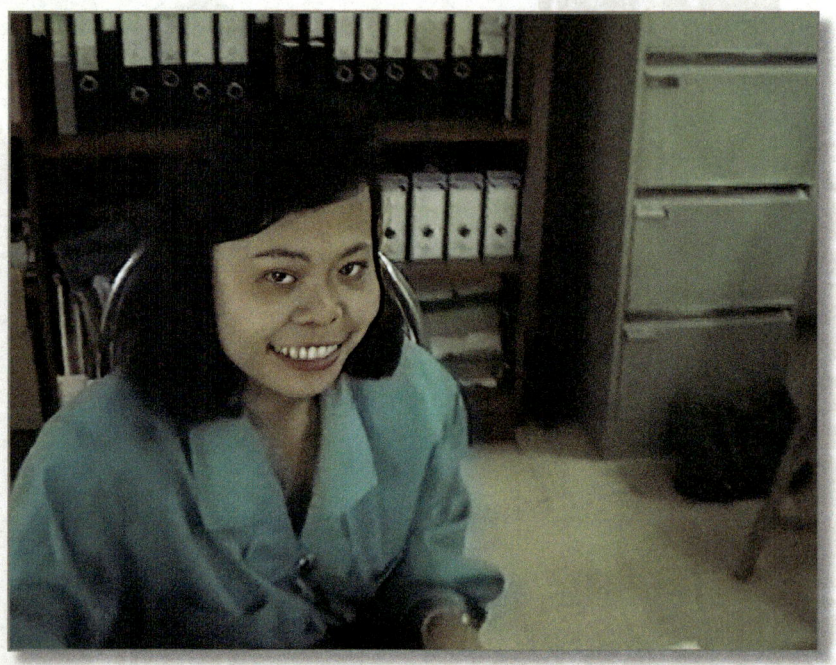

"Eka's on it now. Should have some information soon," Ron replied, taking a leisurely sip of his beer.

What was my initial impression of Ron's setup? Let's just say "professional" wasn't the first word that sprang to mind. The office had the aura of a space that had given up on itself. Paint was peeling, desks were mismatched, and the typewriter in the corner could have been considered an antique even then. Ron himself seemed more invested in his drink than my plight. Was it confidence-inspiring? Not exactly! I was beginning to doubt whether Ron could retrieve a stuck umbrella, let alone my bike.

I consoled myself with the thought that I'd see Dave Jackman later. If Ron was the laid-back beer guy, Dave was supposed to be the organized fixer. Fingers crossed.

At 4:30, I left Ron's office to head to Dave's place in Cinere, about 15 kilometres away. Acef, my driver, was a cheerful, compact man in his mid-forties who seemed to see honking the horn as an art form. He'd beep with abandon, whether or not there was anything in his path, adding a sort of rhythmic charm to the chaos outside.

The day had started sunny, but the skies had clouded over. I paid no mind—until the rain came. And when it came, it came. One moment, dry roads, and the next? Instant flood! Within minutes, streets turned into rivers deep enough to float a canoe. Jakarta's drainage system, if it existed, was clearly taking a sabbatical.

Acef, unfazed, wove the Isuzu Panther minibus through the watery chaos like a man who'd done this a thousand times. Meanwhile, I sat back in awe, marvelling at how a city could transform so quickly and dramatically.

CINERE: GARDEN SUBURBS AND SOMBRERO PHONE BOXES

Cinere was a fascinating place. It reminded me, oddly enough, of Stevenage—if Stevenage had been plonked in the tropics and given a Latin American twist. There were two sides to it: the old and the new.

The old part was all ramshackle stalls and wooden shops, selling everything from cigarettes to knockoff toys. It felt like something out of a dusty Western, complete with a layer of grit and charm. The new part, though, was unexpectedly modern and tidy.

In the middle of this suburban dichotomy, I spotted one of the most peculiar phone boxes I'd ever seen. It had the usual phones-on-a-post setup, but the roof—a giant yellow straw sombrero—was utterly incongruous. Practical, sure, but it looked like it belonged in a theme park rather than a suburban street.

The main drag of Cinere's new town was lined with colourful flower beds that wouldn't have looked out of place in a botanical garden. The tarmacked roads were smooth, a rarity in Jakarta, and the shops, though ordinary, were neatly maintained. At one end of the street loomed an American-style mall, complete with McDonald's, KFC, and even Arby's. Their largest advertisement? - They home delivered. In 1994, in a small town Java, my mind was blown.

DAVE'S HOUSE AND BLACK CURRENCY

Dave Jackman's house was a charming mix of colonial and suburban styles. Thick, dark wood beams contrasted with cool white marble floors, and the décor was a curious blend of modern gadgets and comfortable Western furniture. The house wasn't massive, but it felt grand by English standards, with a veranda that made me long for a climate that didn't turn sitting outside into a frostbite hazard.

I was there to collect four cases of Jim Beam whiskey, courtesy of Remy Indonesia. These weren't for personal indulgence but rather a form of "black currency"—a sweetener for smoothing over bureaucratic hurdles. Whiskey diplomacy, as it were! As we quickly found out, though – alcohol has very little value in a strict Muslim country!

As I sat on the veranda with a beer in hand, the call to prayer echoed through the neighbourhood. Amplified and melodic, it brought a timeless romance to the evening. Moments later, the spell was humorously broken by a vendor on a bicycle, blasting his air trumpet to sell snacks of dubious origin. The sound was reminiscent of a souped-up horn on a boy racer's car—a mix of charm and absurdity.

SERVANTS AND A DIFFERENT WAY OF LIFE

Dave, ever the modest host, casually mentioned the woman pottering about inside was one of his live-in servants. This was an eye-opener. Dave's house was a spacious three-bedroom bungalow, not a sprawling estate, yet he had a full staff: a maid, a gardener, a car cleaner, and a babysitter.

"It's just how things are here," Dave explained, as if it were the most natural thing in the world. The maid, Kus, was a Christian from rural Java who had asked to live with the family in exchange for work. Dave gave her $25 a month—paltry by Western standards but a fortune compared to what the gardener earned. It was a system so foreign to my English sensibilities that I couldn't help but marvel.

DINNER AND FAMILY LIFE

At 8:00, Dave's wife Jen arrived home from work with their seven-year-old daughter in tow. Jen was tall, elegant, and clearly formidable. From what I gathered, she ran their oil company as effectively as a general commands an army. Despite her busy schedule, she changed into casual clothes, organized the household staff with military precision, and had us out the door in no time for dinner.

We ended the evening at a newly opened Indian restaurant,

enjoying great food and even better company. Jakarta, for all its quirks and challenges, was proving to be full of surprises.

PHIL

As we ate, the crew and I began speculating about our sleeping arrangements. Ron's house had some space, but not enough for everyone. Chris, the photographer, and I volunteered to find somewhere else. Honestly, I was relieved. A bit of space from the rest of the crew sounded like a blessing. Chris seemed to feel the same.

The truth is, I didn't quite click with the rest of the team. It wasn't animosity—just different wavelengths. Chris, though, was all right. This seemed to be his first professional assignment, and he had an understated sharpness I liked. Standing about 1.7 meters tall with pale skin that turned pink at the mere suggestion of sun, Chris in his khaki shorts was the image of a classic English colonial civil servant. He was a bit of a loner, or maybe an individualist, but quick-witted and amusing; the rest of the crew? - not so much.

Luckily, Dave Jackman's friend Phil offered a solution: a room in a staff house belonging to an oil company. Staff houses, I learned, were used by long-term contract employees or specialists passing through on their way to oil fields. I imagined something practical—an apartment or, if luck was on my side, a cosy detached house for managers.

We left the restaurant around 11:00 PM armed with detailed directions to the staff house. Detailed, yes, but useless to our taxi driver, who seemed to view them as an elaborate joke. He stopped at least a dozen times to consult passers-by, none of whom seemed any more informed than he was.

By the time we arrived—after countless wrong turns, misunderstandings, and general fannying about—it was well past midnight. The house was behind a high security fence, about 50 meters from the main gate. No bell. No lights. No clue if we were even in the right place.

There we stood, stranded in the dark, shouting and whistling like kids locked out of a school disco. After what felt like an eternity, the garage door opened, and a bleary-eyed young man shuffled out, blinking into the night; so much for their top-tier security!

He stared at us—a group of pale, vaguely European-looking people waving like lunatics outside his gate—before deciding we weren't there to rob him. Without a word, he ambled over, unlocked the gate, and gestured us in. The fact that he didn't ask for proof, or even confirmation of who we were surprised me, but I wasn't about to question our good fortune.

THE MANSION

Once inside, I was stunned. This wasn't just a staff house—it was a Beverly Hills mansion.

The entrance opened into a grand hallway big enough to host a concert. To the left and right were sprawling salons filled with squashy sofas, their arrangement seemingly dictated by a random-number generator. A dining table large enough to seat the United Nations dominated one room. The bedrooms were enormous, with king-size beds, wardrobes you could park a car in, and enough magnolia paint to qualify as a colour monopoly.

The house was perfectly clean but had the hollow feel of a place maintained without care. It wasn't lived in—it was merely passed through. It reminded me of an airport lounge: functional but utterly soulless.

Peering out the back window, I spotted a floodlit swimming pool surrounded by manicured grass and majestic palm trees. It looked like it belonged in a real estate brochure. Yes, it was pristine, inviting, and yet - lifeless. I doubted anyone had ever taken a dip. The eerie emptiness was palpable. Our voices echoed off the walls, the sound unsoftened by any pictures or curtains. I suspected no one, save for Chris, the sleepy security guard, and myself, had set foot in this house for weeks—maybe months.

Dave, bless him, probably didn't realize the scale of what he'd arranged. Still, we'd just have to "make do" with our palatial accommodations.

A GHOSTLY WELCOME

Chris and I ventured into the kitchen, hopeful for a late-night snack or at least a morning coffee. We found the fridge – empty; the cupboards - barren. The silence between us said it all. Survival would have to wait until morning.

We made our way upstairs, each choosing a bedroom from the mansion's endless supply. I flopped onto a king-size bed and stared at the ceiling. No sheets? Who cares? Sleep was far more important than linen logistics. As I drifted off, I couldn't help but feel the strangeness of the place. A mansion built for comfort but devoid of life—ours for the taking. It was surreal, to say the least.

Tomorrow, I thought. Tomorrow we'll figure it all out. For now, the ghostly silence of the house would have to lull me to sleep.

TUESDAY 7 JUNE

ALL HARLEYS ARE BANNED IN INDONESIA

At ten o'clock, Chris and I were picked up by Acef and headed downtown to meet the rest of the crew. When we arrived, we were greeted by some seriously long faces, most belonging to the local Harley enthusiasts we were supposed to discuss the ride to Bali with.

The meeting took place in a sprawling motor dealer's repair yard, where about thirty Harley-Davidsons of every vintage were lined up, each lovingly restored and polished to perfection. Their owners, clad in leather jackets, Harley-branded t-shirts, jeans, and an eclectic mix of bandanas and gold chains, looked like a stereotypical gang of tough bikers. The truth, however, was far less intimidating—these were 9-to-5 businessmen, politicians, and high-ranking police officers on their day off.

And therein lay the problem.

For years, motorcycles with engines over 175cc had been technically illegal in Indonesia. But because these bikes were the playthings of the rich and influential, a little "financial encouragement" ensured the law was rarely enforced.

Until today!

As it turns out, the sudden crackdown on Harleys had nothing to do with traffic regulations and everything to do with politics at the highest level. Apparently, a long-standing rivalry existed between the Chief of Police and the Chief of the Army. The Chief of Police, a Harley enthusiast, had finally been outmanoeuvred by the Chief of the Army, a BMW devotee. Mr. Army decided now was the perfect time to enforce the ban, effectively ruining Mr. Police's fun.

This political feud had spilled into our plans, landing us squarely in the middle of it.

Just as we were digesting this, a convoy of military police arrived. Armed to the teeth, they informed the group that it would be extremely unwise to argue or attempt to ride. Everyone knew the bikes in the yard were technically illegal, many with dodgy number plates and forged documents. They could be confiscated on the spot and likely never seen again.

Despite their tough appearances, these men—usually so powerful—were visibly nervous. They knew when to stay silent. Riding to Bali was now out of the question. Some planned to truck their bikes; others would fly. Meanwhile, I couldn't shake the feeling that this debacle was somehow tied to the trouble I'd been having with customs and my own bike.

Great!

RON DRIVES ME MAD

My frustration was reaching a boiling point. I was desperate to leave Jakarta and begin my journey, but I felt utterly trapped. Every time I voiced my concerns to Ron, all I got was his infuriatingly calm, "Don't worry, mate - these things take time. People here are very sensitive and don't like to be pushed."

I was shaking with worry. I felt imprisoned in a paradise of endless sunshine. While Ron's hospitality was generous, I was losing my mind. Friendly faces surrounded me, but nothing was getting done. My bike was stuck in customs. My visa was expiring. And my funds were dwindling.

Yesterday, I'd been promised we'd visit I.M.I., the motor authority, first thing in the morning to resolve everything. But that, like so many other plans, turned out to be a fantasy. At 10:00 AM, we learned that I.M.I. had called Eka, Ron's assistant, and told her to stop pushing them. Ron was right about one thing—persistence wasn't helping.

Instead, we drafted a letter for Dave Jackman to put on one of his Harley-Davidson Club Indonesia letterheads, requesting I.M.I. expedite the release of my bike. Another letter, written in Indonesian, guaranteed I'd leave the country in two weeks with the bike. Both were faxed to I.M.I., but whether they'd have any effect was anyone's guess.

I couldn't make sense of the system. To my Western mind, it was utterly illogical. Money was running out, and I still had a crew to support. If not for Ron's generosity, I'd be suicidal over hotel bills by now.

Eka was sent to the immigration office to extend our visas. I could only hope she'd have more success than we had so far.

A MYSTERY OF IMPORTANCE

What baffled me most was how my situation seemed to have escalated into a matter of national significance. I.M.I. now claimed they couldn't make a decision until Tommy Suharto, the President's son, returned. Why on earth would someone so high-ranking care where I rode my bike?

Somehow, I'd become a political pawn. British film crews, I learned, had a reputation in Indonesia for stirring up trouble. Documentaries like John Pilger's exposé on the atrocities in Timor had painted British journalists as a thorn in the government's side.

But I wasn't here to uncover corruption or challenge the regime. I just wanted to ride a Harley. Unfortunately, that distinction seemed lost on everyone.

Stuck without a bike, a visa, or a clear way forward, I began to wonder if this entire endeavour was a mistake. Perhaps I should have skipped Jakarta and opted for a more modest adventure—like riding a Vespa from Bedford to Leicester.

WHY AM I SO IMPORTANT?

What I don't understand is why I seem to matter so much. I.M.I. (the motor authority) has now declared they need to wait for Tommy Suharto—the President's son—before they can make any decision about my bike. Tommy Suharto, for goodness sake! Why would someone so high-ranking care where I ride my Harley? Somehow, I've become politically significant. It's absurd.

We suspect this all stems from the fact that we're British. British film crews have a reputation for being a thorn in the Indonesian government's side. People like John Pilger from the BBC have exposed the horrors of East Timor, where countless people were tortured or killed. British journalists are often the ones reporting on corruption and human rights abuses here.

But I'm not here for any of that. I just want to ride a Harley. Unfortunately, they don't seem to know—or care.

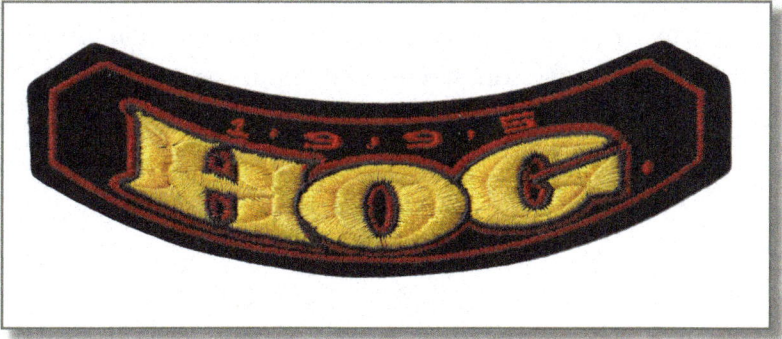

WEDNESDAY 8 JUNE

Wednesday afternoon, with little else to do, we decided to explore Jakarta and film something interesting.

We called Bagu, our Indian-Indonesian production manager, and arranged to meet him at his home in the city centre. Bagu is a fascinating character. Stocky and cheerful, with brown skin and a big smile, he's in his mid-fifties and seems to have lived everywhere and done everything. Originally from Hyderabad, he and his family moved to Indonesia in 1949 after Partition made life dangerous for Hindus in West Pakistan.

Bagu started in the family textile business but quickly grew bored and turned to filmmaking. He's made everything from Indian to Indonesian films, lived in remote parts of Sumatra, became fluent in Cantonese, and added Bahasa Indonesia and several local dialects to his linguistic repertoire. His English is perfect, and his life story sounds like the script for an epic movie. He now lives in a sprawling old house in Jakarta with his wife and teenage son, while his daughter is married to a doctor in York, England. People say he's the best production manager in Indonesia. That remains to be seen, but so far, he's a lovely guy.

DOWNTOWN JAKARTA

We piled into our tiny white minibus—Acef, the driver, me in the passenger seat, and the rest of the crew crammed into the back. Steve, self-appointed boss, barked orders from behind the driver. Paul, our cameraman, grumbled about the logistics of filming from the middle seat, and Sean, our unflappable soundman, managed to stay cheerful despite being squashed. In the back compartment meant for luggage, Chris, our neurotic gofer, shared his latest health worries while Bagu guided us through the chaos.

Our first stop was Dufan Fantasy theme park, where we planned to shoot aerial shots of Jakarta from the top of the big wheel. Bagu negotiated entry—always best done on-site in Indonesia, where bureaucracy eats official requests alive. A $40 bribe got us access, but they still made us buy tickets, probably for plausible deniability if we were caught. Because who wouldn't sneak in a three-foot-long camera and a giant fluffy microphone on a six-foot pole without anyone noticing?

The filming was straightforward—shots of me walking, admiring rides, and watching the buskers. It was innocuous enough, though technically we were still considered "spies" without an official film board representative to accompany us. Bringing a radio microphone into the country is borderline treasonous. The paranoia stems from years of Western journalists exposing atrocities, particularly in East Timor, where Indonesian forces committed unspeakable acts under the guise of suppressing communism.

But I wasn't here to dig into politics. I wanted to show Indonesia as I saw it—a beautiful, friendly country with vibrant culture. Ironically, their resistance was doing more harm to their image than anything I could film. The film board man never showed up anyway.

A CITY WITH CONTRASTS

After the park, we filmed some shots of Jakarta itself. The Monas monument—a towering obelisk with a golden tip—dominated the city centre, while the streets bustled with manic drivers weaving through traffic with incredible precision. Despite their reckless style, I didn't see a single car with a dent. Every vehicle was spotless, a point of pride here.

Vendors swarmed the traffic lights, selling everything from bottled water of dubious origin to bizarre posters, like a teenage boy hawking an image of a New York cop booking a blonde in a 1930s car. Not exactly a spur-of-the-moment purchase.

We wrapped up in Sunda Kelapa, the old colonial harbour. Its colourful Dutch warehouses, Makassar schooners, and lively fish market offered a glimpse into Jakarta's past.

THE BIG WHEEL KEEPS ON TURNING

By 5 PM, I returned to Ron's, heavy-hearted. He was playing poker on his computer, having achieved absolutely nothing all day.

The monotony of my situation reminded me of the big wheel at the park. It spent all day spinning, using enormous energy, yet getting nowhere. That's exactly how I felt.

No bike. No progress. No end in sight. Asking Ron the same questions, getting the same answers - was utterly soul-crushing.

TIME IS RUNNING OUT

The whole reason for being in Indonesia right now was to film the Harley-Davidson festival. We flew into Jakarta to join an exciting ride-out to Bali, where I'd planned to meet fifty bikes here, another eighty in Surabaya, and create a stunning mass entry onto the island. It was supposed to be the spectacular opening sequence of my film.

Instead, political infighting has completely derailed me. What's merely inconvenient for the dozens of Javanese bikers heading to Bali is an outright catastrophe for me. Everything I have—money, resources, reputation—is riding on this project. I've spent a fortune shipping my own Harley and flying in a professional film crew from the UK. On top of that, I've hired a specialist production team here in Indonesia, complete with vehicles and support staff. I'm feeding and housing everyone, running on a budget for five weeks, and I've already lost an entire week.

It's been three days, and now all Harleys are banned from the roads. I still can't believe this is real. How could anyone plan for something like this? In what other country could such a whimsical, immediate law be enacted? It's all because one general wants to ruin another general's pleasure. Utterly insane!

To make matters worse, Harleys—and all large motorcycles, for that matter—have technically been illegal here for years. But the law has never been enforced because these bikes are owned by the wealthy elite: politicians, business tycoons, and the untouchable upper class. This sudden crackdown is a power play, pure and simple. The army has been ordered to enforce the law, likely as a move in someone's private vendetta.

The annual motorcycle festival is a major event, attracting dignitaries and Harley enthusiasts from across the country. Riders on the Bali run include governors and even the national police chief. Yet someone's stepped on the wrong toes, and now the army—who truly hold the reins of power in Indonesia—has decided to flex its muscles.

DEEP TROUBLE

Meanwhile, my bike is still impounded. As a visitor in transit, I should theoretically be immune from this madness. I was supposed to have all the correct paperwork and Ron, my fixer, to ensure everything went smoothly. Yet here I am, with an expensive crew sitting idle, no bike, no ride-out from Jakarta, and no plan for filming in Bali. On top of that, we all have two-week visas that are rapidly expiring.

I'm in deep shit—and there's no shovel in sight.

Steve and I held a crisis meeting to figure out our next move. As far as we know, the festival is still happening. Bali operates with a bit more autonomy, and the army is unlikely to interfere there. Many of the locals are trucking or flying their bikes to Bali, confident that things will go back to normal once they are outside Java.

Obviously, I can't join the ride-out, but we can still record the event. Ron has assured us he'll get my bike released while we're away, and Eka will handle the visa extensions. It's all talk—I've heard these promises before. But at this point, what choice do I have?

THE COST OF MOVING FORWARD

The next hurdle is the cost. Flying the crew to Bali wasn't part of the budget. There are six of us: me, Steve, Paul (cameraman), Sean (soundman), Chris (assistant), and Bagu (production manager and interpreter). Acef, our driver, and his mate will handle the two support vehicles, but that's a gruelling 36-hour non-stop drive.

Financially, it makes more sense for us to drive too. But if we arrive utterly wrecked from the journey, we'll be useless for filming. It's a false economy.

No more dithering. We have to fly. The one o'clock flight tomorrow will get us to Bali by early evening, even accounting for the time difference and inevitable delays. We'll have all of Friday to find the party, film on the beach, and get ourselves organized.

The extra cost? It was roughly $1,000 - painful, yes, but unavoidable. After coming this far, there's no other option.

It must be done!

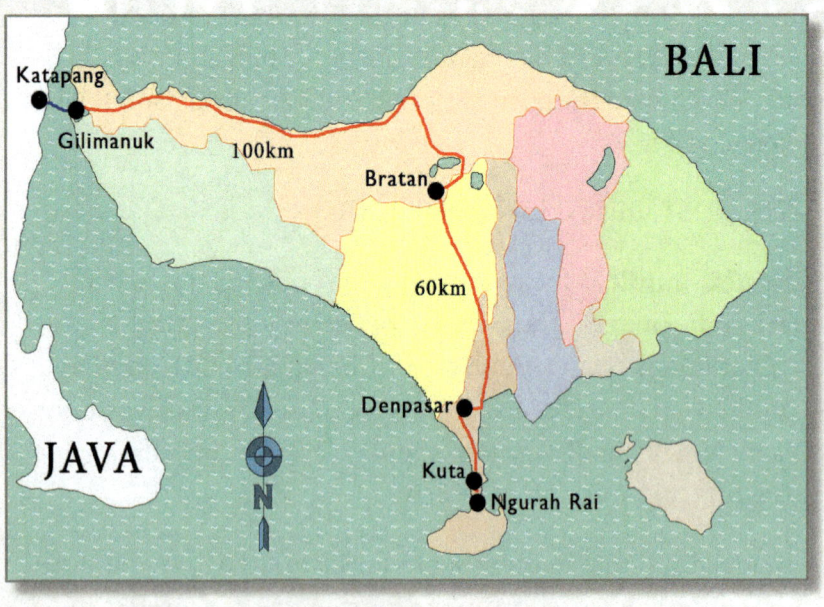

THURSDAY 9 JUNE

I have to admit, my feelings about heading to Bali are mixed. On one hand, I'm relieved to finally be doing something productive. Days of anxious inactivity in Jakarta have driven me to the brink - watching Ron waste hours playing solitaire on his computer, while I'm losing time, money, and sanity has been infuriating. Another day in Jakarta, and I would have exploded.

At least in Bali, we can start filming properly. The theme park we tried to shoot was a complete waste of time. But the nagging frustration remains—my Harley is still trapped in a bureaucratic nightmare. This entire project was meant to centre on a Harley ride from Bali to Bangkok, and at this rate, I might not even get to ride the damn thing, let alone film it. I'm starting to wonder if this venture will become the most expensive "holiday" of my life—one that costs me everything I've got. Failure this early in the game would be disastrous, not just for me but for my investors.

The crew is optimistic, or at least pretending to be. All I hear is "Don't worry. Trauma makes good TV! If it were easy, it'd be boring." Small comfort indeed!

HOLIDAY INN, BALI

Three cheers for Holiday Inn! As one of our sponsors, they've set us up in a hotel that's nothing short of spectacular. The foyer is a masterpiece—a massive space styled like a Balinese village meeting hall, with high, pine-coloured wooden beams forming a pyramid-like structure. Beneath the soaring roof, an expansive platform gives the impression of elders gathering to discuss matters of importance.

The hotel itself is vast—it takes me ten minutes to reach my room. But it's worth the walk. Intricately carved teak doors open into a bright, luxurious suite, complete with a sitting room, two televisions, two balconies, and every comfort imaginable. And best of all? It's free. Not bad at all.

KUTA – THURSDAY NIGHT

Despite the luxury, I'm still pissed off.

I'm pissed off at the bureaucracy. Pissed off at Ron's

incompetence and his irritatingly casual attitude; Pissed off at watching my limited budget vanish on bribes that accomplish nothing; Pissed off at paying a crew of eight to sit around twiddling their thumbs; And most of all, I'm pissed off that I don't have my bike.

Sitting in this beautiful hotel room on this beautiful island doesn't make any of it better. I need a distraction, some light relief to shake off this gloom. I can't face another evening making strained conversation with people I don't know well and don't particularly want to know.

So, I decide to escape.

Kuta is said to be Bali's pleasure capital, a hub of nightlife packed with bars, clubs, and boisterous crowds. According to Lonely Planet, it's "good fun and quite a scene." That's exactly what I need.

LEGIAN STREET

The concierge calls a taxi, and I wait. And wait. The infamous "rubber time" strikes again. After 30 minutes, the cab finally arrives, and I'm off to Legian Street, the supposed heart of the action.

What I find is far from what I expected. The vibrant, bustling nightlife I'd envisioned is practically nonexistent. Most of the bars, clubs, and restaurants are dark and shuttered. Midnight, and Kuta feels like a ghost town.

A dodgy-looking local approaches - offering me dope. I decline, recalling horror stories of tourists landing in Balinese prisons. I ask him where everyone is, and he shrugs. Off-season, he says. He points me to the only two clubs open: the Sari Club and Goa 2000.

Both are dire. I find a handful of drunken Australian surfers straight out of Neighbours—loud, incomprehensible, and utterly unappealing. Not exactly the scene I'd hoped for.

Wandering further, I feel a flicker of unease. The streets are dark, nearly deserted save for a few shady characters and grim-looking women I assume are hookers. Lonely Planet says it's safe, but the eerie quiet is unsettling.

Eventually, I stumble upon a bar that's open. It's a cavernous, dimly lit space with a scattering of tables. Two men play pool in the corner, and a lone barmaid sits behind the counter, engrossed in a tattered book. With nowhere else to go, I order a beer and settle onto a stool.

A CHANCE ENCOUNTER

The beer isn't what I want, but I'm curious about the barmaid's book. It's an ancient English grammar textbook, its cover missing and pages barely holding together. Intrigued, I ask her about it.

Her name is Nok, and she's using the book for college. Over the next hour, she tells me her story. Her English is basic but enthusiastic, and we manage to communicate. She left her parents, farmers from a village 50 kilometres away, at 16 to live with a boyfriend who turned out to be abusive. After four miserable years, she moved in with her grandfather and sister in Kuta.

Now, she attends college by day and works nights at this bar to pay for it. Her dream is to get an office job, something better than tending a nearly empty bar.

I'm impressed by her dedication and hard work. Part of me wonders if her story is a fabricated sob tale—something I've encountered before—but she seems genuine.

I ask if she'd like to come back to my hotel. She politely declines, saying she couldn't possibly do that. Half of me is disappointed, but the other half is relieved. Her refusal only strengthens my belief in her sincerity.

Before I leave, I ask if I can see her again. She's hesitant, explaining that her family is protective, and any prospective suitor must first meet her grandfather. I'm happy to agree. The chance to visit a Balinese family at home is rare. She gives me her address, and I leave the bar, wondering what tomorrow might bring.

 FRIDAY 10 JUNE

NOK'S GRANDFATHER'S HOUSE

I had agreed to be at Nok's house by 9:30 AM. At 8:30, I rang Steve to confirm the day's arrangements and to let him know where I was going. I promised to return by 1:00 PM, at which point we would head to the beach in search of bikini-clad beauties to add some glamour to the start of the film.

Nok lives on the outskirts of Denpasar, the bustling capital of Bali. Although she described it as a "town" last night, it is, in reality, one of the fastest-growing cities in Asia. The small, pleasant, tree-lined streets of a few years ago still exist, but "progress" has brought with it mind-numbing traffic and relentless pollution. Over ten percent of Bali's 2.5 million people now live in Denpasar.

The eight-kilometre journey from Kuta to Denpasar is a chaotic blur where urban sprawl has swallowed the countryside. By 9:00 AM, the narrow single-carriageway road is already a nightmare. Battered diesel trucks cough out choking clouds of pollution as they labour under impossibly heavy loads. Cyclists, dwarfed by towering piles of straw strapped to their bikes, wobble precariously along the edges of the road. Schoolchildren in crisp white uniforms dart across the traffic, their polished shoes glinting in the sunlight. Elderly women shuffle past, moving with a deliberate slowness, while wiry men in nothing but shorts and flip-flops weld scraps of metal by the roadside.

Clusters of market stalls interrupt the monotony of the road, offering a riot of colours and smells. Families perch on rickety stools, selling everything from live chickens to vibrant rolls of fabric. The East may look colourful and romantic, but the reality is a grinding struggle. People here work tirelessly under harsh conditions for very little, while the fortunate few live in untold luxury. No wonder corruption thrives in such disparity.

Seated in my taxi, I eventually escape the urban chaos for a brief stretch of countryside. Rolling fields and lush greenery offer a fleeting sense of tranquillity, but it doesn't last. Five minutes later, Denpasar's outskirts loom once more, and the din of city life returns.

I arrive at a set of traffic lights on the edge of town. Consulting the small scrap of a map Nok had drawn for me, I direct the taxi to take a left turn onto a ring road. A couple of hundred meters later, we veer right, and I ask the driver to stop. After paying, I step out onto the pavement, suddenly feeling disoriented.

The map indicates I should find the "fourth alley," but as I pace up and down the street, I see no sign of it. Alleys stretch out in every direction, none of them labelled. I approach passersby for help, but my scrap of paper seems to baffle them as much as it does me. Their curious, puzzled glances make me acutely aware of how out of place I must seem.

Just as I'm about to give up, I hear someone calling out. Across the street, two girls wave and walk toward me, a large multicoloured plastic shopping bag swinging between them.

One of the girls is Nok, accompanied by her older sister, whose smiling face is marred by a severe case of acne. I explain my predicament, and Nok points to the alley directly behind me, laughing as she gestures for me to follow. There's no sign marking it as number four—perhaps it was stolen, or perhaps street names are deliberately kept mysterious here.

The narrow mud path is flanked by tall, windowless white walls, their only interruptions being the occasional door. Following the girls, I can't help but feel a twinge of unease. My imagination runs wild with images of unseen assailants lying in wait. But a moment later, the morning sun breaks through, and the girls glance back with reassuring smiles.

The alley opens into a dusty courtyard surrounded by neat, white-painted bungalows, each with an elevated concrete veranda. The scene exudes tranquillity, despite the faint hum of traffic in the distance.

On one of the verandas, an elderly man sits in a rattan chair, reading a newspaper. His weathered face and lean frame suggest a life of hard work, but he radiates an air of dignity. He rises to greet me, his sarong swishing around his legs as he offers a firm handshake. This is Nok's grandfather, whose approval I must earn to take his granddaughter out.

The family bustles around discreetly. Her sister disappears into the central bungalow, and other relatives peek out occasionally to observe the intruder. Bare-chested boys in colourful shorts linger curiously, while shy girls in sarongs and cartoon-print t-shirts watch from a distance.

Grandfather and I engage in a pleasant, if unintelligible, conversation, relying on smiles and gestures. Nok returns shortly with a glass of traditional Balinese coffee. Thick, black, and cloyingly sweet, it tastes more like sludge than coffee, but I sip it politely under Grandfather's watchful gaze.

As the morning stretches on, Nok disappears for a shower, leaving me to savour the serene atmosphere. A small white dog sniffs at my feet before retreating to a shady corner, while a bird in a tiny cage chirps faintly above me. I can't help but pity the little creature, confined to its prison.

I reflect on the stark contrast between my world and Nok's. Back home, life revolves around materialism—bigger houses, flashier cars. Here, it's about family and community. Their simple yet well-kept home radiates warmth and pride, a stark departure from the cold individualism I'm used to.

Nok reappears, her freshly washed hair gleaming in the sunlight. She's made an effort to look her best, though her thick black wrap skirt, Disney t-shirt, and clunky shoes are a little mismatched. Still, I compliment her, and she beams.

Bidding farewell to the family, we make our way back through the narrow alley. Her sister walks us to the corner, where we part ways. Minutes later, Nok and I are in a taxi, heading back to the Holiday Inn.

THE BEACH – FRIDAY AFTERNOON

By the time Nok and I return to the hotel, it's about twelve o'clock, giving us an hour before meeting the others. I collect my key from reception, and we make the long trek to my suite at the far end of the complex. For Nok, it's her first time inside one of these grand hotels, and her curiosity is palpable. She's wide-eyed with awe, though too polite to express it outright until I encourage her. Then, like a child discovering treasure, she spends ten minutes investigating every cupboard, door, and corner. The view of the beach from the balcony particularly delights her.

While she explores, I take a quick shower and change. Admittedly, my wardrobe remains consistent—a black T-shirt and shorts—but at least I'm clean and fresh. Once ready, we head back to reception and settle into a cosy corner for a drink. I order a beer; Nok opts for a Coke. We chat lightly about her family, whom I thoroughly enjoyed meeting, and wait for the others to arrive.

Soon, Acef and his mate—the drivers—stride into reception, followed closely by the ever-prompt Bagu. The rest of the team arrives shortly after, burdened with gear and brimming with purpose. Nok greets them shyly, her arm slipping into mine for a touch of security as we head outside to the vans. Our crew now consists of two drivers, Bagu, Steve, Paul, Sean, Chris, Nok, and me. With all the equipment, it's a tight squeeze in the vehicles.

Arriving at the beach is a mixed bag. The day is idyllic: clear skies, soft sand, and stunning scenery. Yet, where we expect throngs of bronzed Aussie beach babes and sculpted six-packed surfers, we find… emptiness. The beach is practically deserted, save for a few sprawled-out tourists whose bodies betray overindulgence in holiday buffets. It's no Baywatch, that's for sure.

Undeterred, we unload the equipment and scout for interesting shots. Scenic panoramas are nice but not enough to make the film captivating. We need people: characters; some event to bring the scene to life.

Bagu remains alert, always watching. Filming in Indonesia without official permits is illegal, and we've taken a calculated risk by operating under the radar. In Jakarta, Ron had shared horror stories of film crews being arrested and held until hefty fines were paid. To avoid this, Bagu takes charge, intercepting beach police the moment we set up our tripod. They approach, shouting and gesturing, clearly unimpressed by our activities. Bagu springs into action, spinning a story about us being invited by the Bali government to film a promotional video. His charm, sprinkled with a few dollars, works wonders. Twenty minutes later, the police lose interest and leave. Crisis averted.

Despite the initial excitement, the beach yields little of cinematic value. We film a few scattered characters—an eccentric woman in a maroon jacket and pink baseball cap who braids my hair for the camera, and a handful of moderately interesting beachgoers. When the woman shows me her handiwork in a small mirror, I'm torn between feeling like a bohemian hunk and a complete twat. Nok finds it hilarious, flicking the beads and giggling as we walk back to the van.

By three-thirty, we call it a day. The boys want to swim, and I'm eager to spend some quiet time with Nok. Back at the hotel, she relaxes, her confidence growing as the day progresses. Her English improves with her ease, and we bond over shared humour and moments of connection.

Unfortunately, Nok has to work tonight, missing the massive Harley-Davidson party I'd hoped she'd attend with me. We have a few hours together before she leaves at seven-thirty, and she makes it clear how she wants to spend them. Her warmth and humour promise that despite the day's minor disappointments, it's still shaping up to be a great one.

CRAZY NIGHT AT PEANUTS

As we approach the centre of Kuta, I sense that Friday night is going to be an unforgettable one. Despite the government's recent crackdown on large engine motorcycles, the turnout at Peanuts Bar on the bustling Kuta strip is staggering. Around three hundred Harleys—Evos, Shovels, Panheads, and an impressive replica of a 1938 Knucklehead—have throbbed their way from Denpasar and surrounding areas. Although many bikes were trucked or flown in due to last-minute restrictions, the enthusiasm of the Harley-Davidson Club of Indonesia and the Indonesian Chapter of the Harley Owners Group is undiminished. This gathering of bikers and machines looks like a scene from a Hollywood movie—which is fitting, as that's exactly what we're here to capture.

Peanuts Bar is owned by the charismatic Nura, a Harley fanatic of the highest order. Over six feet tall and unusually broad for an Indonesian, he struts around in jeans, silver-embellished cowboy boots, a Harley T-shirt, and a black cowboy hat. With twenty-three Harleys to his name, Nura has ensured this is the party of the year. The crowd is a blend of locals, Aussies, Americans, a New Zealander, an Italian, and me. Add in a few hundred curious tourists who stumble upon the scene and quickly realize they've struck gold, and you've got the recipe for an epic night. It's a stark contrast to the desolate emptiness of the previous evening—the calm before the storm.

Peanuts - arguably the largest and loudest bar in Bali - sits at the end of a narrow alley lined with more bikes and bikers. At the entrance, we're greeted by a square bustling with energy. There's a free drinks bar (though it's soon dry), a food zone dishing out mouth-watering Indonesian staples like satay, soup, rice, and fiery chillies. I can't get enough of it; this is the kind of food I could eat every day.

My role tonight is simple: chat naturally with as many people as possible, while the crew films. Naturally, having a bright light and a fluffy microphone hovering over me makes things a little less "natural," but it does help break the ice. The party kicks off with an opening ceremony led by Bali's police chief, a general, flanked by Harley Club dignitaries and a beautifully restored World War II U.S. Army bike. His twenty-minute speech—fifteen minutes too long, in my opinion—earns laughter and applause from the crowd. Then the real party begins.

Muslims may abstain from alcohol, but they certainly don't hold back on having a wild time. Beers appear out of nowhere; I've never drunk so much and still remained upright. I meet John, a bar owner from Buckingham, who's already plastered when we meet and only gets worse. He's a handsome guy in

his thirties with a lively local wife who hands me a Coke…
which turns out to be more Jack Daniels than cola.

The characters here are larger than life. Jake, a pot-bellied
Aussie in his late fifties with a wild grey beard and a wicked
laugh, splits his time between Bali and Australia, living the
dream on his Harley. Then there's Jazz, a local wild child
with chiselled muscles, a leather waistcoat, and a Harley
eagle tattooed across his chest. Despite his intimidating
appearance, he's friendly and helpful, introducing me to
everyone. Frank, the epitome of a wealthy Texas gentleman,
offers us his helicopter if we need it. Meanwhile, Smitty, a
craggy Vietnam vet and bar owner, saves the day by lending
us his Fat Boy—the only one on the island—to resolve our
bike-less predicament for the hotel's photo shoot. The eclectic
mix continues: a straggly Italian with a pilot's leather helmet,
dozens of rock-and-roll-styled locals, and tourists eager for
photos with me and the crew. The energy is infectious.

Around midnight, I wander inside Peanuts Bar proper, buzzing from the night's events. On stage, a scratch band jams rock-and-roll classics with such skill they could rival the originals. The bar's owner, Nura, takes the microphone for a song, followed by his right-hand man, Pete. Both deliver performances that whip the crowd into frenzy. Pete, a stocky Aussie with a signature crocodile hat, is full of drunken charm and infectious bonhomie. We drink together until the early hours.

At one o'clock, I reluctantly leave the party and head to Nok's bar. She greets me with a discreet smile and a kiss on the cheek. Back at the hotel, she's the perfect end to a perfect evening.

Me with Nuru

SATURDAY 11 JUNE

PHOTOCALL WITHOUT A BIKE

At 10:00 AM, anxiety was running high. Patrick Fiat, the manager of the Holiday Inn Bali Hai, was making me nervous. To be fair, he was harassing Steve, who in turn was harassing me. "Who is this Smitty guy?" Steve asked every two minutes. "Can we trust him? He should be here by now!"

The story we had fed Patrick was that my bike was safely garaged at a friend's house nearby. What Patrick didn't know was that my Fat Boy was impounded in Jakarta customs. He also didn't know there was only one Fat Boy on Bali, and that we were relying on a promise made over many beers to a man I'd met twice.

Logically, who in their right mind would lend a $30,000 Harley-Davidson to a virtual stranger? Would you? Yet here we were, standing in front of Patrick and his publicity team, confidently reassuring them that the bike would arrive any minute. Behind Patrick's back, Steve and I were a wreck. Would Smitty show up? Could we trust his word after that drunken promise?

The stakes couldn't be higher. Holiday Inn was sponsoring our accommodations for the entire trip. To let them down on the first day would spell disaster. No bike meant no film, no publicity, and no sponsorship. Patrick would report back to his superiors, who would surely tell other hotels along our route to refuse us. Catastrophe loomed large.

By 10:30, hope was nearly gone. Steve and I were frantically improvising excuses to placate Patrick. "He's on his way," Steve said, "he must have gotten delayed." The truth was, we had no idea where Smitty was staying or even his full name. We'd placed all our bets on a promise made in a bar.

Smitty rescues me

Then, like a miracle, we heard it: a faint rumble in the distance -the unmistakable thunder of a Harley engine. Relief washed over me as Smitty pulled up. Cool as ever, I walked over and greeted him.

"Where've you been? We were worried," I said, careful to sound casual.

"Sorry, Mike," he replied. "The bike was dirty, so I washed and polished it first."

What a guy! Not only was he lending me his pride and joy, but he'd also taken the time to clean it for me. This was Harley brotherhood in action: a complete stranger trusting me with his machine and even playing along by pretending it was mine.

Patrick's mood lifted immediately. We filmed outside the hotel, took promotional photos, and even had the local press snapping shots. Patrick, eager to maximize the moment, suggested I ride the bike through the hotel grounds and park it by the pool for some dramatic footage. The idea was perfect. The pool area, surrounded by palm trees and dotted with sunbathers, was the epitome of glamour.

Riding the Harley through the lush gardens caused quite a stir. The Holiday Inn is one of Bali's most upscale hotels, and guests didn't expect a roaring motorcycle to disrupt their morning tranquillity. I parked by the shimmering blue pool, framed by palm trees. Guests flocked to us, curious and excited.

The Harley's reputation as a "fanny magnet" proved true. Soon, I was surrounded by bikini-clad women eager to pose with me and the bike. German tourists, in particular, were enthusiastic, asking if they'd be on TV or if the film would air in Germany. Mothers, boyfriends, and husbands encouraged their loved ones to strike their best poses. Patrick loved it. I loved it. Everyone was thrilled.

My first taste of stardom was exhilarating. I basked in the attention, fully aware that this was my "15 minutes of fame".

By the end of the shoot, everything was a resounding success. I returned Smitty's bike, and all he wanted in return was a handshake. His generosity embodied the true spirit of Harley-Davidson camaraderie.

FESTIVAL AT NGURAH RAI STADIUM

At 1:30 PM, we set off for Ngurah Rai Stadium to film the Bali bike festival. Though it was supposed to be only 10 kilometres away, it took us a frustrating hour and a half to find it. Bali's maze of closed streets and unhelpful directions turned the journey into an ordeal. Even the local policemen seemed clueless about the stadium's location.

When we finally arrived, it was worth the hassle. The sight of hundreds of Harleys was breathtaking. Unlike in Britain, where most bikes at festivals are relatively new, these were predominantly vintage machines. Beautifully restored duo-glides from the '60s gleamed alongside pristine World War II machines. A stunning replica of a 1943 Knucklehead stole the show.

The event was a whirlwind of stunts, games, and high-energy antics. Riders performed acrobatics, balanced on saddles, and even took bites out of sausages hanging from strings. The atmosphere was electric. A klaxon sounded, and all the bikes roared to life for a ride-out through the countryside. We joined the pack in one of our vans, weaving through traffic under a clear blue sky.

Despite the vibrant festival, I couldn't shake a sense of frustration. I longed to ride alongside the others instead of observing from the sidelines. Sean and Paul, our crew, were efficient but unsociable, and their lack of camaraderie dampened my spirits. I reminded myself to stay positive. The day would end with Nok, whose promises of a lovely evening kept me going.

After a brief roadside stop, the group dispersed with waves and promises to reunite for the next day's festivities. We returned to the hotel, but I couldn't help feeling a little down. Still, tomorrow was another day, and the adventure was far from over.

CUSTOMS

We ring Ron in Jakarta—he reckons he has spoken to the Director of Customs and the bike will be out on Monday. We'll see!

 # SUNDAY 12 JUNE

THE WILDEST RIDE-OUT EVER

Believe me, a six-thirty start after being on the piss until four is very bad news. Apart from Captain Cappuccino (Paul Teverini, our cameraman's temporary nickname) and Bagu, who sensibly went to bed around eleven, the rest of us feel like shit. Chris comes down to reception with a cut forehead and no clue how it happened; Sean has had one hour of sleep in two days; Steve is a little bit vacant. I feel a bit down after a tearful goodbye to Nok. We promise to keep in touch, but both of us know I won't be coming back to Bali—at least not in the foreseeable future. We check out, load the van, and head off to the Ngurah Rai stadium once again for the big ride-out.

It is incredible!

A Bali ride-out you would not believe. You have to see it to believe it. And even then you're not sure. Around three hundred Harleys, one Ariel, one BSA, and one Norton leave the stadium in one huge, thunderous roar. We are flanked all around by siren-screaming military police in jeeps and on bikes, the high-powered squadron speeds through town at sixty miles an hour. Big deal, you say. That's not very fast. But this was no dual carriageway. This was like London in the rush hour. The motorcycle police outriders ruthlessly clear the traffic along our route. Traffic lights are ignored. Side streets are blocked so people cannot enter the road until we have passed.

With no bike, I have to follow in our mini-bus. Acef loves it, driving like a maniac with the police not just ignoring him, but positively encouraging him. It's like racing through Piccadilly, cars and bikes simply scattering before us. Acef, headlights on, foot to the floor, conducts a symphony of horns all around us. The motorcycle police literally force cars out of the way at top speed, lashing out with heavy boots. Those who, through surprise or rebellion, do not move over go home with a dent in the door.

On and on we race. Gradually, the houses thin, and we are in the country, heading for the mountains in the distance. Although the houses become fewer, the traffic lessens only a little. We are now on a small twisting country lane, hedges on one side, and green-terraced rice fields on the other. We are still following the pack which, given that we are in a van and the others are on motorcycles, is somewhat difficult. Often on the wrong side of the road, we occasionally lose our escort. Acef doesn't give a shit, though. He is on a roll, Mr. Monte Carlo Rally, savouring every moment. He is invincible. Hand on horn; drivers coming the other way simply have to move over. He is Mad Max. Adrenaline pumping, we are jumping up and down in our seats. Chris and I shout him on. It is a turn-on, King of the Road.

We catch up with the pack again. A police jeep waves us through. Another police jeep forces oncoming cars and lorries off the road. Remember, we are still on the wrong side of the road, passing all the local traffic. Harley is King here, and we are the courtiers. Higher and higher into the mountains we spiral; whenever we need to turn left or right, a policeman is at the junction to make sure we go the right way. We are travelling through some of the most beautiful, tranquil, serene places on Earth like maniacs. It is wild. It is unreal. It is surreal. It is a turn-on. Fantastic! Amazing! This continues for sixty exhausting miles. We arrive at Bedugul totally wasted. Bloody hell!

After all that excitement, the arrival is an enormous comedown. But then again, anything would be an enormous comedown. I think it will take us half an hour to get back to normal; our hearts are still pumping twenty to the dozen. Phew!

We drive into a field at one of the world's most beautiful locations. A hundred throbbing engines break the tranquillity for a few minutes as everyone finds a good place to park. The whole area is lightly veiled in mist, but through a gap in the trees, I see a wondrous temple, its pyramid roof like a Christmas tree, with ten separate levels reducing to a point at the top. It is built on a promontory in the middle of an ice-cool, clear lake, surrounded by jungle and mountains. The serene lake of Bratan is in the crater of an ancient volcano. As the lake supplies all the water for the local people, the temple was built in honour of the goddess of water, Dewi Danu. There are children fishing for minnows from canoes; another canoe ferries firewood to a settlement on the far side of the lake. Somebody mentions that there is an old Dutch forestry house with a once-magnificent garden buried deep in the jungle. Sadly, we do not have time to visit it. The weather is perfect. Clear blue skies, thirty-degree sunshine, a cooling breeze. Good food, good company, good times.

What a day! And it's only one o'clock.

TO JAVA

We leave Bedugul at two o'clock. Our tight schedule means that, sadly, we have to leave our generous hosts and make for the ferry to Java at Gilimanuk, sixty miles away. Sixty miles of mad traffic and no police escort this time to make life easy. What a lovely road though. Paddy fields, sculptured out of the hillsides in parallel tracks, look like a three-dimensional version of an ordinance survey map. Separating each track, and maybe three metres wide, is a dike half a metre wide. From a distance, they look like hundreds of railway tracks following the contours of a hill. The area between the tracks is filled with water and rice plants. At this time of year, the hills look as though they are covered in foot-high grass. They are very lush, very green. In a week or two, the rice will be harvested; soon after will follow the Rice Festival, an incredibly joyous time for the people of Bali and dedicated to the Rice God, Dewi Sri.

We drop down the mountains all the way to sea level. Right to the sea, in fact! Rice fields run right to the sea edge. Large breakers literally lap the edge of the paddy fields. Not one scrap of cultivatable land is wasted here. We follow the coast for a few miles and head inland again through dense palm tree forests. Not many people now. The occasional little monkey scurries across the road and instantly disappears up a tree. Cutting through the trees are shallow, fast-flowing streams. The water, over thousands of years, has polished the boulders into glass, making the river bed look like it is covered in a carpet of dark, shiny marbles. Volcanic grey, perfectly smooth, they range in size from tiny to two metres in diameter. Beautiful!

All of a sudden we stop. The vehicles in front disappear around a corner. What's this? - A breakdown? - Road works? The ferry queue maybe? No warning that we noticed. No signs. After being stationary for ten minutes, we are directed by a man in a uniform to enter a large dusty area that now appears to be a car park. There appear to be very few cars on Bali. In the ferry terminal, I see only two cars, a white Honda Legend and a white Toyota Carina, surrounded by dozens of minibuses and trucks. As at all ports, vendors wander about plying their wares. Newspapers, cigarettes, bottled water. I try some nuts. They taste like soft peanuts and come wrapped in a brown peapod, with three nuts in each. A small barrow with a glass cabinet is selling fruit salad. Fresh fruit plucked from local trees and cubed. Pineapple, star fruit, a golf ball-sized fruit that looks like a red pepper and tastes like cardboard, and cucumber—quite refreshing but a little strange if you're used to having it in a cheese sandwich. Served in a small plastic dish, the mixture is covered in brown molasses and served, believe it or not, with a very hot chilli sauce and salt. Everything in Bali comes with chilli sauce. Mixed with fruit and molasses, I have to say it is excellent. An upcoming surprise lined up for friends at a dinner party, I can tell you.

The ferry leaves Gilimanuk at five o'clock, arriving at Banyuwangi, on Java, around one hour later. It was a fairly pleasant journey across a fairly pleasant strait, the vista of a traditional cone-shaped volcano being spoiled by the presence of a line of huge pastel green painted oil tanks. At least they are green, a nod to the environment, or a coincidence? On the ferry and because we are filming, we are lucky enough to be treated like VIPs, being allowed to sit on posh, blue-painted wooden benches of the type found halfway along Southend Pier, and situated in a small fenced-off area next to the ship's bridge and away from the rest of the passengers. To pass the time, we are kindly offered some local coffee. Black coffee tasting like the powdery remnants found at the bottom of a

Sugar Puffs box, mixed with the contents of yesterday's ashtray and half a pint of Russian tank sump oil. An acquired taste! The normally conservative Chris drinks his. No one else does.

Crazy way to make a living

As we leave the dock, we see a line of young guys precariously balanced on the wrong side of the protective rail that runs around the ship. Passengers are throwing coins into the sea. Shockingly, one by one, the youngsters dive off the ship and into the murky water, around ten metres below, and search for the coins in the mud. What a desperate way to make a living.

TO BROMO

We drive from Katapang, the entry port for Java, to Bromo largely in the dark. Chris, Bagu, and I are in the second van with Amin, a slightly less practiced driver, shall we say, than

Acef. The road from Pobbolinggo, a small town at the base of Mount Bromo, is forty-five kilometres long and uphill all the way, and gets steeper and steeper and steeper. Around five kilometres from Bromo proper we stop at a gatehouse and pay two thousand rupees each as an entry fee to the volcano rim area, in Bromo National Park. We continue on and up toward our hotel. Four people and lots of luggage were beginning to tell on our tiny vehicle. Amin, I was beginning to think, was far more used to driving on the flat. Long steep hills and hairpin bends are not his bag. Changing gear and slipping the clutch a little too often, Amin struggles to cope with the particularly steep bits. Meanwhile, half a bottle of Jim Beam has taken its toll on Chris. He is fast asleep, deep asleep, snoring and groaning and coughing and moaning with his head on my lap. Sadly, Nok he is not!

A nasty smell and, moments later, the clutch surrenders. We are now stuck on a very dangerous one-in-three slope. It is pitch black, midnight, truly in the middle of nowhere, and we are beginning to slip backwards. Amin is fighting desperately with the now creaking and crunching gearbox. He heaves on the hand-brake with all his strength to stop us disappearing into the deep black abyss that we can't see, let alone avoid. I frantically scream at Chris to wake up. Bagu jumps out. I am shouting at Chris, shaking him, but still he won't wake up. Moaning and going on incoherently in his drunken stupor, slumped on my lap, Chris is preventing me from escaping, and I am not over chuffed. Amin wrestles with the controls trying to save the situation. The other vehicle overtakes us and, seeing our obvious difficulty, quickly pulls up in front. To my mind, behind us would have been a better idea as that would stop us disappearing over the edge. I cannot make that suggestion though, because I still have the demented Chris to cope with. I try to climb over him, open the door, and chuck him out. With a scramble and a tug, I drag him out, half awake, head rolling, and not knowing whether it was Cup Final Day or breakfast time. The others jump out of their van and quickly chock our wheels with lumps of rock. We all run to the back and try to prevent the van from rolling backwards, pushing and shouting all the while to the driver. In his panic, Amin, the dick-head, selects reverse gear, and we all nearly get run over. We scatter and scream as Amin realizes his mistake. With more chocks, brute strength, and some luck, we manage to stop our runaway vehicle. Relieved, we swear a lot and recount our near disaster to the others moment by moment. Remarkably, Chris is now sober. We wait a few minutes for the clutch to cool down. With us all pushing, the clutch still slipping and the engine revving its bollocks off, Amin finally gets it rolling, keeps going, and disappears into the darkness, too afraid to stop.

We now have eight people, one little van with four seats and luggage stuffed into the back - all needing to get to the hotel a few kilometres away. The main worry, of course, is whether all this would be too much for this van. We don't want to burn out another clutch. No worries this time, albeit seriously squashed, with Acef driving, we safely arrive at the Bromo Cottages hotel just after midnight. It was closed. Oh dear, that's a shame we thought! It's dark, cold, we have almost been killed and we're now on the top of a live volcano with nowhere to sleep. Off went our trusty Bagu to sort it out. And he did. The eight of us doubled up, sharing musty, slightly damp, tatty, but it must be said, clean chalets once again Hi-de-Hi style. We are absolutely knackered; over the previous twenty four hours, we'd had a night of drunken revelry, the incredible ride-out, the ferry, driven a few hundred miles and broken down on a volcano. We are now drinking another cup of the delicious Russian sump oil, this time whitened with some white emulsion that had been left in the shed with the lid off. Doesn't taste too bad this time, though – I think I must be getting used to it, or too numb to notice. It is one o'clock. Reveille will need to be at three thirty if we want to film sunrise on Mount Bromo, reputably one of the most sensational sights in the world. I crash into my bed and, just as I fall asleep, am immediately woken up again by a loud banging on the door and someone shouting something incomprehensibly foreign. Oh no, my two hour sleep ration has passed in the wink of an eye, although I reckon this guy has just put the clocks forward to fool me. I wake Chris, who, whilst looking like a ghost, is remarkably cheerful considering the Jim Beam he has recently consumed. We get up and meet everyone else.

MONDAY 13 JUNE

SUNRISE ON THE EDGE OF THE UNIVERSE

We stumble down a cobbled slope toward the cafeteria, our groggy group blending into a bustling hive of sunrise seekers. The contrast is jarring: outside, an oppressive blackness; inside, an explosion of harsh fluorescent lights that sting the eyes. Rows of bright red Formica-topped tables and plastic chairs stretch across the room, evoking memories of a sterile school canteen. The cream-colored walls are broken only by a few tatty posters clinging on with bits of peeling Sellotape. It's cold, uninviting, and, frankly, a shock to the system.

Slumped at the table, heads in hands, we grumble about the ungodly hour and how dreadful we feel—all except for Bagu the Magnificent, who is as annoyingly cheerful as ever. A waiter delivers steaming cups of what can only be described as liquid misery. Its mere appearance is enough to turn the stomach, but I force myself to drink. This morning, I have no choice.

Bagu works his magic and secures six horses to take us to the rim of the volcano. Our two drivers wisely opt to stay behind in bed. Off we go into the darkness, tiny torch beams barely piercing the night as our horses tentatively descend a steep, slippery slope. Hooves falter on the uneven path, eliciting the occasional squeal from startled riders. The unknown looms ominously in the black void beyond the trail.

After ten nerve-wracking minutes, the path flattens out, though visibility remains nonexistent. The horses, seasoned veterans of this route, follow an unseen guide. I can just make out white dots flanking the trail, presumably marking its edges, though I dread to think how narrow the margin for error might be. We press on for over an hour, the monotony of the ride broken only by the discomfort of the saddle and my futile attempts to spot the Southern Cross. Sean calls out directions, but to my untrained eye, the stars blur into one indistinct canvas.

The climb begins anew as the horses navigate a final steep ascent. Ahead, torch beams dance like fireflies, guiding both horses and riders. At last, we reach an improvised base camp, some 200 feet below the volcano's rim. Dismounting, I finally meet my guide; I take his name, Muah, and scrawl it on a scrap of paper. In the dim pre-dawn light, I see our horses tied to wooden posts, a scene straight out of an old Western.

As the sky blushes pink, the guides urge us onward. "Hurry, hurry!" they shout, gesturing toward a staircase of 128 unforgiving steps leading to the rim. Laden with film equipment, we trudge toward the base of the stairs. Around us, a diverse crowd ascends—a mix of pilgrims and local schoolchildren; some elderly women are being assisted by their families, a group of chattering Japanese tourists, a pair of rugged-looking European backpackers and a few laid-back Aussies.

The climb is a gruelling test of endurance. Each step feels like a monumental effort in the thin, sulphurous air. At 8,000 feet above sea level, sleep-deprived and hauling heavy gear, I feel my legs seize up just 20 steps from the top. Sean, ever the motivator, cheers me on: "Just one more step. You're almost there!" But my body feels leaden, each step requiring an almost inhuman effort.

Finally, I reach the summit. In the faint morning light, silhouetted figures jockey for the best vantage points. Some seem unaffected by the climb, but many, like me, are visibly drained. I can't help but think a Stannah stair lift would be a worthy addition to this treacherous ascent.

At certain times of the year, thousands of people jostle for space along the narrow, precarious rim of this hundred-meter-wide volcanic crater. It's a perilous spot to linger. A misstep inward could send you plunging into the fiery abyss, where incessantly burning yellow flames and bubbling white-hot lava would consume you in an instant. Outward, the sheer, dusty conical slope stretches thousands of feet down, an unforgiving tumble. The craggy, ten-foot-wide path is far from safe. Thankfully, today the crowds are sparse, and the risk of being nudged over the edge is minimal.

I am utterly spent. My heart thunders in my chest, as if a mallet-wielding maniac were trying to hammer his way out—a sensation eerily reminiscent of John Hurt's infamous scene in Alien. The sulphurous fumes choke me, stealing the deep breaths I desperately need to recover. Waves of nausea grip me as I struggle to compose myself. Slowly, mercifully, I begin to regain control. The climb has taught me an invaluable lesson: racing at high altitudes is foolish. As it turns out, the rush was unnecessary—we have more than enough time.

As the horizon lightens, the sheer magnitude of our location begins to sink in. Words falter in the face of such natural grandeur. We are standing on the rim of Mount Bromo, one of the world's most active volcanoes, and the scene unfolding before us is otherworldly. To grasp the enormity and splendour, imagine the Grand Canyon, but painted in pumice gray. Yet this is no mere canyon. A delicate, shimmering mist hovers above the vast lower plateau, casting an ethereal, almost enchanted glow over the landscape—a scene straight out of The Lord of the Rings. I

t wouldn't have surprised me to see an army of orcs marching across the flat, dusty plain, their forms emerging ghostlike through the mist. Nearby, another volcano rises, so close you feel you could reach out and touch it. Its perfect conical shape is mesmerizing, its surface etched with the sharp, triangular "teeth" left by its last eruption. The precision is uncanny, more akin to an engineered gear wheel than a product of nature. The rising sun casts deep shadows across its body, accentuating its flawless symmetry and jagged edges.

Being here on Mount Bromo, in this realm of primal power and unearthly beauty, one word reverberates in my mind: WOW.

The wait for sunrise feels interminable, like watching a kettle and willing it to boil. (I can't believe I even thought of something so trivial!) The horizon is steadily brightening, red streaks bleeding into the sky, intensifying with each passing moment. A tingle spreads across the back of my neck, and a shiver runs down my spine. I can't tell if it's the crisp morning air or the anticipation causing it. It's cold, even for me, wrapped in jeans and a leather jacket and used to Britain's dreary weather. Those without coats visibly shiver, clutching themselves for warmth.

As the first sliver of yellow light pierces the horizon, a soft cheer ripples through the gathered crowd. Children bounce with excitement, old women lean into their daughters and granddaughters, and a group of Japanese tourists clap politely.

It's a cool moment, in every sense of the word.

Gunung (or Mount) Bromo is one of the most powerful and awe-inspiring volcanoes in the world. Sitting on its rim feels like peering over the edge of the universe. Below us stretches an expansive, seven-mile-wide sea of lava sand, its surface marked by jagged, conical peaks. At sunrise, the ethereal beauty of the scene is amplified by the swirling morning mist, which drapes the landscape like waves lapping against steep, black cliffs.

The volcano has long been revered by the Javanese people, who view it as a mystical "Fire Mountain." Bromo derives its name from Brahma, the Hindu god of creation, a nod to the region's deep historical ties to the Hindu-Majapahit Empire. Even today, the Tenggerese farmers of the area honour the volcano during the Kesada festival each January or February. They ascend Bromo in a vibrant procession, casting offerings

92

into the crater to appease the volcano's deity. Rice, money, and even live animals are thrown into its depths. Some daring souls venture into the crater itself, risking a fatal fall to catch the offerings—a tradition that allows them to keep whatever they successfully retrieve.

This ritual is rooted in a legend of sacrifice. According to the tale, a 15th-century princess and her husband prayed atop Bromo for children, and the gods answered their prayers— with one chilling condition: their last-born child must be sacrificed. After bearing 25 children, they tried to defy the divine decree, only to face fiery wrath. Ultimately, they yielded, casting their youngest into the crater. Folklore says that the voice of the sacrificed child still echoes, commanding the people to honour this tradition each year.

Standing here, I can't fathom the courage it would take to participate in such a ritual. The heat, the stench of sulphur, the precarious footing—everything about the crater screams danger. The steep, slippery walls make any misstep potentially fatal. And yet, the faith of the Tenggerese persists.

Bromo itself is a crater within a crater, one of four mountains that rise from within the ancient Tengger caldera. Another legend tells of an ogre who, in his obsessive love for a princess, dug the great Tengger crater using half a coconut shell. The king, sceptical of the ogre's determination, tricked him by faking dawn, causing the ogre to abandon his task in despair. The discarded coconut became Mount Batok, and the trench he dug became the sea of lava.

There's something profoundly moving about being here. I've visited many pilgrimage sites—Lourdes, for instance, where faith and tourism blur into an unholy mix of plastic Virgin Marys and mass-produced candles. Despite the sincerity of its visitors, it feels hollow, a place of unfulfilled hope. But here, on Bromo, the balance shifts. The raw power of nature dwarfs human endeavour. The serenity, the magnitude of this place— it's spiritual in a way I've never experienced.

For the next hour, we shoot footage for the film. Steve has me strike "thoughtful" poses, perched in precarious spots to give the illusion of solitary reflection. While I understand his artistic vision, the entire exercise feels hollow, almost disrespectful to the profound emotions this place evokes.

Covered in dust and utterly exhausted, we begin the descent. Finding my guide, Muah, is easy—most of the crowd has already left. By now, the early morning tourist rush is still hours away.

I ride back alone, letting the silence settle over me. The others chat and joke, but I feel disconnected, as though they've missed the point entirely. The narrow paths and the white stones marking our route, which seemed so ominous in the darkness, turn out to be far less treacherous than the rumours suggested. We're in the middle of an expansive plain, and the stones merely mark the most direct route. Not that they're needed; my faithful horse knows the path by heart. After countless trips, he has no intention of getting lost—not with breakfast waiting for him back at base.

THE ORIGINAL 700 YEAR OLD FAT BOY IN PASRADISE

Given that the working title for this trip is Fat Boy in Paradise, one of the most important stops on my journey is to see the monument of the man whose name inspired it. He is King Kertanagara of Singosari, immortalized in a statue created in 1289. Known locally as Joko Dolog or "Fat Boy," the statue resides in Surabaya, just across the road from the East Java Governor's residence.

After a simple breakfast of omelette, bread, and strawberry jam, we set out on a three-hour drive through the lush, green Javanese countryside. Our destination is clear: find Joko Dolog or whatever remains of his memorial. Surabaya, Indonesia's second-largest city, welcomes us with its usual hustle and bustle, and the search for the statue begins.

Acef, our driver, diligently asks locals for directions. Each person seems confident in their guidance, but as we soon discover, their enthusiasm doesn't always align with accuracy. Their friendly, if misleading, instructions result in an impromptu city tour. Still, after a few wrong turns and some persistence, we finally arrive at the site.

At first glance, the statue is modest, far from the grandeur one might expect for the "original Fat Boy in Paradise." Contrary to his nickname, the figure isn't particularly fat—perhaps he was considered portly by the standards of his time. Sitting in the lotus position atop a one-meter-high plinth, the grey stone statue is unadorned save for the faint remnants of gold embellishment that once graced its surface.

The plinth, bearing a neatly carved Sanskrit inscription, rests on a larger marble platform approached by four steps. According to the aged custodian who watches over the statue, the inscription details the history of Java and commemorates the reunification of the island, previously divided into two kingdoms. The statue, originally from Singosari, was transported to Surabaya around three centuries ago and remains a pilgrimage site for some locals. Evidence of this devotion is seen in the two wilted floral garlands draped over the statue, likely placed there a couple of weeks prior. An iron pot filled with burned-out incense sticks sits at its feet, completing the scene.

The statue resides in a 25-metre-square courtyard, which appears to hold ceremonial significance. Scattered around are a number of peculiar head-shaped statues, reminiscent of Easter Island figures but shorter and broader. Their origins may share some connection. The courtyard itself is shaded by an overgrown banyan tree, which, while impressive, casts too much gloom over the area. A touch of pruning would brighten the space considerably.

Encircling the courtyard is a green-painted wrought iron fence with an impressive gate flanked by two weathered, castellated stone pillars. The site, though seemingly insignificant to outsiders, is surprisingly guarded by two caretakers.

The first is an elderly man of about seventy, clad in a well-worn white uniform and baseball cap. He greets me warmly as he opens the gate, his beaming smile revealing a lone tooth. He's small, wizened, and his weathered face seems to wobble with each word he speaks. Using a mix of gestures and broken English, I inquire about the number of visitors the site receives. Smiling broadly, he raises first one finger, then two, confirming that his duties are far from overwhelming.

At the opposite end of the courtyard sits his assistant, presiding over what can only loosely be described as a souvenir shop. The "shop" is a shelf nailed to the back wall of a shed-like structure, displaying two dusty and faded books— likely untouched for decades. The assistant, dressed in a clean but slightly dingy vest, grey trousers, and flip-flops, spends his day idly at a wooden picnic bench. He seems content, though his time might be better spent tending to the courtyard, where wilting flowers and layers of dust lend a tired air to the site.

Despite its worn state, there's a certain charm to this place. Joko Dolog may not impress with grandeur, but as a symbol of Java's history and spiritual traditions, it holds its own quiet significance. The caretakers, with their warm smiles and unhurried demeanour, embody a gentle simplicity that reflects the statue's understated presence.

COMPLETING THE MISSION

From the film's perspective, the most important task here is to document why I've made this journey. The scene begins with me entering the grounds, our aged little friend diligently performing his gate keeping duties. I walk pensively along the dusty path toward Joko Dolog's monument. With one foot on the marble steps, I pause, turn to the camera, and explain the history of the statue and its significance in my story.

We repeat this several times to ensure we capture the perfect take. Additional shots are taken: cutaways of the stone heads, close-ups of plants that appear a bit less withered than the rest, and sweeping views of the courtyard. After wishing the custodians well, we pack up and leave. It's a beautiful, warm, sunny day, and I find myself reflecting on the experience.

While the monument itself feels like something of an anti-climax, this is likely my own doing. In my mind, I had built up Joko Dolog - the Fat Boy in Paradise - to be a grand, towering megalith. I envisioned something akin to Eros at the centre of Piccadilly Circus, set amidst Surabaya's hustle and bustle. But on reflection, he does have his own garden, his own guards, and even a shady banyan tree to relax under. For what it's worth, Joko Dolog is still the heart of my journey.

Harley-Davidson, a partial sponsor of my trip, initially opposed the title Fat Boy in Paradise. Since "Fat Boy" is a registered trademark of theirs - referring to one of their motorcycles - they were understandably cautious about its use in the film. I explained that the title wasn't about their motorcycle but rather homage to this ancient statue. The fact that my motorcycle also happens to be a Fat Boy was purely coincidental. Eventually, they accepted my explanation, but only on the condition that my visit to the original Fat Boy was recorded and included in the film. With today's visit documented, my obligation to Harley-Davidson is now fulfilled.

SURABAYA - Home of the Fat Boy

Surabaya, Indonesia's second-largest city is a sprawling industrial hub with a population of roughly two million. While it serves as East Java's booming capital, it's a city of stark contrasts. Gleaming modern office towers and luxury apartments sit uneasily alongside the grim realities of poverty. The average wage here is pitiful—barely enough to scrape by. A recent story I'd read involved the tragic death of a young woman who campaigned for her colleagues' factory wages to be raised from a measly $1 a day to a still disgraceful $2 a day. The details of her murder remain shrouded in suspicion, and many locals believe that those with power and influence will ensure justice is never served.

This struggle is evident everywhere. Bullock carts laden with produce plod slowly through the dusty streets, relics of a medieval economy trying to survive in a modern age. Thin yet resilient men strain to pedal overloaded becaks—three-wheeled cycle rickshaws—along rutted roads. Rows of corrugated iron shacks are squeezed into every available space between crumbling factories and warehouses. The city is an unvarnished portrait of the "haves" and "have-nots." While the vibrant chaos of becaks, decorated with religious paintings or jangling mementos, adds charm for tourists, life here is visibly hard for its residents. Though becaks are increasingly being banned from city centres as a safety measure, they are still omnipresent, a lifeline for many struggling to make ends meet.

In my opinion, unless you have a specific reason to visit, Surabaya is not a place that rewards casual exploration.

GOOD NEWS FROM RON

The journey to Yogyakarta, the largest city in Central Java, takes a gruelling eight hours. The scorching, sweaty weather makes the trip feel even longer, though the stunning scenery along the way offers some respite. Despite the beauty of the surroundings, the day takes its toll on everyone. Tempers fray as exhaustion sets in, and a dispute breaks out between Steve and Paul over some of the filming decisions.

As usual, Sean steps in as the peacemaker, trying to diffuse the tension. I've noticed that Steve doesn't handle pressure well and tends to overreact. Unfortunately, Paul, being another cameraman, often bears the brunt of these outbursts. With my own concerns to deal with, I decide not to get involved, leaving them to sort out their professional differences.

By the time we arrive at our hotel, the sun has dipped below the horizon. We're all utterly spent. After dragging ourselves to our rooms, I finally manage to shower and savour a refreshing drink. Feeling slightly more human, I head back down to join the others.

That's when I get the news: Ron has made it to Jakarta with the bike! I should feel elated, but until I have all the details, I can't let myself get too excited.

 # TUESDAY 14 JUNE

THE WORLD'S BIGGEST TEMPLE

We arrive at Borobudur around ten-thirty in the morning.
As one of Indonesia's major tourist destinations, its status
is clearly reflected in the gauntlet of shops, stalls, and
enthusiastic vendors that line the approach. The offerings
range from exquisite handmade pieces crafted from local
volcanic stone to truly dreadful items like garish, gold-plated
plastic Buddhas and fans that look like they'd melt in the heat.

An amazing volcanic sculpture of Borobudur 120 x 120cm

Borobudur itself is a different story altogether. The temple is breathtaking—a testament to human imagination and effort. At two hundred meters square at its base, it rises in six square and three circular terraces, wrapping around a hill in the shape of a giant lotus flower, the sacred symbol of Buddha. At its summit, a massive stupa presides over the entire structure. Built around 1,200 years ago, it took approximately a century to complete. Originally painted a golden yellow to catch the sunlight, the grey stone monument that remains today is no less magnificent.

Our guide—a young man with impeccable English grammar but an accent so strong it feels like an aural workout—explains its significance as we approach. The entire temple is a vision of the cosmos, with each level representing a stage of existence, culminating in nirvana at the top. The detail is stunning: more than 400 open-air Buddhas gaze serenely from their chambers, while 72 others sit enshrined in latticed stupas. One Buddha near the main steps is said to bring good luck to anyone who can reach through the lattice and touch its toe. I, naturally, give it a go. Who couldn't use a little cosmic assistance?

The heat is oppressive, and as we climb the steep steps for the umpteenth time to capture every conceivable camera angle, I begin to feel like the temple is testing me. Up and down, left and right—every movement meticulously choreographed to ensure continuity for the final edit. At last, we descend to the lower levels and take a much-needed break on the grass. That's when it hits me: I need to find a toilet.

THE TOILET QUEST

The search begins with a hopeful sign pointing toward the far-right corner of the temple grounds. With the sun beating down on me, I trudge off; muttering prayers to whichever deity oversees restroom facilities. My optimism wanes as I approach a dilapidated wooden structure perched over what appears to be a mushy swamp of dubious drainage.

A cluster of men loiters nearby, their faces a mixture of inscrutable intent and vague menace. Are they guards? Bandits? A secret society of ancient lavatory keepers? Forcing a broad, exaggerated smile (in case friendliness works as currency), I nod politely and edge past them to the door.

Inside, I brace myself for the worst—visions of horrors past in Indonesian public toilets flash before my eyes. But to my amazement, the place is spotless. Not just clean by local standards—pristine by any standards. No foul odours, no suspicious puddles - just a simple, well-maintained toilet.

As I stand there, marvelling at this unexpected oasis, another user informs me in broken English that the men outside are not a threat but rather the most dedicated lavatory attendants I'll ever meet. Apparently, their sole purpose is to ensure the toilet remains in a state of near-divine cleanliness. Feeling a rush of gratitude, I leave a generous tip in the collection plate by the door and return to the group, eager to share the tale of my restroom redemption.

Back at the grass, Chris and Bagu return from fetching a fresh battery, new recording tape, and water—taking their sweet time, as usual. Just as I'm recounting my toilet adventure, a group of schoolchildren arrives, their pristine uniforms gleaming in the midday sun. They chatter excitedly, some brave souls daring to wave at the camera.

The bottle of water Chris hands me is so hot it could double as soup stock, but in the searing heat, it's still the most refreshing thing I've tasted all day. As the kids giggle and point, I sit back and reflect: Borobudur is awe-inspiring, but sometimes it's the unexpected moments—like finding the world's cleanest toilet in the unlikeliest of places—that truly make the journey unforgettable.

A BRIEF TASTE OF FAME

As we relax under the shade of a tree, enjoying the rare respite, it becomes increasingly clear that we are the focal point of a growing buzz among the nearby schoolchildren. Their chatter grows louder, and a few brave ones inch closer, nudged gently by their giggling friends. Their antics amuse me, so I smile warmly in their direction. That turns out to be the signal they were waiting for.

A young girl, with a giggly curtsy and a camera extended in

her outstretched hand, makes her intention unmistakable. She wants a photo—with me. Before I can say a word, two girls sidle up to either side of me, while a third readies the camera, telling her friends to smile. The photo is taken, but that's only the beginning. They swap places, making sure everyone gets a turn, their giggles echoing in the hot air.

Not to be left out, the rest of the group gathers courage and soon engages Steve in the same photo merry-go-round. What starts as a trickle of curious kids quickly turns into a tidal wave. A queue forms. Then another group arrives, and another. Word spreads like wildfire. To them, we must seem like some kind of exotic creatures—a band of long-haired Europeans lugging TV cameras through the heart of Java, a sight as rare as snow on the equator.

Bagu explains that visitors like us, particularly with our unorthodox hairstyles, are an uncommon spectacle in Borobudur. For the thousands of pilgrims and tourists present, our presence is likely a once-in-a-lifetime photo opportunity. While I've had the odd experience of being in someone's holiday snap, such as a Japanese tourist in Trafalgar Square, this—this is on another level.

At first, I can't help but feel flattered. It's not every day someone wants a photo with me, let alone a production line of eager admirers. But after a solid hour of constant posing, my ego begins to sag under the weight of relentless enthusiasm. Steve looks equally exhausted, barely managing a half-smile for the hundredth photo.

Desperate for a way out, we devise a plan: a grand finale. We gather everyone together for one big group shot. Cameras click furiously, capturing the moment, and with polite bows, waves, and as many smiles as we can muster, we make our escape.

Walking back to the car park, I reflect on the surreal experience. It's flattering, no doubt, to bask in the spotlight for a fleeting moment. But I can't help wondering how truly famous people endure this kind of attention day in and day out. The constant scrutiny, the endless selfies, the inability to simply disappear into the background—it must be exhausting.

Blondie's lyrics come to mind: "I'll keep the money, you take the fame." As the heat of Borobudur bears down on us and the prospect of a cold drink grows ever more appealing, I can't think of truer words.

SUICIDE RUN TO JAKARTA

Leaving Borobudur at three in the afternoon, we brace ourselves for the ordeal ahead: a gruelling 15-hour drive to Jakarta. The heat and humidity are relentless, and our cramped Kejang vans—with their spine-jarring suspension, miserable seats, and woeful air-conditioning—do little to lift our spirits.

The first leg of the journey, however, offers a visual reprieve. For two hours, we meander through palm-covered mountain passes on winding country lanes. The vibrant greens of terraced paddy fields stretch as far as the eye can see, contrasting beautifully with the intense blue of the sky. Farmers in broad coolie hats labor under heavy bundles, while wiry men on bicycles navigate impossibly large loads. Chickens, dead and alive, are the cargo of choice. The dead ones dangle like trapeze artists from broomsticks strapped across the bikes, while the live ones squawk indignantly from overcrowded wicker cages. It's a chaotic but mesmerizing scene, as lorries thunder past, missing the cyclists by inches and sending a gale strong enough to rattle the palm trees.

As the sun sets, the idyllic countryside gives way to the true nature of the journey: a high-speed, high-stakes game of vehicular chicken. This mountainous road, with its endless hairpin bends, becomes a treacherous battleground at night. Indonesian truck and bus drivers—paid per trip—are fuelled by a mix of sleep deprivation, cheap stimulants, and pure recklessness. Their bulging, bloodshot eyes glow like headlamps in the dark, a terrifying reflection of their erratic driving.

Time and again, we are forced to the roadside as three sets of headlights rocket toward us, side by side, on what should be a single lane. Blind overtaking on pitch-black curves seems to be the national pastime. At one point, a bus clips our wing mirror as we dive into a hedge to avoid a head-on collision. Our shouts to our own driver to slow down are met with the same recklessness. Whatever madness drives these people, it seems contagious.

By midnight, after five hours of white-knuckle terror, we're utterly drained but too scared to close our eyes. At last, the lights of a roadside café appear at the summit of a long hill, a beacon of respite in the darkness.

The café is a chaotic hive of activity, crammed with trucks, buses, and cars parked in every conceivable direction. The air is thick with diesel fumes, choking out any trace of the cool mountain breeze. As we weave through the smoky labyrinth of snack and cigarette stalls, we enter what passes for a restaurant. It's a scene that would make a health inspector faint: tables that look like they've been salvaged from a landfill, orange plastic chairs sinking into the dirt floor, and food that appears to have been pre-digested.

The menu is an exercise in horror, and I resolve that I'd rather eat a fistful of gravel than touch a meal here. Instead, we stick to bottled Fanta and factory-sealed biscuits, hoping that even this minimal indulgence won't betray our stomachs. The smell of the toilets wafts ominously nearby; pungent enough to knock out anyone who ventures too close.

Despite the discomfort, it's a relief to stretch our legs after hours of being jostled in the vans. I take a short walk, carefully choosing the opposite direction from the fetid toilets, and breathe deeply—well, as deeply as one can in an atmosphere saturated with diesel exhaust.

After the drivers refresh themselves with whatever concoction keeps them awake, we're back on the road. The remainder of the journey passes in a blurry haze of half-sleep and terror. I have no idea what time we finally roll into Jakarta, but I'm too exhausted to care. All I know is that we've survived the madness. For now!

WEDNESDAY 15 JUNE

RON'S DIARY OF EVENTS

The saga of "getting the bike out" finally concluded on Monday, June 13. By that point, I was frantic, envisioning the motorcycle trapped forever in the labyrinth of Indonesian customs. Each day it lingered there added to the mounting costs—storage fees that I, absurdly, was responsible for paying.

To recap: the nightmare began upon our arrival after the dreadful 22-hour journey from Gatwick via Zurich, Abu Dhabi, and Singapore. Exhausted, we were met by Ron, our Aussie fixer, who assured us that the Department of Information (DOI) would assist with clearing both the motorcycle and our camera equipment. That was the theory, anyway.

At Jakarta airport, Ron slipped a few dollars to someone in order to meet us on the customs side. By 5 PM, he was deep in negotiations with customs officials, trying to determine the "price" for their cooperation. Initially, they demanded a laughable $5,000. After an agonizing dance of false smiles and theatrical cajoling, the amount was whittled down to $700—a ludicrous sum for something that should have been free but had been budgeted for nonetheless. I paid the bribe, expecting a swift resolution.

It was not to be.

The camera equipment emerged fairly promptly, but the bike was nowhere to be found. Its exact location became a Kafkaesque riddle: Freight 1? Freight 2? Or, God forbid, "Rush and Handling"—a zone reserved for perishables where the fees could have bankrupted us. The officials seemed to delight in withholding clear answers. What followed was an excruciating series of bureaucratic hurdles that would have made even a chess grandmaster like Karpov weep.

THE CHESSBOARD OF BUREAUCRACY

• Move 1: Obtain a Process Document and locate the bike. Each step involved numerous officials and their insatiable appetite for bribes.

• Move 2: Pay for an airport handling bill and take it to customs to create an Importation File.

• Move 3: Secure an appointment with the customs clearance officer, who asked bluntly, "What's in it for me?" Pay him. Get the file signed.

• Move 4: Another customs officer reviews the documents. Pay him.

• Move 5: Head to the Bond store. Pay porters to search for the bike. Pay again to get a forklift to move it to the customs clearance area.

This absurd pattern repeated itself endlessly. Forklifts came and went, each requiring separate payment. The bike was shunted between International and Domestic customs like a puck in some bureaucratic air hockey game. At one point, the only key to the storage area was missing, prompting us to pay for the lock to be broken—and then for a new lock to replace it.

...And the final indignity? After multiple bribes and inspections, porters had to physically carry the bike the last few meters to our van, each demanding a tip for their efforts. Even the gateman at the exit expected payment to let us leave.

THE AFTERMATH

Ron's triumphant tale of overcoming the odds left us initially impressed but later sceptical. He claimed it cost him $1,000 to "spring the bike," though I now suspect it was far less. His diary of events, while colourful, seems to veer between exaggeration and outright fabrication.

What troubles me most, is not Ron's embellishments, but the broader culture of corruption he so vividly exposed. Indonesia, with its vast natural wealth, is crippled by a system where greed festers at every level. From the powerful skimming millions through shady deals to underpaid workers extorting petty bribes, the cycle perpetuates itself.

Ron's actions leave me wondering: Was he always dishonest, or did the environment corrupt him? Corruption, as they say, corrupts absolutely. Trust, once eroded, is difficult to rebuild.

I can't shake the sadness of it all. In a fairer system, everyone in this country—Ron included—could prosper. Instead, the weight of a corrupt elite bears down on the shoulders of those struggling to make a living. It's a shame, really, that a land so rich in resources is so impoverished in integrity.

THURSDAY 16 JUNE

A WASTED DAY IN PARADISE

Patience is a survival skill in Indonesia. Plans unravel, questions spiral unanswered, and even the simplest tasks stretch into infinity. Today's mission was straightforward: confirm whether a ferry route exists—Dumai to Melaka or Medan to Penang. It should have been a phone call and a clear answer. Instead, Eka, our tireless local ally, spent yet another day chasing shadows. "I must ask the boss," they always say, as though ferry schedules are state secrets. Two days have now become three, and I wonder: is this adventure worth the relentless frustration?

There are moments of brilliance—flickers of joy that pierce through the haze. Memories of Bali's Harley party come rushing back: the laughter, the music, the camaraderie of half-crazed Aussies, and the generosity of Smitty, who lent me his bike. The ride through the mountains, escorted by military police kicking cars out of the way, felt almost otherworldly. Eka, always dependable and glowing with energy, has been my compass in this chaos. And the people—so kind, so giving—make it hard to hold onto bitterness.

Yet the maddening bureaucracy overshadows it all. There's no logic here, no fairness. The threat of arbitrary authority looms large, and corruption permeates every interaction.

The country is a patchwork of haves and have-nots, with the privileged thriving at the expense of the many. Foreigners are seen as bottomless wallets, and the game is to extract as much as possible.

I RIDE MY BIKE - EUPHORIA

Today brought a moment of triumph: I finally rode my Harley on Javanese soil. After days of delays, the bike was reassembled, fuelled, and ready. The engine roared to life, a sound that cut through the frustration and lifted my spirits. Eka, ecstatic and dressed to perfection in her tight t-shirt and jeans, joined me for the inaugural ride. Her excitement was infectious, her arms around my waist a reassuring presence.

The streets of Jakarta, however, are not for the faint-hearted. The chaos is relentless—horns blaring, vehicles swarming like angry bees. A diesel-spewing bus forced me to stop, its

114

choking black smoke nearly making me sick. The pollution here is oppressive, a constant reminder of the city's challenges.

But the Harley turned heads everywhere. Its sheer size and power, illegal for locals to own, made it a spectacle. At the gas station, attendants and onlookers gawked, asking Eka a flurry of questions. When they learned I was riding it to Bangkok, their astonishment turned to admiration.

Our next stop was the Texas Bar, owned by Smitty and Ron. These expat legends have been pillars of support throughout my journey. Smitty, a man of few words, gave his quiet nod of approval. While Eka enjoyed a well-deserved steak, Smitty and Ron warned me about the risks of riding without proper documents. They insisted I call the team to fetch my permits, underscoring the ever-present danger of Indonesia's unpredictable enforcement.

A short ride for fuel turned into an hours-long escapade. Eight miles on the odometer, but a lifetime of stories! The journey today wasn't just about distance; it was a celebration of perseverance, freedom, and the pure joy of being alive.

This is Indonesia: frustrating, intoxicating, and utterly unforgettable.

STEVE STORMS OFF

That evening, we decided to revisit the Jewel of India, the restaurant where we'd enjoyed a fantastic meal with Dave Jackman and his wife upon our arrival in Jakarta. I was finally starting to relax now that the bike was operational, but Steve seemed ready to burst. The stress had clearly taken its toll. While the challenges of this trip were centred on my bike, my dream, and my frustrations, Steve had shouldered the brunt of navigating the bureaucratic quagmire. And in my single-minded focus on my own struggles, I hadn't noticed how much the pressure had been eating at him.

The signs were there, though—his relentless jabs at everyone, the simmering tension that had permeated our days. Each of us was feeling the strain. I was despondent over how little progress we'd made, with only eight miles ridden in over a week. Chris, the stills photographer, felt short-changed, convinced he hadn't been given enough time or freedom to capture the imagery needed for the book. Paul, the cameraman, had been on the receiving end of Steve's frustration, enduring a litany of criticisms about his technical abilities. Only Sean, ever the steady hand, seemed to weather it all, calmly going about his business.

Sensing the mounting tension, I decided to address it head-on. With the bulk of the journey still ahead, the team needed to function cohesively. We couldn't afford internal strife—not when we were aiming to create an award-winning travel film. So, as delicately as I could, I suggested we talk openly about our plans and what we wanted to achieve.

But I hadn't anticipated the bomb I'd just lit.

Steve erupted. He bolted upright, finger jabbing the air as he shouted. "We agreed in London that you're the boss there, and I'm the boss here. So shut up and fuck off!"

His words hit like a slap. The restaurant fell silent.

Steve wasn't done. He railed about how he alone was responsible for making this film, for making decisions, for solving problems. I, apparently, was to stick to riding the bike and leave everything else to him.

We tried to defuse the situation, acknowledging the immense stress he was under and offering to help. But Steve wouldn't hear it.

"You're all cunts!" he screamed, before hurling his chair across the restaurant and storming out.

We sat in stunned silence, the air thick with disbelief. Here we were, at the dawn of an epic adventure, hoping to create something extraordinary, and our director hated us.

My appetite vanished. The dream of a lifetime was rapidly unravelling into a nightmare. The customs ordeal had drained a significant chunk of our budget. My Harley had barely made an appearance on camera, and we were about to embark on a gruelling 4,000-mile journey through some of the most remote regions on Earth—with a fractured team.

Sean, the group's de facto peacemaker, finally broke the silence. He assured us he would have a quiet word with Steve in the morning. Sean had stayed above the fray, steering clear of the bickering, and seemed like the best person to reach Steve.

"Don't worry," Sean said with calm conviction. "It'll be all right in the morning."

I wanted to believe him. But as I sat there, the weight of everything pressing down, it was hard to shake the feeling that our greatest challenge wasn't the road ahead—it was us.

 # FRIDAY 17 JUNE

TRAPPED IN RON´S PRISON

Friday was a day of silent retreat—a collective effort to keep our heads down after the previous night's meltdown. Steve was acting as though nothing had happened, a clear sign of regret for his outburst. I decided it was best to let sleeping dogs lie.

Our focus turned to preparing for tomorrow. The ever-incompetent Ron still hadn't secured all the documentation we needed. True to form, he was spinning yet another tale of how much effort he'd expended on our behalf, claiming he'd had to bribe half of Jakarta to get the bike released. Socially, Ron could be likable, even entertaining. But when it came to business, he was insufferable—deceptive, unreliable, and inept.

His stories were riddled with inconsistencies, which became glaringly obvious whenever Bagu, our translator, spoke with Ron's wife. She, unaware of her husband's fabrications, would innocently reveal the truth, leaving us even more exasperated.

It was becoming painfully clear that Ron's inefficiency had significantly delayed the bike's release. Worse, his clumsy attempts at bribery had likely exacerbated the customs officials' opportunism. Corrupt as they were, they saw Ron for what he was: a gullible foreigner with seemingly deep pockets and no grasp of the local system. If he'd tried to go the legal route, or even been less blatant with his bribes and under-the-table diplomacy, our ordeal may have been much reduced. Instead, his antics had marked us as easy prey.

Ron was a liability, plain and simple.

The most frustrating part of all this was our dependence on him. I lacked the local knowledge and connections to bypass him, and while Steve had learned a lot during this ordeal, those lessons had come at a steep cost. With our dwindling funds, Ron remained an unavoidable fixture in our plans. Staying at his place was the only way we could afford to remain in Jakarta, forcing us to feign gratitude while knowing full well that every extra minute in his orbit was another chance for him to fleece us.

I could hardly stand it.

The thought of tomorrow—finally escaping Ron's grasp—was the only thing keeping me sane. The sooner we hit the road, the sooner we could leave this maddening chapter behind. Tomorrow couldn't come soon enough.

SATURDAY 18 JUNE

TO SUMATRA

Finally, the day had arrived. After days of bureaucratic delays and endless frustrations at Ron's, we were ready to hit the road. By 6:00 a.m., we were packed and waiting. At 6:30, our ride arrived—a twelve-seater bus that seemed more suited to carrying hobbits than a team of eight adults with mountains of luggage. It was small, cramped, and woefully inadequate.

But the show had to go on, and so began the first of many improvisations. Paul needed to film from the back of the bus, but the rear door opened to a limited angle, held in place by fixed shock absorbers. Sean got to work removing these, while I scavenged through Ron's chaotic garage for a prop to hold the door open. After rejecting an overly flexible aluminium boom pole, I unearthed a sturdier steel tube. Sean nested the two poles together for added strength, creating a makeshift prop that passed our rough-road simulation test. With the tripod set in place and bags wedged around it for stability, the back of the bus became an impromptu filming studio.

As always, space was at a premium. With eight people—myself, four crew members, Bagu, and two drivers—plus our gear, we were stuffed into the bus like sardines. The drivers were essential; with so much time lost to customs delays, we needed to cover 1,500 miles in Sumatra in record time, often driving through the night. It pained me to think of sharing the bike or rushing through the journey. This was supposed to be my moment of discovery, but it was quickly becoming a race against the clock.

Meanwhile, the Harley was loaded onto a pickup truck along with spares—two Avon Gangster white-wall tires, belts, plugs, levers, and a spare battery. Lifting a 400-kilogram bike onto the truck without a ramp or forklift took all eight of us, a wooden pallet, and a lot of muscle. Once secured under a blue tarpaulin, the bike was on its way to Merak, our port of departure.

THE ROAD TO MERAK

After squeezing into the bus, our first stop was the rental company to fit a roof rack. Crawling through Jakarta's rush-hour traffic was agonizing, but eventually, the bus returned with what could only be described as a toy roof rack. It was ridiculously small for a vehicle of this size, but it would have to do.

The toll road to Merak offered brief relief—smooth and fast. Unfortunately, it soon gave way to the chaotic, dusty, and unpredictable Indonesian "A" roads, where lunatic truck drivers seemed to rule.

We stopped for lunch at a roadside restaurant in Seang, which could generously be described as peculiar. The tables were a precarious arrangement of mismatched furniture, and when I leaned on one, it collapsed under me. The menu offered little reassurance: dubious chicken dishes served with a bucket of rice and a side of culinary dread. In Indonesia, such places operate on a "pay for what you eat" system, with uneaten food recycled for the next unsuspecting guest. We stuck to rice with curry sauce, washed down with bottled Coke and Sprite, praying for gastrointestinal survival.

The restaurant's toilet was another story entirely. Styled like a cave, complete with dusty potted plants, it seemed almost whimsical—until you stepped inside. What awaited was a damp, stinking corridor leading to what could only be described as the pits of hell. The smell was overwhelming, the conditions unspeakable. Holding my breath, I completed my business in record time and fled. It was a shared trauma that gave us plenty to talk about on the road.

At the port in Merak, Ron's "servant," Woody, met us and directed us to the pickup where the Harley awaited. Unloading it turned out to be surprisingly simple. A group of locals gathered, and with their help, the bike was lifted down in no time.

With the bike safely unloaded and ready to roll, it was time to board the Kota Bumi Ferry to Sumatra. Despite the day's challenges—cramped quarters, logistical hiccups, and questionable roadside cuisine—we were finally on the move. Sumatra, with all its promises and perils, lay ahead.

Now it felt real. The journey had truly begun. Riding up the ramp onto the ferry, I could almost hear the heroic soundtrack playing in my head. The crew worked with precision, capturing every moment: me riding aboard, then dismounting, peeling off my gloves, and strolling towards the passenger decks like a man on a mission—or maybe just someone who knows they're on camera. Meanwhile, Paul and Sean buzzed around like paparazzi, lugging equipment and dangling from odd angles to get the perfect shot. Everything and everyone was filmed—passengers, bits of the boat, panoramic sea vistas—nothing escaped their lenses.

The ferry itself was … let's call it "retro." A roll-on, roll-off relic that looked like it had ferried vehicles across the English Channel in the days when customer comfort was still a radical idea. Mechanically sound? Probably! - And visually? - Well, it could've used a bit of care and attention - or a lot of it. The vehicle deck was a greasy cavern of choking exhaust fumes, a makeshift dormitory for truck drivers napping on their cab roofs to guard against thieves. Sensibly, our drivers stayed there while we ventured upstairs to brave the unknown.

Upstairs, the passenger deck was a sensory assault. Hundreds of people packed onto wooden benches that looked like they'd been sourced from a medieval torture museum. Trash bins—improvised from oil drums—overflowed, with more garbage on the floor than inside. The cafeteria was particularly "special." Two rickety tables hosted piles of questionable vegetables and fly-covered meat, and a young man with a ten-year-old polo shirt and some seriously optimistic hygiene standards chopped chillies with the intensity of a chef on a cooking show—if the cooking show was set on a ferry straight out of your nightmares. His pièce de résistance? An open fire on the deck! Yes, an actual open flame on a crowded ferry. Somewhere, a health and safety officer just fainted.

And then there was the bird - a little, sad, feathered thing hanging in a tiny black cage from the ceiling. Maybe it was the ship's mascot. Maybe it was the chef's pet. Or maybe it was just as trapped as the rest of us. Either way, it wasn't adding to the ambiance.

Vendors wandered the aisles selling everything from bottled water to neon-orange juice that looked like it had been concocted in a chemistry lab. I tried a sip—it was surprisingly tasty, though I wasn't entirely convinced the water was drinkable. I decided to cut my losses and stick to dehydration.

I PILOT THE FERRY

Needing air and a little less claustrophobia, we climbed to the top deck. It wasn't pristine, but at least it had a breeze. Kids ran around giggling, occasionally pausing to mug for the camera. Most were in simple shorts and T-shirts, but then there were those boys—a group of four who looked like they'd wandered off the set of a '90s hip-hop video: baggy jeans - half-way down, oversized sneakers, bomber jackets, and backward baseball caps. On a ferry between Java and Sumatra, they were a surprise.

Spying a white steel ladder leading to the bridge, I felt a sudden wave of boldness. Why not ask to visit the captain? Nothing ventured, nothing gained. Amazingly, the crew greeted us with grins and handshakes. They seemed genuinely thrilled their ship would be part of our film. Within minutes, we had full access.

On the bridge, I was given the captain's seat—a weathered leather throne straight out of an old dentist's office, complete with hydraulic adjustments. But the real thrill came when they handed me the helm. I'm not talking about a quick, ceremonial photo op. No, this was the real deal.

"Five degrees port!" shouted the pilot.

"Ten degrees starboard!" he continued.

I followed his instructions like a pro—or at least like someone trying very hard not to crash. Another crew member stayed glued to the horizon with binoculars, just in case I decided to play chicken with a passing freighter.

And then came the pièce de résistance: I got to sound the foghorn. Twice!. If there's anything more satisfying than blasting a foghorn across the open sea, I don't know what it is.

The two-hour voyage flew by. By the time we docked, I'd developed a new appreciation for ferry captains. Steering across the open sea was exhilarating, but docking? I wisely left that to the professionals. Still, for a couple of hours, I had been the king of the waves.

This wasn't just a ferry crossing. It was an adventure—and one I would never forget.

THROUGH THR SUNDA STRAIT

The strait between Java and Sumatra is a place where history clings to the waves. Once infamous for pirates and adventurers, its wild waters now feel a touch more peaceful— but not by much. As we sail, tiny tropical islands punctuate the horizon, each a picture of paradise with palm trees and white sand beaches. It's the stuff of buried treasure legends, though I suspect any modern pirate would be more interested in smart phones than doubloons.

To our left (or "port" for the nautically inclined) is the legendary Krakatau. Not west of Java as Hollywood would have you believe, but east. This is the site of the most catastrophic volcanic explosion in recorded history. On August 27, 1883, Krakatau erupted with a bang heard over 3,500 kilometres away in Alice Springs, Australia. Ships 6,000 kilometres distant reported ash fall, and the resulting tsunami, over 40 meters high, devastated Java and Sumatra, claiming more than 36,000 lives. The English Channel itself was said to feel the ripple. Today, all that remains is a shadow of its former self, shrouded in mystery—and, on this particular day, shrouded in miserable weather.

I'd long dreamed of seeing Krakatau, but apparently, it had other plans. Rain and heavy clouds obliterated the view. Classic English luck, really. Someday, I'll return, hopefully with better timing and a decent umbrella.

Still, it's been a good day—the first truly good day since we left Gatwick. The prospect of actually going somewhere has lifted everyone's spirits. The squabbling has subsided, largely because Steve's in a better mood. I piloted a ferry across the Sunda Strait (yes, I'm mentioning that again—it was glorious), and soon, I'll be riding my Fat Boy on Asian soil. Not a quick hop to the petrol station, but a proper, epic ride.

From Bakauheni, the Sumatran entry port, to Dumai, where we'll catch a ferry to Malaysia, lies a tantalizing 1,500 miles of road; and the highlight? - crossing the equator on a Harley-Davidson. Not many can say they've done that – if anyone. Certainly, nobody in the Harley community knew of anyone – not even the legendary Bill Davidson, when I asked him at the

Harley festival in the Southport, in the north west of England. Most of the equator is ocean, and where it does pass over land, Harleys are as rare as snowstorms. A magical moment awaits.

INTO THE JUNGLE

The road starts modestly, lined with roadside vendors peddling snacks and trinkets. Their stalls range from charming new rattan huts with golden thatched roofs to haphazard shacks slapped together from driftwood and rusting corrugated iron. Truck-stop restaurants add their own charm—or horror, depending on your perspective. These dim, windowless dens, lacking electricity and refrigeration, are enough to test even the hardiest of stomachs.

Soon, the road bursts into lush jungle. The massive palms and thick, impenetrable foliage stretch endlessly toward distant mountains. The scenery is spectacular, but the sun—hovering just so in the sky—seems intent on frying my retinas. Even with my trusty Ray-Bans, the glare is blinding. Twenty kilometres in, my eyes ache, and I'm beginning to worry. How will I manage another 2000?

The Trans-Sumatran Highway is a marvel of practicality—a ruler-straight path cut through the jungle. Riding it feels like being in a classic movie: a lone man and his machine, chasing the sunset. I'm overwhelmed by the moment. This is why I came all this way. The hardships, the delays, the aggravations—it's all worth it.

I start to sing. Badly! Not that it matters—there's no one to hear me except the jungle, and it doesn't seem to mind. Emboldened, I shout into the wilderness, my voice swallowed by the dense green expanse. The crew is close behind, but in my mind, I'm utterly alone, lost in the freedom of the ride.

A GLIMPSE OF LIFE

The road twists and turns through sweeping bends, vast rubber plantations, and sleepy villages. Farmers wobble past on bicycles overloaded with greenery, their bundles comically large, like sofas on two wheels. Chickens dart across the road, narrowly avoiding disaster. Villagers sit outside their homes, watching the world go by, while children—beautiful, wide-eyed, and motionless—stand like statues at the roadside.

Teenage boys shout and wave, their energy a stark contrast to the quiet toil of their elders. Here, life seems both beautiful and impossibly hard. With little industry, most scrape by on smallholdings or plantations, earning just enough to survive. It's paradise, but with a price.

DRUNK ON THE MOMENT

As the miles roll by, I'm intoxicated—not by alcohol, but by the sheer joy of being here, in this place, on this bike. I came for moments like this, and now that they're here, they feel even sweeter than I imagined.

It's not perfect—my eyes ache, and I know there are challenges ahead. But for now, as the jungle envelops me and the road stretches endlessly forward, I feel invincible. This is freedom. This is adventure. This is why we ride.

THE MOST INCREDIBLE SUNSET EVER

As sunset approaches, we suddenly find ourselves on a coast road. And I do mean suddenly. One moment, we're engulfed in dense jungle, the next, we turn a corner and—bam!—the sea is right there, lapping at the road's edge like it owns the place. The transition is so abrupt it feels like we've stumbled into a whole new world.

The water stretches out like molten glass, reflecting the fiery hues of the sinking sun. Somewhere along this stretch, I just know there's a spot that'll make the perfect photograph—the kind that doesn't just capture a moment but tells a story. It doesn't take long to find it.

We pull into a small fishing village, and it feels like stepping into a postcard. Before us is a breathtaking panorama: dozens of tiny volcanic islands scattered across the sea, their silhouettes fading into the hazy horizon like emerald stepping stones to nowhere. One, in particular, catches my eye—a perfectly domed green island, rising majestically about 500 metres offshore.

The beach here is less sand and more suggestion, with the water gently nudging against the shore. Frail-looking blue-painted canoes are lined up side by side, some even stacked precariously atop one another. These slender boats, with their twin masts and outriders, seem almost too delicate for the challenges of the open sea. Yet, you can feel the weight of generations in their design—crafted with experience, not luxury.

A little farther out, slightly larger boats bob gently, their tiny cabins offering scant protection from the elements. I spot a lone fisherman hauling in a basket from the water, silhouetted against the shimmering sea like a character out of a dream. The sun continues its slow descent, and here, near the equator, dusk is fleeting—a fiery climax followed by an almost instant curtain of night.

As we set up to capture this scene, the village seems to awaken. Out of nowhere, we're surrounded. Laughing and smiling, the villagers form an eager crowd, with the children squeezing through the gaps to get the best view. Unlike some of the more chaotic interactions we've had on this trip, these villagers keep a respectful distance, watching with quiet fascination as we work.

We don't have long; exhaustion is setting in after a long day. But before we leave, we take a few shots of me silhouetted against the sinking sun, my Harley providing a perfect contrast to the natural beauty around us. Then, with a quick nod to the adults, we invite the children to join us.

That's all the encouragement they need. With whoops of joy, they rush down, giggling and jostling for position around the enormous bike. It's bigger than most of them, but they're fearless, grinning ear to ear as they pose for the camera.

For a moment, everything else fades away—the miles we've travelled, the challenges we've faced, the ones still ahead. In this idyllic little village, with the sun dipping below the horizon and the laughter of children ringing in the air, life feels as simple and as perfect as a picture.

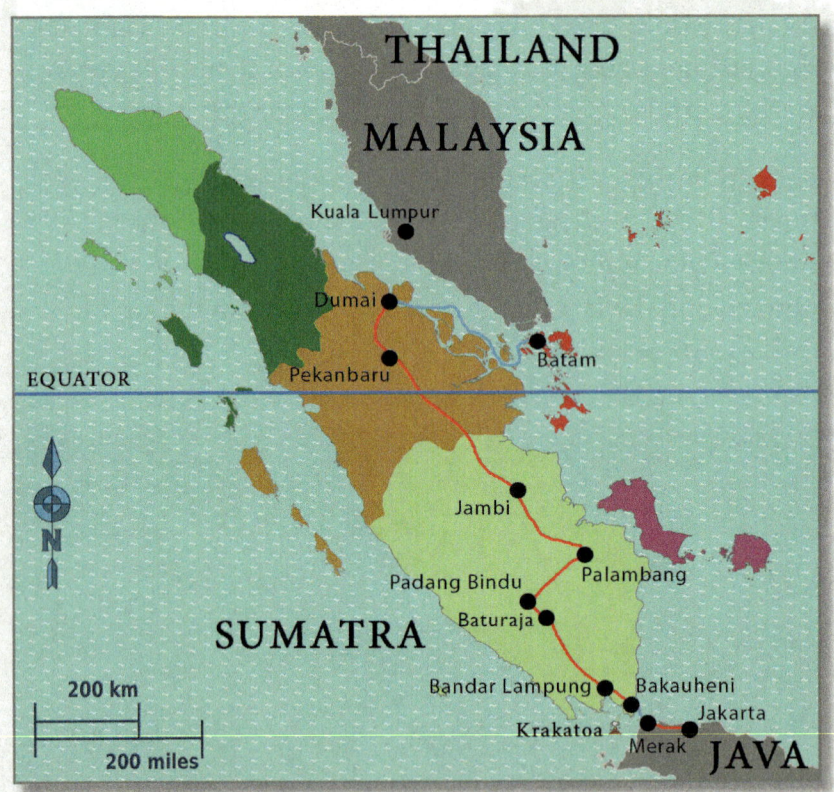

CIRCUMCISION

After spending the night in the luxury of the Sheraton Hotel in Bandar Lampung, it's time to get back on the road. The journey starts slow—our bus is just about knackered. Fully loaded with people and luggage, it sometimes struggles to

132

manage 15 miles per hour on the slightest gradient. When I follow the bus, its clapped-out diesel engine occasionally coughs and splatters me with black gunge if I forget and ride too close. Going uphill, I overtake and wait at the top. It's a proper pain in the backside, though I reckon I'm lucky—at least I'm out in the fresh air. I can't imagine the discomfort of those crammed inside the lumbering beast.

This slow slog continues for about an hour until we pass through a small village where traffic grinds to a halt. A procession of around fifty people is making its way down the road, creating a short tailback in both directions. Half a dozen men, clearly tasked with traffic control, are waving vehicles to a stop—a wise move to protect the marchers from the maniacs who usually barrel through these villages without a thought for what (or who) might be in their path. Judging by the impatient honking from some drivers in the queue, the caution is more than justified.

The parade is a dazzling spectacle. Brightly dressed men, many in vibrant blue shirts, carry tall, semi-spherical sunshades of red and white cotton. Others hold bouquets of sticks adorned with small paper flags, adding to the celebratory air.

Curious, I weave past the stationary vehicles to get a closer look. The parade has almost reached its destination—a collection of large, red, open-sided tents set up in an open space behind a mud wall by the roadside. Intrigued by what seems to be an important event, I park up and investigate.

A man in his fifties, apparently the chief organiser, greets me warmly and ushers me through a white-pillared entrance. Inside, the entire village seems to have turned out to celebrate. Hundreds of people, dressed in their finest attire, fill the space.

Most of the men wear traditional costumes: colorful shirts, loose trousers, and black fez-like hats.

The central tent, a bright orange structure roughly forty feet long, serves as the focal point. Around eighty men stand solemnly in rows, hands clasped in front of them. A long white tablecloth runs down the middle, dotted with small silver bowls containing spices and condiments for the meal to follow. Outside, more guests mill about, sipping orange juice from glasses neatly arranged on trestle tables.

THE BRAVE LADS

As I approach the tent, I notice four small boys—perhaps six to ten years old—being led into a nearby building. They're dressed in ceremonial robes: immaculate white shirts paired with red and green shawls embroidered in gold. Their regal attire reminds me of the Three Wise Men from a nativity play, though here there are four, not three. The first two boys wear pyramid-shaped golden crowns, while the smaller ones behind sport cylindrical headpieces that resemble Christmas cake bands.

This is clearly a momentous occasion, but the boys don't look particularly thrilled about it. Their solemn expressions, framed by a wailing chant in the background, betray a mix of fear and trepidation. It doesn't take long to learn the reason for their nerves: this is their passage into manhood, marked by the traditional circumcision ceremony.

We're invited to attend the festivities, though thankfully not to participate! The atmosphere has the vibe of a church fête. Elderly women sit on benches, dressed in their best shawls and sarongs, while children play quietly, perhaps mindful that it could be their turn next. Watching this unfold, I can't help but feel a pang of gratitude for my Church of England upbringing, where the gravest threat at a church fête was falling off the donkey in the derby. Here in Sumatra, it's a far more public affair to lose your most cherished bit of foreskin.

An elderly man in a neat black blazer and matching hat invites me to follow him. He leads me through a crowd of women into a brightly decorated room at the back of the building. Tinsel and streamers hang from the ceiling, adding to the festive air. At one end of the room, the four boys huddle together in front of a large red wall hanging. The smallest lad, wide-eyed with fear, stares out at the crowd. His piercing white eyes, set against his olive complexion, remind me of my son at six years old. My heart aches for him. This isn't a sterile hospital procedure with a reassuring surgeon; this is a tent in the middle of the Sumatran jungle.

I know the tradition has been honed over centuries, and I

understand that some form of anaesthetic is used these days. But still, I can't help but feel for the little guy. Never has a child needed a hand to hold more than he does now.

I formally shake hands with each of the boys, trying to offer some encouragement, though I'm unsure whether it's for their benefit or mine. The elderly man laughs, sensing my unease.

Back in the main tent, the men prepare for the celebratory feast. They sit cross-legged on colourful carpets and rattan mats, ready to share a meal that marks this significant milestone. The women, meanwhile, gather outside to exchange smiles and laughter, clearly proud of their sons and grandsons.

REFLECTION

As I leave, I reflect on the day's events. It's a reminder of how deeply communal life is here, where milestones are celebrated with the entire village, blending solemnity and festivity. Though vastly different from the quiet privacy of similar rites in the West, there's something profoundly moving about this shared experience. While I wouldn't have traded places with those boys for anything, I feel privileged to have witnessed their courage—and the rich culture that celebrates it.

Leaving the celebration is a surprisingly emotional experience. As I prepare to go, I'm presented with a small but touching gift—an egg wrapped in paper. I'm told it's an honour for them to have had us in their village. In response, I express how deeply privileged I feel to have been welcomed so warmly into their community.

Nearby, I notice a "money tree," a bouquet of sticks adorned with 100-rupiah notes, forming colourful little flags. These, I realize, were the same decorations carried during the procession earlier. Assuming they're gifts for the boys, I offer a few notes of my own. They accept them but seem unsure of what to do with them. For a moment, I worry I've made a cultural faux pas. After all their kindness and hospitality, the last thing I want is to offend.

Thankfully, it's soon explained that the flags are a token of good luck and prosperity, traditionally gifted to honored guests. Relieved, I leave with warm smiles, vigorous handshakes, and waves from the villagers. It's a moment I'll carry with me for a long time—a heartfelt reminder of human connection and generosity.

The notes from the flags presented to me

Meanwhile, Bagu, ever resourceful, has wandered off during our visit and struck up a deal with a local man. The result? - A small pickup truck, complete with its owner as the driver, rented for a few hours. This is a godsend for filming. Not only will it allow the crew to capture varied angles, but I can finally escape the noxious diesel fumes of our battered bus.

Our luck holds as we hit the road again. Just ten minutes later, we roll into a bustling little town, and there, sitting outside a restaurant, are the local biker boys. As I rumble past, I see their jaws drop. Big bikes like mine are banned here, so the sight of a Harley-Davidson in their midst is pure fantasy brought to life.

I wave for them to join me, and in an instant, they're off in a frenzy of revving engines and a Le Mans-style start. What follows is a spontaneous spectacle of wheelies, stunts, and weaving antics as they proudly show off for the camera.

We pull up at the far end of town to chat, and I take in the group. They're a rough-and-ready lot—like pirates straight out of the South China Sea—with gap-toothed grins, weathered skin, and bandanas completing the look. Their bikes, however, steal the show.

These are twenty-year-old Kawasakis transformed by pure passion and ingenuity into "Easy Rider" dream machines. Without access to chrome, handlebars are meticulously hand-painted silver. Scraps of leather are fashioned into hand grips, adorned with whatever embellishments they could scavenge. It's creativity born of necessity, and the result is nothing short of extraordinary.

One rider catches my eye—he's astride a classic: a 1965 BMW R26, single-cylinder, in original condition. The green paintwork is tired and dull, but with a little T-cutting, it would gleam like new. In this tropical climate, rust doesn't stand a chance, and it's a testament to the bike's durability and the owner's care.

The Lampung Motorcycle Club is a ragtag group of true enthusiasts. They may not have much in the way of resources, but their love for motorcycles is boundless, transcending barriers of geography and circumstance. Sharing a moment with them, I'm reminded that passion is universal, whether it's for a gleaming Harley or a lovingly restored relic.

BITS DROP OFF

The day begins perfectly. Riding through lush green countryside and into a small village, I feel a profound sense of contentment. The sky is an endless blue, the sun is shining, and the world feels alive. Little children laugh and play in the streets, while an elderly lady sits in her garden, glancing up as I ride by. It's one of those rare moments when everything feels right.

Back on the open road, the bike hums through vast green rubber plantations and stretches of untamed jungle. The rhythm is perfect—until something strikes my left foot. Startled, I glance down but see nothing. Was it a pebble, maybe? It's wise to stop and check. Pulling over, I give the bike a once-over but find nothing amiss. Up ahead, the bus has also stopped, so I mount up and signal that everything's fine, overtaking them as we continue.

A mile or so later, we approach a steel bridge spanning a ravine. As usual, I apply the front brake gently. Clonk. My heart skips a beat. That sound is never good.

I signal frantically to the bus, glide to a stop, and inspect the damage. It doesn't take long to discover the issue—a brake calliper bolt has vanished, leaving the mechanism barely secured by the second bolt, which itself is hanging on by a single thread. The earlier "pebble" was, in fact, a critical piece of my bike.

After explaining the problem to the crew, I recall where it likely happened and decide to head back to the village. Tightening the remaining bolt, I retrace my path and arrive at the spot. An elderly man, neatly dressed and pottering in his garden, greets me with a smile. Using exaggerated gestures, I explain my predicament. To my astonishment, he understands and assures me that there's no problem—his son has the bolt!

THE SEARCH FOR THE BOLT

As the bus pulls up, I recount my minor miracle. By now, the entire village has gathered, curious to see what's going on. The man's son soon returns, proudly carrying... a nut and bolt. Not the nut and bolt—just a nut and bolt. Clearly, something was lost in translation.

I ask Bagu to enlist the villagers' help in searching for the missing part. Together, we form a human chain, combing the area like a search party. Back and forth we go, scanning the ground meticulously. Alas, no luck. A brake calliper bolt is a specialized, double-threaded shoulder bolt—not the sort of thing you can replace easily, let alone in rural Sumatra.

With no other options, I improvise. Using the bolt provided by the man's son and a couple of washers he happened to have, I fashion a temporary fix. It's a solid seven-out-of-ten bodge job, good enough to keep the brakes functional until I can reach a Harley dealership in Kuala Lumpur.

Grateful for the villagers' assistance, I thank them profusely before we set off again.

ONWARD – AT A SNAIL'S PACE

The day drags on. After a brief stop to capture the sunset over a rubber plantation—a stunning view of the highway snaking through trees that stand like thousands of green soldiers— we press forward. Twelve hours on the road, and we've only covered 200 miles. The light is fading, and the potholed road grows treacherous. Twice, I've been forced into the bushes by reckless lorries. Continuing would be madness.

We reach the small town of Batu Raja and settle on Hotel Kenana II for the night. It's more "Holiday Out" than "Holiday Inn," but it's the best option available. The foyer is clean but spartan, save for two large framed photos of the Indonesian

President.

My room is modest: twin beds, aging mahogany-coloured furniture, and air conditioning that must have been state-of-the-art in 1970. The bathroom, however, leaves much to be desired, with its broken tiles, a faintly mouldy smell, and a squat toilet with two foot pads instead of a bowl. Balancing is an acquired skill, and the absence of toilet paper is a challenge for the uninitiated. Here, a plastic scoop and tub of water are the tools of the trade. I try to embrace the "when in Rome" mindset but find myself yearning for a roll of Andrex and a proper seat.

The hotel staff are wonderfully courteous. Concerned for my bike's safety, they insist it be parked in the foyer under watchful eyes. That kind of hospitality would never happen at a Holiday Inn.

A BRUSH WITH TROPICAL ILLNESS

Steve isn't feeling well. In fact, he's convinced he has something dire. Armed with a thermometer and the Living Planet guide to tropical diseases, he diagnoses himself with typhoid or malaria. The thermometer suggests otherwise— according to it, he's dead. More likely, he just has a cold.

While Steve rests, Paul, Bagu, and I venture out to a local café. Sean and Chris stay behind, looking dubious about our chances of surviving the meal. We order jackfruit curry and rice. Jackfruit, I learn, is an extraordinary plant. When mature, it's the largest tree-borne fruit in the world, about the size of a rugby ball. As a fruit, it's sweet and tender. Before maturity, it's a vegetable used in curries. The curry is delicious, and I make a mental note to try ripe jackfruit someday.

Satiated, we return to the hotel for an early night. It's been a long day, but despite the challenges, it's one I'll remember fondly.

MONDAY 20 JUNE

DESPERATELY BEHIND SCHEDULE

It's decision time. The debacle in Jakarta has left us miles behind schedule and dangerously over budget. As the days pass, it becomes increasingly clear how Ron's incompetence has landed us in this mess. His tall tales about knowing Tommy Suharto and the importance of the I.M.I. letter were just that—tall tales. The real necessity is the carnet, an internationally recognized document that guarantees our entry and exit from a country.

As if that weren't enough, Ron's story about bribing customs officials was pure fiction—a failed attempt to siphon more money from us. His scam fell apart because neither he nor Mrs. Ron could get their stories straight. It's frustrating because, deep down, Ron is a genuinely nice and hospitable man. Unfortunately, niceness doesn't compensate for his lack of business acumen—or common sense.

If we're to make Bangkok by July 4th for the Harley party I've been hearing about, we need to cut inland, bypassing Sumatra's mountainous terrain. On paper, the inland route has its advantages. First, it's flatter, which is a blessing for our wheezing old bus. Second, it's shorter—just 250 miles from Batu Raja to Palembang to Jambi. In theory, this could be done in a day.

144

But then there's the uncertainty. Our map, supposedly only a couple of years old, shows no road across the swamp to Dumai. Locals insist a new road has been built. While a phone call to the police in Jambi would confirm this in minutes, Steve—ever in his "hope over planning" mode—prefers to gamble on word of mouth.

This lack of organization is maddening. We're constantly reacting to crises instead of planning ahead. Malaysia, for instance, is an afterthought. We have no clear itinerary, no confirmation of anyone meeting us, and no updates for Harley-Davidson, Holiday Inn, or Jim Beam. The latter still doesn't know where to send the promised product.

I'm especially worried about Dumai. If we're delayed there or in Melaka, it'll cost us precious time and money. Ron, of course, promised to handle the documentation, but given his track record, I doubt it's been sorted. Steve assures me Ron took care of it before we left, but experience says otherwise. I can't hold my tongue any longer—this needs addressing today.

PADANG CUISINE

Sumatra has introduced me to Padang cuisine, a style of cooking from West Sumatra that's spread throughout Indonesia. Padang restaurants follow a unique system: pre-cooked dishes are laid out on the table alongside a large bowl of rice. You only pay for what you eat; the rest is taken away.

The dishes are as diverse as they are flavourful:

• Fish curry, with chunks of white fish in an ochre, medium-spiced sauce.

• Deep-fried chicken, coated in curry dust—crispy skinned, though often tough.

- Jackfruit curry, made from the massive, spiky fruit that looks like a green hedgehog. Cooked jackfruit tastes like a mix between potato and melon.

- Morning glory, a leafy vegetable resembling oversized watercress, with a flavour akin to spinach.

- A dark prawn curry, rich with garlic and chillies.

At first, I was sceptical. How long has this food been sitting out? But I've learned to trust my instincts—and Bagu's recommendations. Closing your mind to the "what-ifs" is part of the experience, and the flavours make the gamble worthwhile. My stomach has handled it all beautifully.

In most places, the absence of refrigerators suggests the food is fresh, though a few flies and lukewarm portions are par for the course. Roadside stalls, however, are a safe bet. The fresh fruit—pineapple, banana, coconut, and star fruit—is delicious, and there's always plenty of variety.

One culinary surprise was Sumatrans' treatment of cucumber. Biologically, I know it's a fruit, much like a tomato. But culturally, I associate it with salads or sandwiches. Here, cucumber often accompanies banana and coconut in fruit platters. It's a curious combination, but I've come to embrace it as part of the adventure.

Truck stops, on the other hand, are a different story. Some are decidedly suspect, and even I have my limits.

THE WASHER-WOMEN

Leaving Buturaja behind, we head north along one of the little black roads marked on the map. After the horrors of the Trans-Sumatran Highway—a supposed "main route" littered with craters and dust—it's hard to imagine what these lesser roads will bring. According to our guidebook, white roads might be tarmacked, but black roads are usually dirt. Considering how bad the "red" road was, the thought of worse is daunting. Thankfully, it hasn't rained in a week. Mud and floods might be the only thing more impassable than the T-S.H.

We pass through villages that seem frozen in time. Wooden bungalows are built on sturdy brick pillars, ready to channel floodwaters during monsoon season. Each garden is tidy, with hard-baked earth replacing lawns and fruit-bearing trees— bananas, pineapples—encircling the homes. The wealth of a village is easy to gauge: the better-off ones boast well-built homes, clean streets, and maybe a mini-bus or motorbike under a lean-to. The poorer ones tell their story through peeling paint, neglected yards, and rubbish piles.

For now, the road is a revelation—newly paved and smooth. The sun glints off countless tiny reflective stones embedded in the tarmac, creating the illusion of a black Milky Way stretching into the horizon. Riding along this "carpet of stars," with the sun on my face and a refreshing breeze, I feel a rare moment of bliss.

Our goal is Jambi, but the rush is sapping the joy from the journey. Stopping to explore isn't an option, and we resort to quick snapshots, feigning connection to places we barely pause to notice. Steve's grumpiness about time is constant, while Chris frets over safety at every turn.

Near Meadulo, on the way to Palembang, we cross a small bridge over a river. Below, a cluster of wooden houses lines the riverbanks, some elevated on brick pillars, others closer to the ground. In the river, a dozen or so women wash clothes—a vibrant tableau of daily life.

The scene is mesmerizing. Fully dressed to preserve their modesty, the women wear flowing, brightly colored saris, their movements both purposeful and serene. Some stand waist-deep in the water, while others place their supplies— soap, shampoo, laundry powder—on a raft of lashed-together wooden planks floating nearby. Their ages span generations, from sprightly young girls to grandmothers with practiced hands.

The moment feels cinematic, like a scene from Mutiny on the Bounty when the crew first sets eyes on Tahiti. Adding to the surreal charm, a young man passes by on a cart with solid wooden wheels, pulled by a giant white ox with impressive horns. The timeless simplicity of it all is enchanting.

Before long, the entire village has materialized to inspect the strangers on the bridge. Children chatter excitedly, and young men gather around us, all smiles and curiosity. Their warmth is infectious, and I find myself grinning back.

The washer-women remain focused, not in the slightessed distracted by the commotion above them. Perhaps they're unaware of the scene unfolding on the bridge—or maybe they just don't care. Meanwhile, we attempt to film: me riding into the village, out of the village, and so on. The villagers' unfiltered joy at our presence is heart-warming. I wish I could stay longer. This place feels special, untouched by the rush and chaos of the outside world.

But, as always, time pushes us onward. After forty-five minutes, I wave goodbye to the gathered crowd and ride on, reluctant to leave.

INTO THE HEART OF SUMATRA

The road stretches ahead, winding through rolling hills and lush greenery. The jungle here isn't what I'd imagined. There are no tangled vines or draping ivies. No deep, dark mysteries. No echoes of Johnny Weissmuller's Tarzan. Instead, it's a landscape of striking beauty: vibrant, rolling hills and expansive panoramas.

The true essence of the jungle reveals itself when I stop and kill the engine. It's in the sounds—the screech of monkeys, the melodic calls of birds, and the faint rustle of unseen creatures. And it's in the smells: a rich, fertile scent that feels alive. This isn't the earthy aroma of English farmland with its silage and manure. It's a heady mix of green, living plants, occasionally punctuated by the smoky tang of burning wood.

The air is clear and fresh, free of pollution except for the occasional black puff from our tired old bus. I stay ahead to escape it, savouring the sensory feast around me.

Sumatra continues to surprise and enchant, even as the journey presses onward.

NO PETROL IN THE JUNGLE

The tranquillity of a few hundred miles of jungle is intoxicating. Just one man on his bike, riding the unbroken path ahead, venturing into the unknown, savoring the thrill of going where no Harley Fat Boy has gone before. But these iron horses need feeding, and their appetite isn't satisfied by fruit plucked from jungle trees. As I climb yet another hill, the bike stutters and coughs—a telltale phut-phut, indicating a near-empty tank. I lean to the left, reach beneath the tank, and switch to the reserve. That buys me maybe 20 miles, a few more if I ride with a feather's touch.

Except this isn't five miles outside Cirencester. There's no AA hotline, no roadside café with a handy pump. I'm in the middle of the middle of nowhere—real nowhere. There is jungle to the left, jungle to the right, and endless road snaking ahead.

I flag the bus to relay my predicament, but there's no reassurance there. Their fuel situation is no better—needle well into the black, running on vapours. A tiny thought needles my brain: Why hasn't Steve, the self-proclaimed king of organization, thought to pack a spare can or two of fuel?; especially given that we're on a road so obscure it doesn't even appear on our map.

The butterflies in my stomach grow to the size of bin lids. With every hill, I scan the horizon, hoping for salvation. I see just jungle, more jungle and then a bit more jungle.

I remind myself of the worst-case scenario: one of us hitchhikes to the nearest town, grabs a can, and comes back. That would hardly be a catastrophe - Right? Except I can't recall seeing another vehicle on this road – ever! The prospect of being stranded in an endless sea of green feels far less hypothetical with every passing mile.

A GLIMMER OF HOPE

At the top of a long, winding hill, the road bends left—and suddenly, a village. Relief washes over me like cool rain on a hot day.

And there, in the middle of this tiny settlement, salvation: a petrol station. Well, "petrol station" might be overstating it. Beside the road stands a wooden hut, little more than a makeshift stall with an open front, patched roof, and weathered sides. It looks barely permanent, as though a strong gust might blow it away.

The offerings are eclectic: tins of sardines, warm water bottles, a pair of second-hand Chopper bike wheels, and, on a cracked Formica-topped table, the prize—petrol and diesel. Plastic cans, labelled in fading felt-tip pen, and holding one, five, or ten litres of this life-saving elixir.

The bus pulls up as I dismount, parking on the verge beside the stall. A teenage boy in an oil-stained t-shirt and shorts steps forward with the confidence of someone who knows he holds the key to survival. Using a large funnel for the bus and a smaller one for me, he carefully transfers the liquid gold into our tanks.

As he works, I take a moment to inspect the bike for damage from the brutal Trans-Sumatran switchbacks. Sure enough, a chrome screw securing the passenger seat to the rear fender is missing—rattled loose somewhere along the way. A small circle of paint, no bigger than a one-penny coin, has chipped off from the vibrations. I cover it with a strip of gaffer tape to prevent further wear and silently curse the road's relentless battering.

I stretch my legs, resensitising parts of my body that no gaffer tape could ever protect. With the bike refuelled, a smile creeps back onto my face. The jungle may test my resolve, but with a full tank, I feel invincible again.

The road beckons. I swing my leg over the saddle, rev the engine, and once more ride forward into the unknown.

PALEMBANG

Roughly 150 miles from Baturaja lies Palembang, the industrial hub and sprawling epicentre of South Sumatra, where all roads inevitably converge.

I have a sneaking suspicion that Bagu orchestrated our route through this dense, bustling city. As we navigate its chaotic streets, he tells me stories of the seven years he spent living here in the early 1960s. Back then, he recalls, Palembang felt like a different world—remote, isolated, and predominantly Chinese-speaking. In fact, he says he came close to forgetting his native Urdu during his time here.

But the Palembang of Bagu's memory is unrecognizable now. The city, Indonesia's second-largest on Sumatra with a population nearing 700,000, has evolved dramatically, driven primarily by its burgeoning petrochemical industry. The promise of work has drawn countless rural migrants to this industrial powerhouse, diluting the once-dominant Chinese community.

Palembang's cultural upheaval can also be traced to the violent events of 1965. In the wake of an attempted coup, the city saw a brutal purge of its Chinese population. Many fled to Hong Kong, China, or Macau, while those who stayed were forced to assimilate, taking Indonesian names and abandoning their Buddhist or Taoist beliefs for Islam or Christianity. The Chinese schools were shuttered; newspapers ceased, and even today, Chinese characters remain banned from public signage.

Modern Palembang is a chaotic mosaic of development. Crossing the Musi River via the imposing Ampera Bridge, we are greeted by an extraordinary sight: a mishmash of wooden shacks, corrugated metal roofs, and improvised shelters crammed together along both banks. Some structures extend precariously into the river, propped on spindly stilts that seem barely capable of withstanding the water's rise during floods. Amid this patchwork, more permanent buildings attempt to assert themselves, their tiled roofs standing in stark contrast to the polythene and rusted iron surrounding them.

Navigating deeper into the city reveals a strange juxtaposition of the old and the new. Dusty streets lined with aging, ramshackle shop-houses give way to gleaming glass skyscrapers that feel oddly out of place against this backdrop of Indo-Oriental grit. The modern buildings, no doubt built to dubious standards, rise like islands of ambition in a sea of unregulated sprawl. Electrical wires dangle hazardously overhead, forming chaotic webs between buildings, their precarious loops a testament to the city's haphazard growth.

The streets teem with life. Pedal-powered trishaws dominate the roads, their paint faded and their drivers sweating under the midday sun. They move at a leisurely pace, some ferrying passengers while others wait in clusters, their drivers reclining in the shade or chatting by roadside stalls selling coconuts and fried snacks.

At one intersection, I spot two children sitting on a narrow central reservation. The older of the two, barefoot and wearing ragged clothes, can't be more than eight years old. They dangle their legs toward the passing vehicles, completely unfazed by the danger. The drivers, equally indifferent, weave around them without a second glance, while the children sit, staring into space with expressions of quiet resignation.

After hours of weaving through Palembang's noisy, polluted streets, we finally leave its grip. The cacophony of honking horns fades, replaced by the serene sounds of the jungle. The air clears, and the road stretches ahead, winding through lush greenery. Here, the jungle asserts its dominance. Invisible monkeys screech from the treetops, and the dense foliage emits an earthy, vibrant scent.

As the sun dips lower, it filters through the splayed palm leaves, creating a strobe-like effect that plays tricks on my eyes. The flashing light makes my head throb, but I press on, grateful to leave behind the chaos of Palembang—a city that seems to encapsulate the frenetic, unbalanced pulse of modern Indonesia.

CUCUMBER

The jungle stretches endlessly, a verdant maze under a blazing sun. The air is thick and oppressive—a classic mad dogs and Englishmen scenario. The road cuts through an ocean of green, broken only by the occasional clearing. In one such gap, two shacks stand on either side of the road, their faded wood blending into the dusty surroundings.

On the right, an old woman sits behind a modest stall. Her offerings are humble: bananas and cucumbers - both treated as fruit here. Moments later, the van pulls up, and I ask Bagu to grab me something to eat. He eyes the bananas with suspicion and opts for cucumbers instead. Biting into one himself, he hands me the rest, dismissing my preference for thinly sliced cucumber sandwiches as quaint absurdity. His look says it all.

While Bagu's occupied, I attempt conversation with three men lounging under the shade of a veranda. Their faces, tanned and weathered, reflect both amusement and bemusement as they listen to me. Using a mix of gestures, broken phrases, and a map, I glean that we're near Merlung, a small town about halfway to Jambi. After a few photos and polite smiles, we're back on the road.

The map marks this route as "variable quality," but it's a pleasant surprise. The smooth black tarmac and painted white lines rival any British "A" road. Choosing this path over the highway was a stroke of luck.

The miles roll on, each one affirming my reason for this journey. While the bus passengers endure stifling heat and sticky discomfort, I revel in the wind, the sun, and the unbroken road ahead. This is why I came here: freedom. The Harley hums beneath me, carving through landscapes where no Fat Boy has ventured before. It's the antidote to Jakarta's bureaucracy, the strained crew dynamics, and the maddening inefficiency of this production.

Villages dot the journey, their inhabitants pouring out like waves as we arrive. To them, we're a travelling circus—a strange blond man on a massive bike, accompanied by a foreign film crew. They touch the Harley, stroke its chrome, and offer cigarettes with beaming smiles. Sometimes, it's profoundly moving. Other times, it's overwhelming, their curiosity manifesting as a swarm of fifty or more, trailing me like an invisible chain.

By the time we reach Jambi, night has fallen. It's nearly ten when we secure rooms at a three-star hotel, and I barely register the modest $30-a-night rate. After freshening up, we gather in the hotel's cool marble restaurant. It's cavernous and empty, save for us.

We clear out their stock of cold beer and finally place a food order. Bagu's selection seems overly ambitious for the late hour, but I let it slide. The day's frustrations weigh heavily: Steve is irritable from illness; the desperately under-powered van slows our progress; and I feel tethered by the crew's inefficiencies. My Harley might be my Fat Boy, but this hardly feels like paradise.

The food takes forever. By 12:30 a.m., nearly two hours after ordering, my patience is threadbare. When the dishes finally arrive, I'm too angry to eat. Steve is too sick, and Sean and Chris scrutinize the meal as if it's laced with tropical diseases. Only Bagu and Paul make an effort, but most of the food goes untouched.

Frustrated and exhausted, I retreat to my room. Sleep doesn't bring relief, only the lingering weight of another long day ahead.

 # TUESDAY 21 JUNE

THIEF

I can't shake the gnawing anxiety about Dumai. Will we actually be able to leave Indonesia from there? Will there even be a ferry waiting? I've grown to love the warmth of this country—its people, its lush landscapes, the spicy food, and even the unrelenting sun—but the bureaucracy terrifies me. It's an impenetrable wall of rules and paperwork that I can't navigate. Without Bagu to smooth things over, to decipher, to negotiate, Dumai feels like a gamble with impossible odds.

What if the necessary paperwork hasn't arrived? What if it's lost in some bureaucratic purgatory? Steve brushes off my concerns, accuses me of worrying too much. But it's not just worry; it's the helplessness that eats at me. I'm used to being in control, calling the shots. Here, I'm a passenger in my own story, and I hate it.

There's no confirmed fixer waiting for us in Malaysia. Bagu still hasn't located him. Has Ron even faxed the exit certificates to Dumai? Every unknown mounts up onto the last, and I can't stop the spiral. Will we run out of money before we hit Bangkok? Will I grow old here, trapped in this purgatory of unresolved paperwork and stalled plans?

And Steve...his sullen moods are the perfect storm cloud

to my hurricane of frustration. Today's the day I have to fix this—if only for my sanity.

The day doesn't get off to a good start. My Handy cam bag is missing. The camera itself is safe, but without the charger, it's as good as useless. Panic sharpens my edges as I start knocking on doors, asking everyone. Nothing! The van is torn apart, every corner searched. Twice! Three times! Nothing!

Bagu makes the call to the hotel in Baturaja. Nothing either. I'm trying to keep my temper in check, but it's a losing battle. I comb through the van again, as though it'll magically appear if I glare at the mess hard enough. And then—there it is - on Steve's floor.

"Sorry," he mumbles, utterly insincere.

Arsehole!!

We're finally on the road to Pakanbaru at nine, stopping a short way up for petrol. That's when I notice it. The chrome cap, at the end of my handlebar grip, is gone. A small thing, really - just a decorative piece with the Harley-Davidson bar and shield logo. But it was mine.

That's why the alarm went off at 6 am; someone had stolen it.

Three days, three problems: the brake calliper, the seat-retaining screw, and now the grip cap. All small, solvable issues, but the pattern is depressing. If trouble insists on following me, I hope it continues to arrive in bite-sized pieces. Anything bigger, and I'm not sure how much more of this I can take.

TO PAKANBARU

The morning starts with a bit of creative flair. We're clamping the Handy cam onto poles, attaching it directly to the bike, and capturing odd angles—close-ups of the headlight, the handlebars, and sweeping views from the saddle. It feels like trying to make art out of chaos. The weather, thankfully, is still perfect.

The roads remain good, though I'm growing weary of the jungle. Sumatra seems to be an endless green expanse, stretching for over a thousand miles, almost entirely cloaked in dense rainforest. It's stunning, yes, but there's such a thing as too much jungle. Winding roads that lift us into the hills are a welcome relief. Up here, the panoramas stretch endlessly, offering views far more inspiring than the relentless press of trees.

Chris, meanwhile, is descending into his own personal misery. His stomach has turned against him, and he's convinced he's on the brink of contracting every tropical disease known to man. Mosquitoes, food, water, even the very air—he sees them all as enemies. Chris survives on an arsenal of Dia-reez and would probably bathe in DDT if given the chance. He loathes the toilets, balks at bathing with a scoop from a water tank, and looks as though he'd sell his soul for a proper hot shower. He's more Surrey suburbia than the intrepid explorer of Bandung.

We stop at the top of a hill to film some road footage. The bus becomes our makeshift dolly. The camera is mounted on the roof, facing backward, and Paul climbs up to operate it. Perched precariously between the roof rack and a saddle cam—a beanbag-like contraption for stabilizing the camera on uneven surfaces—he looks anything but secure. Three metres off the ground, swaying with every turn of the van, Paul signals the driver and we're off.

I follow close behind on the bike, weaving in and out of the camera's frame, testing different angles. It's a beautiful day. The sun blazes in a cloudless sky, the temperature hovers around ninety degrees, and there's no helmet law to stifle the feeling of freedom. This is bliss. If only England could be like this—a perpetual summer to lift the spirits and evaporate troubles, at least for a while.

After about ten minutes, we call it a wrap. Paul's had enough of playing stuntman for one day, and he's confident he's captured some good footage.

Chris, however, is still in agony. His stomach cramps are relentless, and he's moaning louder than the cicadas in the jungle. He's desperate, but no amount of desperation will drive him into the wilderness to relieve himself. To Chris, the jungle is a death-trap full of snakes, mosquitoes, and every creepy crawly imaginable, all lying in wait to target him specifically. I try to reassure him, but he's beyond consolation.

He refuses to "go" unless he can find a proper sit-down toilet, porcelain pristine, with a roll of Andrex on standby. I've been lucky so far. I've eaten just about everything, from street food to roadside snacks, and I've avoided trouble. Fingers crossed it stays that way. Chris, on the other hand, looks ready to give up the whole adventure for the promise of a clean bathroom and a day free of his imagined maladies.

Adventure, it seems, isn't everyone's cup of tea.

CLEAR THE AIR TIME

By the time we pull into the gravel car park of a roadside restaurant around five o'clock, we're eight hours into the day's journey. Everyone is cramped, sweating, and irritable, but this is the nicest spot we've seen in miles. The restaurant is open-fronted and slightly rundown, but it feels respectable—clean tables, fairly new white polypropylene garden chairs, and, most importantly, shade.

The solitude of the bike has been my saving grace today, but I know a confrontation is brewing. It's time to clear the air.

This trip has strayed far from its promise. Fat Boy in Paradise was meant to be an adventure, not a slog. Paradise isn't endless logistical cock-ups or an oppressive atmosphere. Paradise isn't racing through a country without experiencing it. Indonesia is rich in scenery, culture, and history, but I feel like it's slipping through my fingers. I wanted to connect with people, visit their homes, and share their meals. I wanted to see temples, wash in a jungle river, and immerse myself in a once-in-a-lifetime journey. Instead, I'm stuck in a relentless dash, missing everything meaningful.

Inside, the others return from the restaurant, grumbling. There are only four cold beers, and they're fed up with chicken and rice. Tough luck—it's what's available.

I pull Steve aside for a quiet word. Calmly, I explain how I'm feeling. He immediately explodes.

"You don't trust me," he snaps. "You don't trust my ability to handle this project!" He insists I focus on riding the bike and leave the rest to him. "On a project this complex, things will change. Things will go wrong. But that's what makes great television. The drama in Jakarta, no bike in Bali, the magnificence of Bromo, the race to Dumai—it's all part of the story."

He has a point. Chaos does make for compelling TV. This trip has been a rollercoaster, and we're only a third of the way through. Strangely, the outburst seems to relax him. The tension drains from his face, and for the first time in days, we share a calm moment. A beer, a few words, and the air is cleared.

The day doesn't end there. After fifteen difficult hours, we finally reach Pakanbaru at midnight. The last fifty miles have been the worst yet, the roads pitted and punishing. None of us has eaten—no breakfast, no lunch, and no dinner.

There's work to do. Steve has to call our shipping agent in England about the Malaysian permits, while Bagu chases his contact in Kuala Lumpur. We still don't know if Ron has handled the exit documents. The drivers go off to refuel the van, and I park the bike near the phone office, thankful it's still open.

Within minutes, a crowd of over a hundred people gathers around me. They press in close, shoulder to shoulder, silent and staring. Their curiosity is palpable, almost reverent. Some stroke the bike, their fingers tracing its curves like it's a relic from another world.

Despite the sheer number of people, I don't feel threatened. Their interest is genuine, their smiles warm. Most are dressed in vests and crumpled trousers, their faces friendly, their teeth often the only giveaway of age. One elderly man, thin and deeply wrinkled, grins with two remaining brown stumps—a seven-ten split of teeth.

A young man steps forward, eager to practice his halting English. He asks me where I'm from, where I'm going. It's clear he's savouring this rare opportunity to speak with a foreigner. He tells me he's learning English in evening classes after work, his determination impressive.

This region, from Palembang to Pakanbaru, has a strong Chinese influence. Bagu often says that Palembang in the 1960s was entirely Chinese. Though the area retains a Chinese look, the population boom and government policies have made Bahasa Indonesia the dominant language. There's harmony among people here—Chinese and Indonesian, blending cultures and intermarrying. It's a shame the government doesn't reflect this same tolerance; Chinese cultural expression feels muted, with little writing or cuisine visible.

After the calls and faxes, we grab beef sandwiches at the only open restaurant. It's past one in the morning, but the journey isn't over yet. Dumai awaits us. Rest will have to wait.

MEGA POTHOLES

Night riding has its charms. The air is cooler, the roads are quieter, and there's a certain intimacy to the jungle at night. The darkness is absolute—no streetlights here, just the occasional glow of the moon.

But then, there are the road works. They appear suddenly, un-announced, and perilous, with no reflective cones, no safety barriers, no blinking lights - just gaping holes, appearing with-out warning. Occasionally, a large excavation is marked with a dark tree stump or a concrete block, placed smack in the middle of the road—a rudimentary alert system that's more hazard than help. How anyone is supposed to spot these in pitch-black conditions is beyond me.

Some of these chasms stretch across the road like a fissure

from an earthquake. The smaller ones—six inches wide—can be ridden over with a jolting bumpity-bump that shakes your confidence but leaves you intact. Others feature sudden six-inch drop-offs where the tarmac ends abruptly; leading into gravel pits that stretch for a hundred meters or more. (Yes, I switch between metric and imperial. Don't ask—it's just how my mind works!) Exiting these pits on a big, low-slung Harley takes patience, precision, and occasionally a bit of luck.

Usually, I get some kind of warning—perhaps a flicker of brake lights ahead or a vehicle flashing its right indicator to signal a hazard. But not always!

One night, the warning didn't come.

I was cruising at a comfortable forty, savouring the serenity of the ride. The moon was high, casting silver light over the treetops, which stood silhouetted against a star-filled sky. The jungle whispered around me: the rhythmic hum of crickets, the occasional rustle of leaves, and the gentle murmur of distant water. The Harley's steady pop-pop-pop provided a reassuring rhythm, like a heartbeat in the quiet night.

Then, out of nowhere, chaos.

I hit something—an unseen pit or a hidden drop—and was suddenly airborne.

One moment, I was savoring the night's tranquillity; the next, I was flying above the saddle, legs flailing, clinging desperately to the handlebars. It felt like I was competing in the finals of the Nevada Rodeo, riding a bucking bronco rather than a Fat Boy. My heart pounded, my brain raced, and every organ inside me felt like it had been shaken loose.

It was over in seconds, but it felt like an eternity.

The Harley landed hard but steady, like the sturdy beast it is. I slowed down, hands trembling, my pulse racing. My first instinct was to pull over and catch my breath, but I pressed on, vowing to be hyper-vigilant for the rest of the night.

The jungle at night is no friend to the complacent. It offers beauty and tranquillity, sure—but only to those who are ready for the unexpected.

 # WEDNESDAY 22 JUNE

BIKE GIVES UP THE GHOST

The road from Pakanbaru to Dumai is a torment disguised as a highway—150 miles of betrayal. Smooth stretches of tarmac lull you into false confidence before plunging you into a rutted abyss. Deep trenches and jagged edges lurk without warning, ready to shake rider and machine alike. Then there are the trucks—hulking, relentless beasts driven by men paid by the load. They thunder along, head-on or overtaking, horns blaring with a single message: Move or suffer.

We left Pakanbaru at 2 a.m., the darkness a cloak over the road's treachery. In the absence of streetlights, the jungle around us becomes a black void, swallowing every hazard. The Harley handles the chaos better than I do, its low centre of gravity giving it a reassuring steadiness, but the relentless jolts and vibrations grind me down. Every trench feels like a personal attack.

Twenty hours on the road, and I am spent. My shoulders throb, my thighs ache, and my saddle-sore backside burns with each mile. The clutch hand I once took for granted now screams with blistered rebellion. My focus flickers, my vision blurs. I can barely think.

The distance to Dumai taunts me: seventy-five miles. I slow

to a crawl, hoping that might stave off the inevitable. But the exhaustion is winning. My eyelids grow heavier with every bump and curve. I feel myself slipping into micro-sleeps, only to jolt awake with a panicked gasp.

I talk to myself out loud, desperate for any semblance of focus. Stay awake. Stay awake. Dumai isn't far. Stay awake.

It doesn't help. Words give way to songs, and soon I'm belting out anything that comes to mind. But for reasons I can't fathom, the only song I truly remember is "I Saw Her Standing There" by The Beatles.

I sing it over and over, the lyrics looping like a broken record. When I try to switch songs, they all dissolve back into I Saw Her Standing There. It becomes a strange sort of madness.

When even singing fails, I start shouting. Not words—just guttural, primal screams into the endless jungle. It's absurd, really. Part of me is hoping for a miracle, some knight in shining armour—or perhaps an overly curious monkey—to leap out and rescue me from this nightmare.

And then, a miracle actually happens.

The bus pulls up beside me, and Paul leans out of the window, his expression calm as ever. "Want me to take over for a bit?" he asks casually, as if he hasn't just offered to save my life.

The relief is overwhelming. "Yes," I croak, nodding furiously. "Please."

I hand over the bike and stumble into the bus. The cramped, crowded interior feels like the lap of luxury compared to the hell I've endured. The moment I sit down, I'm out cold.

For the first time in hours, I'm not fighting. For the first time, I feel safe.

A MIRACLE

Even through the haze of exhaustion, a creeping sense of unease stirs in my foggy mind. Something isn't right. I try to ignore it, clinging to sleep, but the nagging feeling persists.

Reluctantly, I force one eye open. The dim morning light filters through the bus window, revealing a surreal and unsettling scene. The world outside reminds me of an abandoned set from a post-apocalyptic, old, sci-fi film. Bare, lifeless tree trunks stand like solemn monuments, their branches long gone, guarding the impenetrable jungle beyond.

Below, dense ferns and bushes form an unbroken carpet. Occasionally, a muddy track snakes into the undergrowth, flanked by neatly stacked logs. Everything is shrouded in mist, bathed in a grey light that robs the landscape of any warmth. The slight chill in the air sends a shiver down my spine.

I stumble out of the bus, bleary-eyed and disoriented. The piercing wail of the bike's alarm slams into my ears, relentless and unforgiving. It's unresponsive, a dead hulk, screaming into the stillness.

Half-asleep, I fumble with the alarm buttons, trying every sequence I know. Nothing! We push the bike up the road, attempting a bump start, but it remains stubbornly lifeless. I try disconnecting the alarm and removing a spark plug—still no spark.

We're stranded in the middle of nowhere, twenty miles from Dumai. The ferry leaves in less than three hours. Exhaustion crashes over me like a wave. I slump against the bike, defeated.

And then, as if by divine intervention, a low rumble cuts through the jungle stillness. A battered pick-up truck emerges from the mist, its headlights barely piercing the grey haze. Without hesitation, the driver pulls over. Bagu springs into action, negotiating with the driver in rapid-fire Indonesian. Within moments, a deal is struck. A flurry of activity follows: the bike is hoisted onto the truck bed, secured with ropes, and we're on the road again.

I sit in stunned silence, watching the jungle blur past. A complete stranger, appearing at the exact moment of crisis, has offered help without hesitation. It feels miraculous, almost too perfect to be true.

This trip has tested me in every way imaginable, but it has also shown me the extraordinary resilience of people. Even in the most inhospitable corners of the world, there's always someone willing to help.

Unbelievable! Absolutely unbelievable!

TO DUMAI

Mr. Pick-up, like every other driver in Indonesia, was a complete maniac. The bike, weighing a hefty four hundred kilos, was precariously balanced on its side stand in the small truck bed. With no way to strap it down, Paul and I had to sit on either side, steadying it as best we could.In such circumstances, you'd think the driver might exercise a little caution. Not this guy. He tore down the jungle road flat out, navigating a treacherous mix of dirt, tarmac, and potholes that could swallow a small car. The Pertamina petrol tanker Kamikaze squad roared past in the opposite direction, their sheer size and speed leaving us clinging to the bike for dear life.

The truck bed was a nightmare. We sat on corrugated wheel arches, dented and sharp, each bump sending me airborne. The bigger the pothole, the higher I flew—and the harder I crashed back down. It felt like being in a sidecar motocross race, both of us hanging out and hanging on, desperate not to topple over.

"Twenty-five kilometres," the milestone read. Only half an hour more of this torture. I shouted into the jungle, "A decent road, and my kingdom for a decent road!" Paul didn't respond, his face locked in a grimace of concentrated anguish.

As the light grew stronger, the driver seemed to gain better control—or perhaps the road improved slightly. Finally, we reached a dual carriageway. Though it could have used a steamroller, it felt like heaven compared to what we'd endured.

We passed sprawling Pertamina refineries, their chimneys

stretching into the sky. These industrial giants were the source of the region's wealth—and the lunatic tanker drivers we'd spent hours dodging.

As we approached Dumai, the road became smoother, flanked by neatly cultivated central reservations blooming with colourful flowers. It was a stark contrast to the scruffy villages we'd passed. In Indonesia, official spaces are always pristine. Council offices gleam with fresh paint, statues are meticulously maintained, and main roads are litter-free—though you suspect the rubbish is merely swept into the backstreets.

First impressions of Dumai were surprising. Avenues lined with trees and elegant houses spoke of affluence. Expensive foreign cars—a rare sight in Sumatra—glided past, symbols of success.

And then, suddenly, the scene shifted. The polished roads gave way to an untidy, unmade stretch riddled with waterlogged potholes. It looked like a Klondike boomtown from an old John Wayne movie, the streets a sea of mud. People trudged through the mire, splashing from one dry spot to another.

As we navigated this muddy chaos, I glanced behind and was astonished to see the crew bus only a short distance away. I'd worried we might lose each other in Dumai's maze, but there they were, as if by some unspoken agreement, trailing in our wake.

For all its chaos, Dumai had a strange charm—a place of contradictions, where affluence and adversity existed side by side. And after the ordeal we'd just endured, simply arriving felt like a triumph.

We all stop together and Bagu and Steve jump out to enquire where the ferry office is. Soon established, we turn right and head onto a suburban dual carriageway, both sides having a motley selection of shop houses and roadside stalls. We pull over after a quarter of a mile and stop on a wide dusty hard shoulder that doubles as a car park and market stall area in the centre of town. A hundred yards ahead is a large crossroads, the main shopping street going off to the right.

It's surreal how quickly things escalate. Within seconds, we're surrounded by a noisy, energetic mob—an army of curious locals, mostly young men and boys. They chatter excitedly, jostling forward to catch a glimpse of the bike. For many, it's likely the first time they've seen such a massive machine up close, and they're eager to touch, feel, and inspect every inch of it.

The immediate task, though, is to get the bike off the truck. Our saviour, the pickup driver, has other commitments

174

and needs to leave. We hand him 10,000 rupiah along with heartfelt thanks. By now, we're seasoned veterans at unloading the bike; it's off the truck in no time, much to the amazement of our audience.

It's nine-thirty. We've made it—with half an hour to spare.

Steve and Bagu push their way through the dense throng and cross the busy street toward a once-white series of shop houses. Above one doorway, a faded sign with a red-and-black painted boat marks the Pelni Ferry Office. They vanish into the dark space, hopefully to secure tickets for our crossing to Malacca, Malaysia.

But something feels off.

We've been unnervingly lucky so far. Twenty hours of non-stop driving, a breakdown in the middle of nowhere, and yet, miraculously, we're here on time. My gut churns with unease. I can't shake the suspicion that Ron has once again dropped the ball and failed to fax the necessary documents.

Minutes crawl by. I glance around and realize the others have wandered off, leaving me stranded with the bike. I catch a glimpse of Sean's towering frame above the much shorter locals as he disappears into the shadows across the road. Left sitting side-saddle on the Harley, I try—and fail—to ignore the relentless chatter of the crowd that swarms around me.

Surrendering to their curiosity, I brace myself for the inevitable interrogation. The questions come in rapid-fire succession—or rather, the same three questions repeated endlessly:

- "Where you from?"

- "Har-ry-Davidson?"

- "How much cost?"

It's the last question that always trips me up. Should I answer with the price in England; or the equivalent in U.S. dollars? Or what it might be worth here in Indonesia? I never know what's appropriate, especially when faced with people who clearly have far less material wealth. The awkwardness gnaws at me. No matter what I say, I feel like I'm either boasting or underselling, and both options are equally uncomfortable.

NO FERRY

As the crowd presses closer, I glance back at the ferry office. The wait is unbearable. I long for some indication—anything—to tell me what's happening.

It was nearly half an hour before Steve returned, bearing news I hadn't anticipated—a twist in this rollercoaster of a journey that no one could have foreseen.

"The ferry's broken down," he announced.

I stared at him, disbelieving. "What? No ferry?"

"No ferry," he confirmed, shrugging helplessly. "The bloody thing's knackered."

I slumped against the bike, letting the absurdity of the situation sink in. After everything we'd endured to get here—the endless waiting in Jakarta for confirmation that this ferry even existed, the countless phone calls to Pelni offices, the punishing journey from Jambi, the sacrifices, including missing the equator crossing at Bukittinggi—all of it now felt utterly wasted. And to top it all off, the damned ferry had broken down.

Steve, this time optimistic, added, "Bagu and I will try to figure out our next move."

I barely heard him. What grated most wasn't the ferry but the missed equator crossing. Through a combination of bad luck, poor planning, and sheer stupidity, I had lost my one chance to photograph the Harley straddling the line of the Earth's divide. Instead of the grand celebration I'd envisioned—a cinematic moment, complete with echoes of a naval crossing ceremony—it had become a non-event. I had crossed the equator unnoticed, in pitch darkness, and that memory would haunt me for years.

With the ferry saga clearly set to drag on, we decided to move the bike across the road and park it outside the Pelni office. A gap in the centre divider offered a path, so I fetched Sean, our tallest and strongest crewmember, to help push. Getting to the bike was an ordeal in itself. A gaggle of kids surrounded it, their curious hands eagerly exploring every inch. With a lot of polite "excuse me's" and some gentle elbowing, I eased the Harley off its stand. The crowd parted reluctantly, forming a narrow corridor for us to manoeuvre through.

At the road's edge, we paused, waiting for a break in the traffic. As I stood there, I couldn't help but notice the town's character. Dumai felt like a quintessential frontier town— dusty, humid, and chaotic. It had the energy of an old Mexican border settlement, the kind you'd expect to find in an old cowboy movie. Seedy buildings lined the streets, while vendors peddled their wares in a cacophony of voices. This town, I thought, was made for my Fat Boy—perfect for cruising. If only it weren't dead on its wheels.

Crossing the street was a far cry from cruising. It was more bruisin' than cruisin', a graceless waddle as we dragged the bike through the gap in the median.

PAY NOW!

By the time we parked outside the Pelni office, most of my curious entourage had melted away. Alone with the bike, I decided to give the repairs another shot. Opening the saddlebag, I immediately noticed something amiss: the buckle was undone, and my sunglasses case was empty. Someone had stolen my prescription sunglasses. My second brush with theft in Indonesia, the first being in Jambi. At least the thief would discover they were useless without my astigmatism.

Once again, I removed the saddle and stared hopelessly at the tangle of wires. I'd followed the alarm installer's instructions to the letter so many times, yet bypassing the system had always eluded me.

First things first: I needed jump leads to test the battery. A shop nearby caught my eye—an ironmonger's, with a chaotic array of tools, pots, and rope hanging from the ceiling. It seemed promising.

I approached the counter and tried to explain what I needed. My gesticulations and rudimentary sketches only seemed to confuse the lady behind the counter. She summoned a friend, and after more pantomime, they disappeared into the back. A glimmer of hope surfaced when she returned, brandishing massive leads—fit for jump-starting a tank.

"Can I try them first?" I asked.

"You must buy," she replied curtly.

promised to meet him in an hour.

BAGU LEAVES

As I approached the City Hotel, I spotted Steve, Sean, Paul, Chris, and Bagu gathered outside. The two drivers were meticulously combing through the van to ensure nothing had been forgotten. Steve's questionable organizational skills were no longer a debate. Bagu's time with us had come to an end, and from here on out, Steve had to step up. Yet morale was low, and confidence in his leadership was thinner than Dumai's petrol fumes.

Bagu's departure was surprisingly emotional. For almost three weeks, we'd relied on his resourcefulness, honesty, and calm under pressure. He'd become more than just a Production Manager; he was a friend. We shook hands, embraced, and promised to stay in touch, even though we both knew how such promises usually go. Climbing into the bus with a wave, he was gone, leaving us to face the uncertain road ahead.

I stood there for a moment, a thousand doubts swirling in my mind.

"Well, here we are," I thought grimly:

Booked on a boat that might never arrive, bound for a destination that might not lead to Malaysia. My Harley, dead as a stone, wasn't helping matters. The schedule was in tatters, the budget was shot, and we had no contingency. Worse, our exit documents were valid only for Dumai, not Batam, and we were now surrounded by corrupt officials with no interpreter to smooth things over.

Would you be worried? I most certainly was.

But life, chaotic as it was, had to go on. To distract myself, I decided to take Jukman up on his offer. For the equivalent of two pounds, we rented his friend's ancient Suzuki moped and set off. Riding as a passenger proved to be a challenge; the moped had only one footrest, leaving my left leg swinging awkwardly. I couldn't let it dangle—it would scrape the ground. Instead, I had to keep it bent at an excruciating angle. After several minutes of discomfort, I asked Jukman to pull over. A quick inspection revealed a small hexagon-headed bolt near the frame, just big enough to balance my foot. It wasn't perfect, and I had to be cautious not to clip the spokes, but it was better than losing a toe or two.

For the next thirty minutes, we cruised through Dumai. Passing the City Hotel, we rode down the clean, whitewashed avenue of government offices, which stood in stark contrast to much of the town. Beyond the city centre, we turned onto a tree-lined dual carriageway, shaded by coconut palms. Underneath the trees, a handful of food vendors sold snacks from wooden carts, their colourful umbrellas offering respite from the sun.

Across the road, an enormous petrochemical plant loomed. The refinery was immaculately maintained, with gleaming white walls and a towering chimney that burned off waste gas in a flickering orange flame. Unlike most industrial sites in Indonesia, this one exuded efficiency and wealth—a testament to its American operators.

Strangely, in a town dominated by this international presence, I hadn't seen a single foreigner. According to Jukman, the expatriates lived in a self-contained enclave, rarely interacting with the locals. Isolated in their Uncle Sam bubble, they were as much strangers to Dumai as I was.

wasn't cheap, but it was the best option in town.

Time was short, and I returned to the Honda dealer. The service technician had arrived and, to my relief, produced a set of jump leads. These were comically undersized, designed for the mopeds that dominated the local streets, but they were better than nothing. He kindly loaned them to me, and I promised to return them promptly.

Back at the Pelni office, I removed the saddle once again. I instructed our driver to reposition the crew bus as close to the Harley as possible, allowing the diminutive jump leads to stretch between the two batteries. With everything connected, I hit the starter switch. Nothing! The Harley remained lifeless, utterly immobilized.

This only reinforced my suspicion: the alarm system was the culprit. It had to be bypassed, but how? I'd exhausted every trick I could think of.

I decided I needed connector blocks to rewire the system more methodically. After pushing the Harley into a corridor of the Pelni building for safekeeping, I set out to find an electrical shop.

Passing a group of teenagers lounging in a doorway, I decided to ask for directions. One of them, to my surprise, spoke excellent English and knew exactly what I needed. Following his instructions, I found a shop just past the traffic lights. The owner sold me two connector blocks and a handful of replacement fuses for a couple of quid. Feeling oddly optimistic, I thanked the boys on my way back, and they wished me luck.

Armed with my new tools, I stripped down the wiring

again. Each wire was carefully labelled with masking tape as I snipped and rejoined them using the connector blocks. Following the alarm installer's instructions to the letter, I tested the system. Still nothing! Frustrated, I tried every conceivable wiring combination, yet the alarm refused to be bypassed.

In any other situation, this would be a testament to the system's security—a thief would find it nearly impossible to steal the bike. But in the middle of Sumatra, it felt more like a curse. My suspicion grew that the installer had left out a crucial step, and being thousands of miles away from anyone who could help, I was well and truly stuck.

Defeated, I reassembled the bike, resigning myself to the hope that a Harley dealer in Malaysia could fix it. That is, if I ever made it there.

After returning the undersized jump leads to the Honda man, I passed the trio of boys who had helped me earlier. They waved me over, eager for an update. "Crap," I said, shaking my head. "Total failure!"

One of the boys, Jukman, was the most conversational in English and saw this as a golden opportunity to practice. About twenty years old, he was one of many young men in Dumai facing the harsh reality of unemployment. Despite the town's wealth from its petrochemical industry and port, jobs were scarce, with too many hopefuls flooding in from surrounding villages. Jukman was luckier than most. He lived with his brother's family—an extended household supported by his brother's modest success as a merchant and exporter.

Jukman, eager to share his town with me, proposed a tour. I explained I needed to return to the hotel for a while but promised to meet him in an hour.

BAGU LEAVES

As I approached the City Hotel, I spotted Steve, Sean, Paul, Chris, and Bagu gathered outside. The two drivers were meticulously combing through the van to ensure nothing had been forgotten. Steve's questionable organizational skills were no longer a debate. Bagu's time with us had come to an end, and from here on out, Steve had to step up. Yet morale was low, and confidence in his leadership was thinner than Dumai's petrol fumes.

Bagu's departure was surprisingly emotional. For almost three weeks, we'd relied on his resourcefulness, honesty, and calm under pressure. He'd become more than just a Production Manager; he was a friend. We shook hands, embraced, and promised to stay in touch, even though we both knew how such promises usually go. Climbing into the bus with a wave, he was gone, leaving us to face the uncertain road ahead.

I stood there for a moment, a thousand doubts swirling in my mind.

"Well, here we are," I thought grimly:

Booked on a boat that might never arrive, bound for a destination that might not lead to Malaysia. My Harley, dead as a stone, wasn't helping matters. The schedule was in tatters, the budget was shot, and we had no contingency. Worse, our exit documents were valid only for Dumai, not Batam, and we were now surrounded by corrupt officials with no interpreter to smooth things over.

Would you be worried? I most certainly was.

But life, chaotic as it was, had to go on. To distract myself, I decided to take Jukman up on his offer. For the equivalent of two pounds, we rented his friend's ancient Suzuki moped and set off. Riding as a passenger proved to be a challenge; the moped had only one footrest, leaving my left leg swinging awkwardly. I couldn't let it dangle—it would scrape the ground. Instead, I had to keep it bent at an excruciating angle. After several minutes of discomfort, I asked Jukman to pull over. A quick inspection revealed a small hexagon-headed bolt near the frame, just big enough to balance my foot. It wasn't perfect, and I had to be cautious not to clip the spokes, but it was better than losing a toe or two.

For the next thirty minutes, we cruised through Dumai. Passing the City Hotel, we rode down the clean, whitewashed avenue of government offices, which stood in stark contrast to much of the town. Beyond the city centre, we turned onto a tree-lined dual carriageway, shaded by coconut palms. Underneath the trees, a handful of food vendors sold snacks from wooden carts, their colourful umbrellas offering respite from the sun.

Across the road, an enormous petrochemical plant loomed. The refinery was immaculately maintained, with gleaming white walls and a towering chimney that burned off waste gas in a flickering orange flame. Unlike most industrial sites in Indonesia, this one exuded efficiency and wealth—a testament to its American operators.

Strangely, in a town dominated by this international presence, I hadn't seen a single foreigner. According to Jukman, the expatriates lived in a self-contained enclave, rarely interacting with the locals. Isolated in their Uncle Sam bubble, they were as much strangers to Dumai as I was.

"If they fit, I'll pay," I reasoned.

"Pay now," she insisted.

I pointed to the bike parked right outside. "I'm not taking them anywhere. I just want to see if they fit!"

"Pay now."

It was exasperating. The leads looked absurdly oversized, and I doubted they'd work. But the woman wouldn't budge. Even when I offered to rent them for a few minutes, she stood her ground. "Ten dollars," she demanded.

"Fine," I said, "but only if they fit!"

Her answer was the same: "Pay now."

Frustrated, I realized I was getting nowhere. Her stubbornness wasn't just unhelpful—it was bad business. Why would I risk paying for something that might not work? Still, not wanting to burn my only lead on leads, I backed off.

"I'll be back," I said, retreating to the sound of yet another "Pay now!" echoing behind me.

Standing outside the ironmonger's shop, I was at a crossroads. My pride didn't want to part with ten dollars for oversized jump leads I couldn't even test, yet I couldn't proceed without them. I scanned the street for inspiration and spotted a Honda dealership at the far end of the road. With a glimmer of hope, I walked over.

Inside, I discovered it was merely a showroom, devoid of a workshop. The man behind the desk listened to my request with a bemused expression and confessed he had no idea what I needed. However, he assured me the service technician would return in thirty minutes and promised to ask him. With nothing else to do, I drifted back to the Pelni office to check on the ferry situation.

The news was as grim as expected. The broken ferry wouldn't be operational for at least a week, which, in Indonesian "rubber time," could mean anything from weeks to months. Bagu, resourceful as ever, had uncovered an alternative: a hydrofoil to Melaka. Unfortunately, it was strictly for passengers—no bikes allowed. The only viable option was a boat to Batam Island near Singapore, with a potential onward connection to Malaysia.

The word "potential" loomed heavily. Indonesian logistics had a way of stringing travellers along, one false lead at a time, until the buck had been passed beyond reach. Official documents served more as vague suggestions than binding agreements, and timetables adhered to the same philosophy. In other words, the route from Batam to Malaysia might not even exist, and by the time we discovered the truth, we'd be too far from Dumai to complain.

Regardless, our hands were tied. The Batam ferry was our only way out, allegedly departing at 8:00 AM the next morning. Tickets were booked, but an uneasy feeling gnawed at me.

To complicate matters, today marked the end of Bagu's contract. Throughout this chaotic journey, he'd been our rock, deftly navigating the bureaucratic minefields and bailing us out of trouble. Now, with no backup plan, he had to leave. He'd arranged for a Malaysian contact to meet us in Melaka, but with our detour through Batam, that plan was now in shambles. Bagu, ever professional, booked us into the City Hotel—a modest but decent establishment just a few doors down from the Pelni office. At thirty dollars per person, it

As we rode on, I couldn't help but feel that Dumai, with its contrasts and contradictions, was a microcosm of the journey itself—chaotic, unpredictable, and strangely fascinating.

THE SMELLIEST FRUIT IN THE WORLD

As we cruised past the food stalls, my stomach reminded me it hadn't had a decent meal in hours. Suddenly, I had an overwhelming urge to try durian. The fruit's infamy had been following me across Southeast Asia, and now seemed the perfect time to see what all the fuss was about.

I mentioned it to Jukman, who immediately knew the place. "The best fruit in Dumai," he promised, pointing me toward a stall near the crossroads in the centre of town.

Durian has a reputation like no other food. In every hotel I've stayed at, its presence is strictly banned, complete with official-looking "no durian" signs resembling no-smoking placards, except with the silhouette of the fruit instead of a cigarette. The fruit itself is bizarre—about the size of a bowling ball, covered in a spiky yellow-green shell that makes it look like a weapon from medieval times.

But it's the smell that makes durian legendary, or infamous. The odour is often compared to sweaty gym socks left in a swamp, baked in the sun with a hint of overripe sweetness. To many Westerners, that's enough to avoid it completely - but not me. I'd heard the tales, seen the signs, and now I had to taste this so-called "King of Fruits" for myself.

The moment the spiky shell was cracked open, its infamous aroma hit me like a wave. I braced myself as the vendor revealed the fruit's innards: several large stones encased in a creamy, golden-yellow paste. Cautiously, I scooped a bit with my fingers and tasted it.

The verdict? - it was incredible. The flavour was rich, sweet, and custard-like, with a slight nuttiness. It was unlike anything I'd ever eaten, and instantly I understood why it was so beloved in the region. Forget the smell—this was one of the most extraordinary things I'd ever tasted. To anyone traveling through Asia, my advice is simple: pack a clothespin for your nose and dive in.

We sat on small stools by the roadside, the durian feast spread out in front of us. The stall wasn't exactly inviting—wedged between the road and a foul-smelling ditch, with a rickety, rotting plank bridge leading to a dilapidated residence behind it. Yet, with Jukman guiding the experience, I couldn't have cared less about the setting.

The stall was about three meters long, bursting with rambutans, bananas, golf-ball-sized red fruits I didn't recognize, and, of course, heaps of durians at the front. Next door, the stallholder's mother-in-law presided over a smaller stall selling green coconuts, sweets, and biscuits.

As we ate, I watched her expertly crack open a coconut with a machete. She worked with incredible grace, spinning the fruit in her left hand as her blade flashed through the air. Each strike chipped away a layer of the coconut until its top was a sharp pyramid. With one final, precise chop, she sliced almost all the way through the peak, leaving a small hinged lid.

I sipped the fresh coconut water through a straw, its cool sweetness perfectly complementing the creamy richness of the durian. Despite the odd setting—the smell of the ditch mingling with the aroma of the durian—it was one of those moments where everything felt just right.

The King of Fruits had won me over.

CHECK OUT THE DOCK

Having finished my drink, I hand the coconut back to the stallholder. With a practiced motion, she rips off the lid, chops the nut neatly in half, and hands it back to me with an old army spoon to scoop out the moist, sweet flesh. It's simple but satisfying—a small luxury for just a few dollars. The durian was pricey, but worth every penny; the coconut cost next to nothing.

Back on the moped, we resume our tour, heading to the dock. Jukman is eager to show me its significance to Dumai, and I want to scope it out before the morning.

The ride there is rough, testing my endurance on the battered old moped. While Dumai's main streets are paved and manageable, the potholed road leading to the dock is another story. Each jolt sends me bouncing on the torn saddle, struggling to balance with one foot precariously placed on a bolt and the other dangling uncomfortably. It's far from ideal, but I remind myself this is part of the adventure.

The dock itself is a simple concrete slab, roughly a hundred meters long and thirty wide. To the right sits a small white boat—the passenger ferry to Melaka. Seeing its size, I finally understand why my motorcycle couldn't come aboard; there's simply no space for it. While frustrating, it's a relief to know practicality, not bureaucracy, is what redirected us to Batam.

Dominating the jetty is a massive, rusty cargo ship. Everything about it—hull, superstructure, bolts—is covered in a deep layer of corrosion. Despite its decrepit appearance, it's clearly still in use, though I can't imagine life aboard is anything but grim. The thought of Chris encountering its facilities brings a faint smile to my face.

We exit the dock and head back onto smoother roads, leaving the bustle of the port behind. As the dust settles and the warm air carries the faint scent of rain, I take in my surroundings. Dumai is not a tourist hub, but that's precisely its charm. It's a working town, unvarnished and authentic, where locals go about their lives unaffected by the artificiality of mass tourism.

The Lonely Planet dismisses Dumai as "strictly a one-street town where the only thing you can do is catch the ferry," but to me, that simplicity is its appeal. The warmth and hospitality here feel genuine, untouched by the greed and pretense that often accompany tourism.

Dumai lies in Riau Province, an area rich in oil, tin, and bauxite. Despite its industrial significance, much of the surrounding landscape remains pristine jungle and mangrove swamps. This contrast between natural abundance and industrial development is striking. American-run refineries dominate the skyline, their pipelines connecting distant oil fields to Dumai's bustling port.

I can't help but wish I had more time. If not for the pressures of the journey and the responsibilities of the film crew, I would venture deeper into the jungle, where elephants, tigers, and rhinos still roam free. For now, I feel privileged to witness this slice of real Sumatra, a place where nature, industry, and history intersect in ways few travellers ever experience.

After a brief respite, I'd almost forgotten how challenging it is to ride on the back of Jukman's moped. On the smooth, tarmacked roads in the centre of town, it's manageable—I can balance my left foot on the small bolt that serves as a makeshift foot peg without too much trouble. But the bumpy, unpaved road leading to the dock is a different story entirely. It's a jarring, bone-rattling ride that feels more like a moped obstacle course. With nothing to hold onto and my leg swinging awkwardly, I'm bounced around on the worn-out saddle like laundry in a spin cycle.

When we finally arrive, about ten minutes later, I feel as if I've been on the road all day—my backside sore, my legs aching, and every joint shaken loose. I'm relieved to hop off and collect myself.

The dock is simple: a concrete slab roughly 100 meters long and 30 meters wide. To the right, a small white boat bobs gently on the water. This, I'm told, is the passenger ferry to Melaka. Seeing it now, I understand why they couldn't take us. It's tiny, and there's no practical way it could have accommodated my bike, let alone transported it safely across open sea. At least I now know it was practicality, not red tape that redirected us to Batam.

Taking up most of the jetty is a massive cargo ship, a hulking, rusty giant. Its hull, superstructure, and even the smallest bolts are cloaked in a thick layer of corrosion. It's a vast, crumbling relic that seems one step away from retirement, yet clearly still operational. Life aboard that ship must be grim—hardly a haven of creature comforts. As I eye it, I can't help but chuckle, wondering how Chris would cope with the state of their facilities.

Back on the moped, we putter along the jetty, dodging more potholes, testing my balance, and further punishing my already tender backside.

The road eventually improves, becoming smoother but

dustier. Despite the distant threat of rain, with a few black clouds gathering on the horizon, it remains warm and pleasant. Though I complain about the discomfort, deep down I'm relishing this adventure. Dumai isn't some sanitized tourist destination. It's a real, gritty Sumatran town, a functioning port bustling with ordinary people. There's no gloss or manufactured charm here—just authenticity. I feel privileged to witness this slice of life, a place untouched by the commercialism that often erodes local culture.

The Lonely Planet guide dismisses Dumai as "strictly a one-street town where the only thing you can do is catch the ferry." To me, that's an asset, not a flaw. Here, the hospitality is genuine, untainted by tourism's greed.

Dumai lies in Riau province, a region rich in natural resources like oil, tin, and bauxite. Exploitation of these riches began just 30 years ago. Even now, only a fraction of the dense rainforest has been cleared, leaving most of the land covered in jungle and mangrove swamps. While Dumai itself thrives as a growing port for the Pertamina refinery, the surrounding wilderness remains largely untouched.

This area has a tumultuous history, marked by piracy, violence, and tribal conflicts. Yet deep in the jungle, nomadic and animistic tribes still live as they have for centuries.

For two centuries before World War II, the Dutch claimed Riau—then known as Siak—as a colony, though they showed little interest in governing or developing it, their focus was merely to rid the surrounding seas of pirates. It wasn't until American engineers discovered oil near Pakanbaru that the region's potential was realized. Today, pipelines connect the oil fields to Dumai's refineries, allowing tankers to export the province's wealth to the world.

I wish I could linger here longer, free from the pressures of the journey, the film, and the responsibility of managing a film crew. If I had the time, I'd venture deeper into Sumatra's jungle heart, where tigers, elephants, bears, tapirs, and the elusive hairy rhinoceros still roam freely.

But for now, I'm content to absorb the essence of this town—a glimpse of a Sumatra few travellers ever see.

THE HOUSING ESTATE

It's past five o'clock, and I decide to return to the hotel to check if there's been any news. When I mention this to Jukman, he nods but insists on showing me one last part of town. We turn off into what appears to be a housing estate—a peculiar mishmash at that.

The narrow streets buzz with life: kids playing, mothers bustling about, and neighbours chatting. What catches my attention is the striking contrast in the houses. Luxury bungalows with grand verandas and enormous satellite dishes stand cheek-by-jowl with dilapidated wooden shacks, their corrugated iron roofs sagging under the weight of years. Between them runs an open sewer, a grimy channel cluttered with plastic, rotting food, wandering chickens, and less mentionable debris.

As we weave through tight alleys, I find myself brushing past lines of people carrying their washing or shopping. The deeper we go into this labyrinth, the more out of place I feel, aware of the curious stares following us. "Who is this long-haired blonde outsider invading our space?" their eyes seem to ask. The unfamiliarity is disorienting, and I can't help but feel uneasy. Anything could happen here, I think, and no one would ever know.

Shaking off my nerves, I ask Jukman how much farther. "Only a few minutes," he says without looking back, "just around the corner."

We cross a creaky log bridge spanning yet another fetid stream, and suddenly we're back on the main road. Relief washes over me as I recognize the far end of Jalan Jenderal Sudirman, where my hotel is located.

Dismounting the moped, I rub my aching backside, grateful to stretch my legs. Jukman makes me promise to meet him later for dinner. He's eager to introduce me to authentic Sumatran cuisine and even more eager for me to join him at a karaoke bar afterward. "Great entertainment and great girls," he assures me with a grin. His enthusiasm is infectious, but I can't resist teasing him about his determination to practice English. I reassure him I'll be there and thank him for his kindness and the insights he's shared about Dumai.

At the hotel, the trio of young women behind the reception desk greets me with bright smiles. I ask for my key, "Number three, please." One girl repeats the number as she writes it down, her smile never faltering. I hold up three fingers to confirm, feeling a pang of guilt for not attempting Bahasa Indonesia. The middle girl murmurs, "Tiga," and the key is passed along like a ceremonial handoff. The smiles persist.

As I retreat to my room, I reflect on the unparalleled guest-to-staff ratio: four receptionists for one traveller. Even the grandest hotels couldn't rival that.

AT JUKMMAN´S FAMILY HOME

By 7:30 sharp, I'm outside Jalan Sudirman No. 399, where kids playing nearby dispatch a messenger to fetch Jukman. He soon appears, brimming with excitement, and ushers me inside to meet his family.

His brother's home is a typical shop house, though the shop area doubles as a cluttered lock-up garage. Stepping over ladders and timber, we enter the living quarters, a stark contrast to the disarray outside. The room is immaculate, its cool tiled floor and whitewashed walls softened by vibrant rugs and sparse but tasteful furniture. A coffee table sits near a modest sofa, and a dark wooden sideboard lines the wall.

Jukman's brother, Mansyur Damanik, soon joins us. Modestly dressed but adorned with gold jewellery and flashy rings, he exudes a quiet air of success. Mansyur is a trader, buying timber in Sumatra and selling it in Malaysia. Through Jukman's translations, he explains he doesn't make a fortune but earns enough to support his extended family. Their closeness is palpable.

One by one, family members trickle into the room. Children, siblings, and in-laws greet me warmly. A young woman cradling a baby briefly appears, retrieving something from the sideboard before disappearing upstairs. Though I catch glimpses of her, the men barely acknowledge her presence—a subtle insight into traditional gender dynamics.

POWER CUT AND DINNER

As coffee arrives, the room is plunged into darkness. The power cut is no surprise, I'm told; it's a nightly ritual in Dumai. By the light of a Zippo, candles are quickly distributed, their soft glow casting an otherworldly charm over the room.

Concerned the outage might extend to our dinner plans, we

step outside to survey the situation. To the left, the street is shrouded in darkness. To the right, lights flicker reassuringly in the distance. The restaurant, it seems, is unaffected.

I thank Mansyur for his hospitality, shaking his hand and passing him the candle before bidding him goodnight. As we head toward the restaurant, I'm struck once again by the warmth and resilience of the people I've encountered. Dumai may not have the glitz of a tourist destination, but it has a depth and authenticity that's hard to find anywhere else.

The 'Pak Datuk' is a traditional Padang restaurant, much like those we had experienced throughout our journey, but more upmarket. This is obviously Jukman's favourite place and one into which he ventures only when someone else is paying.

I suggest he choose the dishes. I want something typical of the area, preferably with fish and chicken. Our waiter turns out to be the owner. Jukman explains who I am and asks for his recommendations. Mr Mudo is very pleased to help, and brings a delicious range of dishes, together with the largest bowl of rice I have ever seen. As with all Padang restaurants, many more dishes arrive than you actually need; the idea being to eat what you want and leave the rest. The untouched plates are then returned to the cooking area at the front of the restaurant and passed on to other tables, later on. This is not as bad as it sounds. Everything here is fresh and clean. The cooking is for all to see, just done in advance to save time.

I choose the spicy Udang Prawn, some boiled chicken, a grilled hake fish, and some Odour Fruit. This is a vegetable, so called because of the dreadful breath it gives you afterwards. Delicious to eat, but suspect in company. Mr Mudo recommends a supply of peppermints to follow.

194

Together with a couple of bottles of beer and Aqua, the local bottled water; the whole bill came to 16,200 Rupiah or about £4.50. And that's for two people, remember.

Now approaching nine, it is time for the Karaoke Club. I must confess to absolutely hating karaoke; probably due, in part, to the fact that I have a voice like shit. Add to that my innate British reserve and the fact that I am stone cold sober and you have one reluctant Karaoke Club visitor.

Repeatedly, I ask Jukman if there is somewhere else we could go. He assures me this is the only club in town and very good it is too. He was sure I would have fun.

We wander back to his brother's place to collect the moped. My offer of a taxi was rejected on the grounds that he thinks they cost too much money. I actually would have liked to ride in a becak, (a pedal powered tri-shaw), but the driver (if that is the right word seeing as he is also the engine) asks for so much money - about 50,000 Rupiah (£15) for a half mile journey, it is ridiculous. At that price I would have been taken for a ride!

The Karaoke Club car park is packed, and largely with new cars. This is obviously the place to be. We pull into a space in the middle of a row of around twenty mopeds. Compared to the odd naked light bulb and the dim street lights everywhere else in town, this is like Las Vegas. Flashing lights, taxis coming and going, stacks of becaks parked in a ramshackle mess at the corner, loads of the local male youth just generally hanging around. I pay the entrance fee of 10,000 Rupiah for the two of us to someone sat at a table in the doorway and get an ink stamp on the wrist in return.

Inside, the place is reminiscent of a seventies club in the

north of England; a terrace of upholstered benches and wooden tables which lead down to, and face, the dance floor, at the rear of which is the disco unit. The back of the stage is decorated with those metallic ribbons that shimmer when the lights flash on them. Above, and at strategic places around the room, were television screens that broadcast the video discs and karaoke lyrics.

So far, the place is about a quarter full, and filling up fast. A girl with a small notepad and pencil walks around taking karaoke requests. After she has collected a few, she passes them to the operator, sat behind a console in the far back left hand corner of the room. It is very well organised. A second girl is responsible for the radio mike, passing it to whoever's turn it is. There is no shortage of takers. It is very popular. Some stay where they are, sing part of a song and pass it on. Others believe they are stars - grab the microphone, run down to the stage and truly perform to the audience. Almost without exception they are excruciating. My crappy voice would sound like a choir of angels compared to some of these boys. The crowd like it though, cheering and whistling, oblivious to the fact that some of the participants seem to be singing a completely different song to the one on the screen.

At ten o'clock it's show time. The master of ceremonies, resplendent in a bright green satin shirt, bounces on to explain the proceedings. Jukman explains we are to have a beauty parade; a sort of Miss Dumai contest. To enthusiastic applause, it begins. No swimsuits unfortunately. This is a Muslim country, so propriety must be observed. Not so strict so all the contestants were dressed in black from head to foot so all we could judge was the eye slit, but nevertheless very sober.

All the girls have their best party frocks on and strut their stuff across the stage. The crowd once again whoop and cheer. I can't for the life of me suss out who is winning. The contestants just keep walking around; and around and around again.

After about three quarters of an hour, and still with no obvious impression of how things are going, the M.C. announces it is now the men's turn.

I can't believe this: an endless procession of John Travoltas appear from nowhere, walk round the stage, give a twirl and disappear again - all for no obvious reason. As far as I can make out, the girls haven't been judged yet.

I have never been so bored in all my life. To watch a bunch of poseurs in flared trousers and shiny shirts flouncing around a stage is seriously dull. It is never ending. And I mean never ending. They are still appearing from nowhere at eleven thirty with no end in sight. Where do all these guys come from? No judging, no whittling down to the final eight, nothing; I cannot not see the purpose.

These are no Chippendales, I promise you. They are just ordinary guys off the street.

I have to leave. I am losing my mind.

I politely express my desire to leave and Jukman nods. We haven't spoken for about half an hour anyway. It is too noisy to have a conversation in here, so perhaps he is just as fed up as me.

He takes me back to the hotel; I collect my room key from the ever smiling girls, and go upstairs. There is no sign of the others, so I assume they have drunk the place dry and gone to bed.

REFLECTIONS

As I approach the end of the first stage of this adventure, my emotions are a tangled mix of relief, regret, and a lingering sense of wonder. On one hand, I am desperate to leave Indonesia. The bureaucratic quagmire I've been navigating— endless forms, stamps, and approvals—has left me frazzled. The constant dread that my prized Harley-Davidson might remain trapped in customs hangs over me like a storm cloud. This stress has robbed me of the ability to fully relax and immerse myself in the journey.

Yet, for all the frustrations, Indonesia has captivated me. The chaos of Jakarta may have disrupted our schedule, forcing us to race through Sumatra, but even at this hurried pace; I've glimpsed the island's raw beauty. Sumatra is truly one of the world's last unspoiled paradises, with landscapes that take your breath away and people whose warmth and generosity defy description.

I've done something few can claim—crossed the equator on a Harley-Davidson. It's a milestone I should've celebrated, but in the pitch-black of night, it passed unnoticed. That missed moment epitomizes this leg of the trip: extraordinary experiences overshadowed by time constraints and logistical hurdles. If only I had more time. If only I had more money. If only!

Before departing, I thanked Jukman for his kindness and companionship. His eagerness to share his world and his genuine hospitality made a chaotic journey infinitely more bearable. I shook his hand, wished him well, and accepted a scrap of paper with his address scrawled on it. "Promise to write," he insisted.

As I leave, a single thought stays with me: I'll be back. Someday, I'll return—not as a hurried traveller, but as someone ready to explore Indonesia's wonders at a pace they deserve. Until then, these memories will have to suffice—a bittersweet reminder of the beauty I left behind.

The ferry that does not exist!

 # THURSDAY 23 JUNE

VOYAGE ON THE FERRY OF DEATH

What I imagined would happen…

For the long boat trip from Dumai to Batam I expected a ship - a Pelni liner with decks, restaurants, cabins and all the rest of it. Believing what was described in my travel guide in great detail, I thought I had a good idea what it was all about. Boring, tedious and a long way – yes; but, I could take the opportunity to relax, lie on the deck in the sunshine, chat up the captain as we had done previously from Bali to Java and Java to Sumatra. Maybe steer the ship for a little bit; make the most of it.

What actually happened…

A mini-bus collects us and the luggage from the City Hotel at eight o'clock for the short trip to the docks. I had reccied the day before, so I knew the way onto the wharf was over one of the two steel bridges. I had seen the Melaka ferry and assumed that's where we would go. Unfortunately the bus couldn't get to our wharf. The ruts in the road were so deep; we had to stop a hundred yards away. A porter with a boy-scout-sized wooden handcart with two bicycle wheels was readily available for the last leg, charging a reasonable 5,000 rupiah (about £1.50). He transferred our mountain of luggage and off we went. I couldn't see the ship, so just followed the crowd onto the jetty. "Should be here now", I thought, as it leaves in an hour.

I couldn't see it because it was lower than the jetty. Not a ship, but a large, white speed boat; a thirty metre long sleek looking craft with seats on two levels.

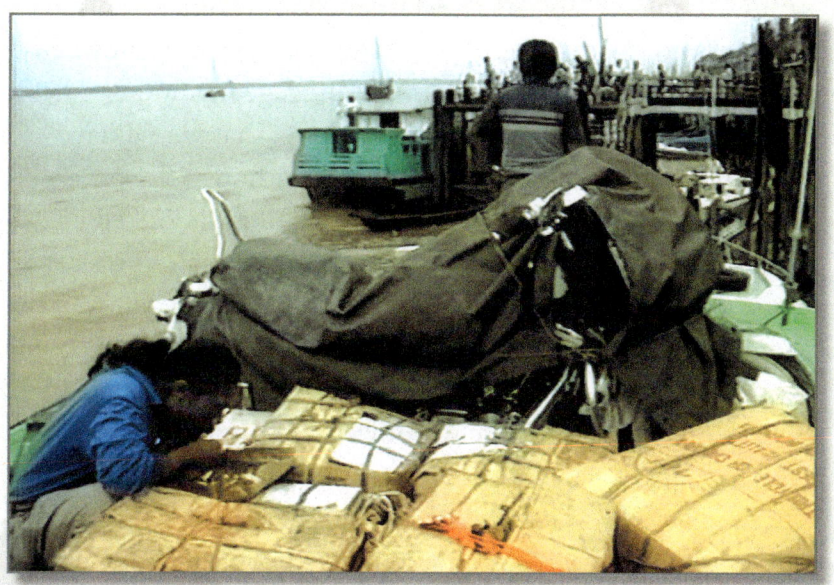

The bike was already loaded on the roof, alongside an old bicycle, both having been collected from the ferry office in the early hours. They had put it the wrong way round on the pallet so couldn't get the straps to fit. Steve and I took over and quickly sorted it out.

Our luggage was loaded into the hold and we went to take our seats. Well, first impressions can be misleading, and this time I got the prize for making the biggest mistake. No lifeboat drill here. No point; it was scary. Claustrophobic would be an understatement. We entered a small door to the upper deck which consisted of around one hundred, rather tired, brown aircraft seats, crowded together with a narrow isle in between. To the right of the front seats was a narrow stairway leading to the forward lower deck. First Class - so the sign said – with slightly better, grey aircraft seats. There were forty eight of them; still crowded, still with a narrow isle. People were filing in - lots of people. Not the one hundred and fifty to fill the seats, though, more like five hundred. They were stood up, sat down, piled high - on the stairs; sat on wooden stools in the gangway. Everywhere! A mother and two kids crowded in one seat, Granny and their entire luggage in another. There was one consolation though, no smoking; that would have made it like the black hole of Calcutta, without a doubt. I looked around. The cabin was so squished in, it looked like a tube train in the Tokyo rush hour. Here though - no safety exits. No safety exits at all. Literally, the only way out was the way we came in. Downstairs were over a hundred people with access to one small, narrow stairway, already cluttered with people. The porthole windows were tiny. No bigger than saucers. I was not happy; I felt very, very claustrophobic. There was nothing I could do except accept it. It was bad news. Upstairs was a sea of humanity - people everywhere. There were old grannies, screaming kids, whole families that looked like they were surrounded by the entire contents of their home. Not an inch to move. With no safety exits there either, it was seriously dangerous, one day there will be a major disaster. But not today, I hope.

As we waited to leave, vendors came on board selling food and water. Squeezing through the throng with their trays of goodies was an art form. I bought two chocolate sandwiches for a few Rupiah and tucked in. As usual, Sean and the others thought I was mad to eat something of unknown origin. I didn't care, they were delicious. I wish I had bought another.

We left Dumai, heading for Batam Island, off the coast of Singapore. The death boat actually turned out to be a water bus, hugging the coast and stopping at a number of islands on route. Bengalis, Padang and Karimun were all ports of call. Vendors boarded to sell snacks and drinks, whooping and shouting to let passengers know who they were and what they sold. I bought a plastic bag with something in it for 2,000 rupiah (£0.60p). A reasonable price for a lucky dip, I thought. It turned out to be a tasty package of boiled rice and a small piece of curried chicken. The small bag of water that accompanied it I did not touch. Best keep to a bottle of Aqua - always.

For entertainment, a television and video had thoughtfully been provided, bolted high up the wall at the front end of the cabin. Through the journey numerous members of the crew fiddled with them, generally to no avail. Dodgy fifth generation copy videos of no fixed story and no sound presented a colourful, yet abstract moving picture to look at. Just a blurry picture hung on a wall. The stereo was of better quality, but only pumped out an endlessly repeating, single cassette of Indonesian pop music. Strangely, this included disco versions of Auld Lang Syne and Ging Gang Gooley. Disco-camp-fire beat, maybe!

Nine hours we were on that boat. Nine interminable hours, during which I forced myself to think of anything except what would happen in the event of an accident. There was absolutely no way out. It was actually time well spent for me. I was behind on this journal and needed to catch up.

ARRIVAL AT BATAM ISLAND

A Comedy of Chaos

Arriving at Batam Island, the gateway between Indonesia and its more cosmopolitan neighbours was like stepping into an elaborate exercise in organized confusion. As the boat docked under the equatorial sky, where daylight turns into night faster than the flick of a switch, the true absurdity of our situation began to unfold.

Imagine a cramped, floating death-trap disgorging 500 passengers, a mountain of luggage, and my Harley-Davidson onto a floating dock smaller than the average backyard patio. This dock, crowded with families eager to welcome relatives, was connected to solid ground by a rickety wooden gangplank. A mere twenty yards long, the gangplank wobbled under the weight of every step and felt like a metaphor for the precariousness of the entire operation.

Disembarking Madness...

The system for unloading was both simple and heart-stoppingly chaotic. Luggage wasn't unloaded into a designated area or transported by conveyor belt. Instead, a man at the boat's door grabbed parcels from the hold, held them aloft, and shouted for the owner. If you recognized your bag, you raised a hand. The parcel was then launched through the air towards you—often caught, sometimes not. Standing next to someone with bad hand-eye coordination felt like a death wish.

Meanwhile, Sean, towering like a rugby colossus among the petite crowd, muscled his way to the front. Steve, ever resourceful, went back aboard to chat with the captain, leaving me to watch this chaotic luggage lottery unfold.

The real problem, however, was the Harley. In Dumai, loading it onto the roof of the boat was easy, as the wharf was level with the roof. Here, the dock was level with the deck, leaving the bike stranded three meters above where it needed to be. If that wasn't challenging enough, a corrugated tin roof hanging a meter above the boat complicated matters further.

The porters in their numbered blue uniforms—official yet somehow unofficial—turned up demanding quick decisions. The bike couldn't stay on the boat as it prepared to leave, yet getting it onto dry land seemed an impossible task. Forty U.S. dollars later, we had a deal: they would unload the bike to the road. Easy in theory; a logistical nightmare in practice!

Enter James...

Amid the chaos, James appeared—a mysterious local with a decent grasp of English. He claimed to have no ulterior motive, only to be in the right place at the right time. His story about waiting for friends who never arrived was suspicious, but we had bigger problems to deal with. We needed transport: a car for us and a truck for the bike. James, self-appointed problem solver, assured us he could arrange it.

SCARY REMOVAL OF BIKE FROM FERRY

Directing operations by moonlight and a tiny flashlight, I faced the first task: releasing the straps holding the bike to the pallet. The straps were tricky, so I tackled them myself. Once loosened, the wheels still held the bike steady, but coordinated pulling from my enthusiastic - if clueless - porters separated it from the pallet. Stage one complete.

Next, we had to move the bike from the higher roof to the lower one. Three planks were found to protect the boat's windscreen, but the first test of their strength was laughable. Stacking them improved stability, but the setup was far from ideal—a narrow, slippery 45-degree slope on a moving boat, in the dark. With rope tied to the bike's front crash bars and porters bracing at the rear, I mounted the bike, holding the brake and praying no passing boat would cause a swell.

The descent began cautiously. I edged the front wheel onto the planks and slowly eased forward until the back wheel hit the ramp. Balancing precariously, I feared a fierce wave would send me crashing into the cabin below. Behind me, someone shouted, "Satu, dua, tiga!" A heave from the porters lifted the back wheel, and the bike slid rapidly to the lower roof. Relief was short-lived; the real challenge was yet to come.

The boat and jetty swayed independently, making the next move treacherous. Attempting to roll the bike across narrow planks was out of the question. The decision was made: strap the bike back onto the pallet and lower it, like a castle drawbridge, onto the jetty. With slightly better lighting on the lower deck, we rigged ropes to the bike and pallet. Half the team stood on the jetty; the rest remained aboard to ease the descent.

Inch by inch, the pallet slid forward until it tipped past the boat's edge. My heart raced as frantic shouts and gestures accompanied the delicate operation. At the fulcrum point, the bike dangled momentarily before the jetty crew took the weight. The boat swayed, drifting dangerously from the dock, but the porters acted swiftly, lowering the bike until it touched the jetty.

Finally, with the bike safely on solid ground, it was wheeled off the pallet and across a narrow, rickety gangplank to the dock. Compared to the earlier ordeal, this final task felt like a breeze. As I followed, numb with stress and relief, the boat was already departing, leaving me and my iron horse to recover from the chaos.

Meanwhile...

CUSTOMS STORY

We told James we needed to get to the ferry for Malaysia. He nodded confidently, claiming to work in the travel agency business.

"There's a ferry at eight tonight," he said. I couldn't believe our luck—a godsend, surely!

"Are you sure? Tonight?!"

He nodded again. "Yes, but the port is thirty minutes from here."

We checked the time: 18:30. Ninety minutes. If we could somehow get the bike down, we'd just make it. James explained our urgency to the captain. Calling him over, they exchanged rapid-fire Indonesian. The captain gestured dismissively.

From the shadows, a fat customs officer emerged. He had a long, wispy Fu Man Chu moustache, like something out of a cartoon. He barked something at the captain, which James translated as:

"He wants to see the papers for the bike."

"Why?" Steve asked. "It hasn't left the country. It's still in Indonesia!"

The customs officer shuffled closer, his face impassive.

James turned back to Steve. "He says you need special papers to get the bike off."

"Why?" Steve repeated, louder this time.

His expression apologetic, James shrugged. "I think he wants money."

James and a wiry boy guided Steve to the customs office, a decrepit room straight out of a noir film: two battered desks, a filing cabinet that might have survived World War I, and a flickering fluorescent light casting a sickly green glow.

One officer was sprawled in a chair, his feet propped on a desk, snoring lightly. Steve coughed loudly, jolting him awake. He sat up, slicking back greasy hair and adjusting his uniform like a schoolboy caught napping in class.

James launched into a rapid explanation. The officer listened, uninterested, until James mentioned the bike. At this, his demeanour changed. He leaned forward, his moustache twitching.

"They say you have to pay," James relayed.

"Pay?" Steve spluttered. "We haven't left the country! The bike came from Dumai and is still in Indonesia!"

James spoke again. The officer remained unimpressed. James turned back to Steve. "They still say you have to pay."

"How much?"

The officer stood and, with a theatrical flourish, shut the door. James hesitated, and then turned to Steve.

"Four hundred dollars."

"What?! Four hundred dollars?!" Steve's voice echoed in the shabby office. "You've got to be joking. I don't have that kind of money. No way."

The customs officer looked up, his expression unreadable. James tried again:

"How much do you want to pay?"

Steve rifled through his wallet, heart racing. "Fifty," he said finally. "Forty in US dollars, the rest in rupiah. That's it."

James relayed the offer, gesturing emphatically. The room erupted into an animated debate. The officer scowled, muttering under his breath. Seizing the moment, Steve held out the money, as if to say - This is all you're getting.

After what felt like an eternity, they grudgingly agreed.

Steve added one condition. "I need my paperwork stamped."

At this, the officer recoiled, visibly alarmed.

"What's the problem?" Steve asked James.

"They're internal customs," James explained. "The bike needs clearance from international customs before you can leave for Malaysia."

Steve stared at him in disbelief. "You mean there's another set of customs waiting to bleed me dry?"

They flatly refused to stamp anything, scribbling a half-hearted note on a scrap of paper instead. Twelve words for fifty bucks. The note looked like it had been torn from a roll of toilet paper—and was probably just as useful.

FINAL MOMENTS

By now, the dock was quieter, most passengers having already left. The luggage formed a neat pile thanks to Chris's efforts, and the bike, after much sweat and improvisation, was finally on solid ground.

As we prepared for the next leg of our journey, I reflected on the sheer absurdity of the day. What should have been a simple disembarkation had turned into a master class in chaos management. Yet somehow, through a mix of stubborn determination and blind luck, we had survived another chapter of this adventure.

The Harley was safe, our belongings were intact, and we were still standing. As I watched James barter for transport in the dim glow of the equatorial night, I couldn't help but think: maybe, just maybe, this journey would eventually find its rhythm. Or maybe not...

TERMINAL

While all this was going on, Steve and James were organising transport to the international ferry terminal. If you remember, this is about twenty five kilometres away, and we have only forty five minutes to get there. Unlikely, I say. In pitch black, I am standing next to the bike and pallet when round the corner I see a pair of headlights approaching. It is the pick-up truck. A minute or so later, another set of headlights accompanied by a rattling noise and some squeaks appears. This time it is car. Through the dim ambient light caused by the headlights I can see that these vehicles are not exactly in perfect condition. Runners, yes, but only just. Beggars can't be choosers, however, and I am grateful James has managed to get a pick-up and a car so quickly. Standing next to the bike, a thought comes over me. You never know, so, hope against hope, I put the key in, turn on the ignition and press the starter. It was vibration, after all, that killed the bike, and so maybe the endless shaking it received on the ferry rattled back whatever was rattled loose. No chance. It is still as dead as a dodo. "Right, get the bike up, no poncing about, we must be gone!" As the bike is loaded, our team of porters are bringing the rest of the gear from the jetty - big stuff in the pick-up, small stuff in the car. After a bit of argy-bargery over the deal, I end up giving the porters sixty dollars for their trouble. A lot of money, but by the end there must have been twenty of them so three dollars each is hardly excessive. They had worked hard and carefully, and the bike was safely aboard the pick-up. Although fifty percent up on the original price, I didn't feel ripped off.

Grateful as I am, I have to say that the transport James has located is shagged out. The pick-up is a mid-seventies Datsun with a bench seat so knackered, that wherever I sit, a spring stuck up my arse. The driver is constantly smoking some evil smelling local cigarette, but considerately keeps the windows down. Least I think he was being considerate. It may have been simply because they didn't wind up any more. I sit in the middle and James sits by the other open window. The likelihood of us reaching the ferry terminal in time diminishes by the second. Top speed of our trusty steed is all of twenty five miles an hour, so allowing for some traffic I reckon it would take fifteen minutes longer than we have to get there. The roads are fairly good, though. They are certainly better than in the other parts of Indonesia we have visited. Probably due, in part, to the fact this is a tourist island for Singaporeans, whose wealth has financed a relatively boom economy.

James is directing the driver who, I reckon, has no more idea of where we are going than me - Up hill, down dale, turn left, turn right - it's a long way when you're in a hurry. Every few seconds I look in the mirror to check that Steve and the crew are still behind us. All I can see, of course, is two dazzling headlights which I assume is them. I keep checking nevertheless.

Finally we enter the ferry area and, following the signs, we head for the main gate. Unbelievably, we still have five minutes to go. As usual I've been dealt all the low cards because we get there and find the main gate locked. A man in a fancy uniform saunters out of his hut and points back the way we came. What he said I don't know, but the general gist is, go somewhere else. Waving to the car behind, we tell them to turn round and follow us. Off we go, through what seems to be a sparsely occupied trading estate and back into the countryside. There are no street lights and no signs. Hopefully James knows where he is going, because no-one else does. Eventually we come to a T-junction with a chain link fence facing us. We turn left, follow the fence and look for the gate. A hundred yards or so and there it is, open and lit by a tiny dim light. Success! In we go and park in front of what looks like the terminal building with signs saying 'Arrival', 'Departure' and the dreaded 'Customs'. The pick-up and the car have travelled in tandem so we all arrive together. Not too difficult, I suppose, at the speeds we were managing. As Steve enters the Terminal Building to see what the score is, a man in an important looking uniform asks us to move our vehicles. Not unreasonable as we've blocked the walkway between the Arrival and Departure doors and the dock, thirty metres in front. James and I get out as the driver moves the pick-up out of the way, parking a short way away at the end of the terminal building.

There is no boat parked here, so, assuming we are in the right place, it is apparent we have either missed it........or there was never one in the first place. We were told so much crap in

Jakarta and Dumai about ferries, my guess is the latter.

We hang about for half an hour. Steve has disappeared inside the building, so the rest of us have no idea what is going on. Apart from anything else, I am starving. The last thing I ate was the funny little bag of rice I bought on the Dumai ferry at eleven o'clock this morning. It is now nine. Just outside the gate a stallholder is selling satay, (chicken on a stick, smothered in peanut sauce) and a very enticing aroma is wafting my way. Problem is -no money. No Indonesian money anyway. We had all expected to be out of the country by now so are totally rupiah-less. I leave the others moaning about something (as usual) and go off to find James, who very kindly lends me the 1000 rupiah (about 30p) I need to buy some food.

Eventually Steve returns, his carnet and document-filled briefcase under his arm, looking very stern. There never was a boat to Malaysia, he explains darkly - once again we were given a bum steer. The same old story!

"There is a ferry to Malaysia from Dumai, you must return there."

"The Dumai ferry is not working, that is why we are here."

"You must leave from Dumai. That is shown on your documents.", the official insists.

"We wanted to leave from Dumai, but there is no boat, it is broken. We can only leave from here."

"There is no ferry to Malaysia. You must go to Singapore then to Malaysia."

"We cannot, we have no papers for Singapore."

"You must go to Singapore. There are many ferries that go to Singapore, many take motorcycles."

"We cannot, we have no documents, we must go to Malaysia from Batam Island. Dumai officials said it was the only way. Why were we told that?"

"Tomorrow!"

"What do you mean tomorrow? So there is a ferry?" "Yes, but it will not take motorcycles, only passengers."

"When is the ferry tomorrow?"

"Eight o'clock." "How can we get on it?" "No motorcycles, impossible."

Indonesia has been full of conversations like this. Essentially, they are all too worried to make a decision. Everything must be referred up the ladder. Punishment can very harsh on anyone who makes a mistake. Often resulting in instant dismissal, there is certainly great personal embarrassment and "loss of face". "Loss of face" is a bit like being sent to Coventry, but a hundred times worse. It is the worst thing that can happen to someone in many parts of Asia. It was loss of face that drove so many Japanese generals to suicide when they lost battles in World War II. The best way to avoid the likelihood of this happening is to take no responsibility. It can never, therefore, be your fault. Always pass the buck. To be on the receiving end of all this crap is frustrating and expensive. Frustrating, because it always takes so long to establish the truth and expensive because only bucks stop the buck being passed. American greenbacks have great memory restoring capabilities in Indonesia. The smell of some was, it seems, perking up our local ferry official.

He has now gone off to consult with his colleagues, no doubt to establish how much they can screw us for. All we can do is stand around and wait, and wait, and wait. Again, the longer we are made to wait the easier it will probably be to squeeze money out of us.

After half an hour Steve is called back into the office and the door behind him firmly shut. Another half an hour goes by. Not a bad sign. At least it means they are talking. And talking generally means how much, rather than no way.

HARBOUR MASTER MUST APPROVE

To cut a long boring story short, when Steve returns; "yes" we can leave; "yes", they will accept our paperwork; "yes", there is a ferry to Malaysia; "maybe", we can put a motorcycle on it. But the harbour Master needs to give his permission. He, however, is at home. It is, ten o'clock at night, after all. Can we get hold of him - please? You say the ferry leaves at eight and the Harbour Master starts work at nine, so that's too late. OK, we can go to his house.

Remarkably, he is not at all pissed off at us disturbing him, and yes it is alright by him; providing the ferry captain agrees. It is, after all, a passenger ferry and there may be no space for a motorcycle. The decision rests with the captain. The Harbour Master is thanked for his help and we leave. Basically, all we can now do is find a local hotel, as close as possible to the terminal, and go to bed. Not quite. The bike and the camera gear must go to a bonded store for the night and be looked after by security guards. How much? "Very cheap, very efficient, very secure", he assures us. It is very clear there is no option, so off we go to the bonded store. It all looks a bit dodgy to me. Half a dozen shady looking characters sitting around an old brown wooden table at the front of an anonymous looking large concrete shed. True, it was surrounded by a chain link fence with an official looking sign on it, but, to be honest, it was very dark and late at night and so it could have said 'Battersea Dogs Home' in Indonesian for all I knew.

We unload the truck and the car and stack everything neatly in the foyer (I use that term loosely) of the store. The boss man makes it very clear to the workers that they are to look after this stuff and nothing must go missing. Sensibly they ask for an inventory. I write out two which we both sign, retaining one copy each. With reservations, but no choice, I leave.

As uncomfortable as I am about leaving my cherished possession in the custody of some very dubious looking characters, I now have to concentrate on the next job in hand. We are all very tired and need to find somewhere to sleep. It is now almost eleven, and what an eventful day we have had. It started with nine hours on the 'death ferry', squashed in a first class cabin with about as much luxury and comfort as the Roman galley Spartacus spent some time on. Arriving at our destination life does not improve - I am then confronted with a low dock and a high bike. Solve that one move onto the next problem: transport. Each time I feel a little closer to salvation, but each time another difficult situation pops up its ugly head. You think I would learn. Ever the optimist I think 'Great, got that sorted, now I can relax!'

Of course I can't. Each day, each moment of every day, seems to present new difficulties. What I failed to realise, but am now beginning to appreciate, is how complex this journey is. In retrospect (I hope) it is what will have made it all worthwhile. Even as widely travelled as I am, I was not prepared for the culture shock. Visiting a country as a tourist is one thing, trying to untangle the mysteries of bureaucracy and get an official to do something a little out of the ordinary is quite different.

THE SYSTEM

I later learned that shortly after my time in Jakarta, headlines in Italy erupted over a foreigner acquiring Lamborghini—a brand synonymous with Italian design and flair. The buyer? - Tommy Suharto. Where he got the money is a mystery.

This epitomized a truth about Indonesia: corruption is woven into its fabric. The example set from the top is that it's perfectly acceptable to take whatever you can from wherever you can get it. Rules and regulations exist, but only as tools for profit.

It's not just dishonesty; it's a system. Bureaucracy in Indonesia is like a giant jigsaw puzzle where each official holds one piece. Earning a government salary isn't enough to support a family, so each official sells their piece for as much as possible. By spreading these fragments across a web of nepotism, they ensure that any single task involves as many people as possible. Great for them – not so good for me!

A PLACE TO CRASH

Using the bonded store as our makeshift compass, we eventually found a fairly new, bland hotel: the Nan Tonga View. Steve negotiated the price—$50 for a twin room—and booked three. Steve and Chris shared, Sean and Paul paired up and, as paymaster, I got a room to myself.

Exhausted but unwilling to turn in without a drink, we decided to check out a nearby bar. After quick showers (where the dirt of the day turned the water black), we followed the receptionist's directions: turn right, skirt the perimeter, and look for the neon lights of the Ski-Club.

The tropical rain shower didn't bother us too much—warm and fleeting—but the large, unseen puddles did. By the time we reached the club, each of us had one soggy, squelching shoe.

THE SKI-CLUB EXPERIENCE

From the outside, the Ski-Club looked like a seedy massage parlour in a dodgy part of Manchester. Graffiti-covered walls and an unkempt façade didn't exactly scream "welcome." Still, after the day we'd had, a drink felt necessary to dilute the stress oozing from every pore.

Inside was a time warp to the early 1970s: sticky carpets, flashing disco lights, ultraviolet tubes, and a faintly desperate air. We were greeted by a stocky lad—Little Richard's doppelganger—who ushered us to a table. No sooner had we sat down than three girls descended, eager for us to buy them drinks.

The problem was, as we were the only customers, they clearly saw us as their last shot of the night. Unfortunately for them, their "car boot sale chic" didn't quite align with our tastes. After a polite but firm decline, they left, disappointed.

Chris, looking every bit the colonial adventurer in his khakis, became the next target—for Little Richard. Misreading Chris's stoic English reserve as interest, he scooted closer, offering awkward small talk and unsubtle suggestions. Meanwhile, the steward received a scolding for not corralling more girls to our table.

Eventually, two more reluctant young women were sent to join us. Their disinterest was palpable; they sized us up, shook their heads, and walked off.

"Well, that's a first," I muttered to Steve. "We have been rejected by a hooker! Really speaks to how terrible we must look." We laughed, but it was a low moment.

Chris, visibly annoyed by Little Richard's persistence, finally reached his limit. We settled the bill and left, relieved to escape the uncomfortable vibe that lingered in the club.

On our soggy trudge back to the hotel, we speculated about what fresh chaos the morning would bring. Despite our fatigue, sleep seemed a distant hope.

As we reached the lobby, I muttered to no one in particular:

"Please, God, just get me out of this country."

SICK WITH WORRY

Right now, I am physically sick with worry.

I woke at 5:30 a.m., feeling even worse than when I collapsed into bed four and a half hours earlier. The bike—my once-prized machine—is stashed in the port security building, battered and broken. Over the thousand miles it was permitted to travel on Indonesian roads, it's been a disaster: a brake calliper bolt vanished, the seat lost its retaining bolt, a chrome handlebar grip was stolen, the electrics failed, and just last night, I discovered the front speedometer cable had snapped.

This country seems to take delight in grinding me down. A week of bureaucratic hell just to get the bike into Jakarta, four days of riding, and three more trying—and failing—to escape.

The authorities said I could leave from Dumai. Then they said no, it must be Medan. Then it was Dumai again. Fine, so I went to Dumai, enduring roads so appalling they broke the bike.

Then in Dumai, the ferry was broken - so, off to Batam Island. On Batam, they informed me I'd need to go to Singapore. But I had no papers for Singapore, and they wouldn't let me in. The only route to Malaysia was a passenger ferry—no motorbikes allowed.

"Go back to Dumai," they said.

"No point," I replied. "There's no ferry there."

I am losing my mind.

After hours of wrangling with customs officials, they finally conceded that my paperwork was in order and gave me permission to leave. Relief? Hardly! The ferry operators refused to let the bike on board—they only transport passengers.

More negotiations ensued. Eventually, they agreed that if the Harbour Master gave permission, the bike could board. Off I went to his house at 10 p.m. He was at home with his wife and kids, and—miracle of miracles—he agreed, provided the vessel's captain consented.

And now, here I am, sick with anxiety, hoping for a sympathetic captain.

STILL HOLDING BACK

I haven't called home. They'll sense the tension in my voice, and I don't want my family to worry. I'll call when I'm in Malaysia.

If I ever get there.

 # FRIDAY 24 JUNE

NO JAMES

I had asked James to meet us at the hotel with a van and a pick-up by 6:30. Judging by his reluctance at the mere suggestion, I wasn't optimistic about punctuality, but I figured he might still manage quarter to seven.

Six-thirty came and went. So did quarter to seven. By seven o'clock, panic had set in. The ferry to Malaysia was supposed to leave at eight. Although the port was just five minutes away, we were stranded. The bike was still locked up in the customs shed, and we needed transport—not just for the bike, but for all of us and our luggage. Tickets still had to be purchased, assuming we could convince the captain to load the bike onto a ferry that ostensibly didn't take bikes. Customs clearance for the bike and the camera gear loomed over us as an unthinkable hurdle.

What were the odds of accomplishing all this in forty-five minutes?

Exactly!

The hotel had a pick-up and a van parked in its lot. Pleas for help at the front desk were met with smiles and blank stares— the kind of response I've come to dread. Were they completely clueless, or was this their polite way of saying, "Tough luck, you're on your own"?

I turned to the one who seemed marginally in charge. His stature was exaggeratedly diminutive, thanks to the recessed floor behind the counter—a clever design trick to make even the shortest guests feel towering. But this wasn't about ego. I needed action.

He was a shiny sort, with a young Nicholas Parsons vibe: thin, polished, and constantly smiling, as if his face might split in two. His neck was so thin that when he turned to confer with his colleague, his shirt collar stayed put.

"We desperately need a van," I explained, fighting the churn in my stomach to stay outwardly calm.

He smiled.

"We only have forty-five minutes to catch our ferry!"

He smiled wider.

Even though his English was perfectly fine—this was a tourist area for Singaporeans—I slowed my speech for emphasis. "Please, we need your van and pick-up."

"No driver. Driver asleep," he replied, still grinning.

"Wake him up. Please."

"No keys. Can't find keys. Only one driver. Pick-up okay. Mini-bus okay. One driver only."

It was maddening. Outside, Steve was running up and down the street, hunting for alternative transport. If we could find a pick-up truck in the middle of the Sumatran jungle at six in the morning, surely we could manage it here.

After what felt like an eternity of pleading, "Smiley" finally agreed to call the driver and wake him. His colleague meandered off in search of the elusive keys - neither seemed to grasp the concept of urgency.

It's a delicate dance in Southeast Asia. Losing your temper is not only undignified but counterproductive. People here avoid confrontation at all costs. Even if they're furious, they won't yell—they'll simply walk away. And when they do, you've lost.

Eventually, the driver picked up the phone and agreed to come over "right away." Meanwhile, the key-finder returned with a set that didn't fit. Back he went, unfazed. When the driver finally arrived, he trotted over with a second set of keys. Miraculously, they worked—for the pick-up truck, at least. There were still no keys for the van, but at this point, beggars couldn't be choosers.

We loaded our luggage and the crew into the back of the pick-up and set off. I found Steve, still searching frantically, and waved him over. Instead of running to the gate, he vaulted the perimeter fence, shaving precious seconds.

Still no James!

At the customs yard, my stomach churned as new anxieties bubbled up. Would the bike still be there? Would it be intact? Would they release it as agreed? And how much would this cost?

To my shock and relief, everything went smoothly. The bike and equipment were loaded onto the truck in record time. A few dollars exchanged hands, and within five minutes, we were back on the road, clinging to our luggage as we rattled toward the dock.

When we arrived at the terminal, it was deserted. The supposed eight o'clock ferry was clearly another case of "no problem" nonsense. We could do nothing but wait and hope. Hope that a ferry to Malaysia actually existed. Hope that we'd be allowed on it.

Three weeks of this madness had pushed me to the brink. Geronimo might have said, "Man speaks with forked tongue." Here, they use the entire cutlery set.

WRONG DOCUMENTS

By 8:30, the first uniforms begin to appear, as clueless as I anticipated. Eventually, a familiar face emerges—a grinning opportunist who's clearly thrilled at the prospect of how much he can extort from me today.

The latest update: the ferry will now leave at 11. The Harbour Master is expected to sign the necessary papers at 9:30. Of course, this timeline is as fluid as everything else here.

Steve is ushered into the office, where he's surrounded by four uniformed officials. The door closes behind him, signalling the start of another round of heavy negotiations.

The obstacles are laid out like a game of bureaucratic whack-a-mole. The ferry, they remind us, is a passenger ferry. Loading the bike will be "very difficult." We'll need a crane, they say. We'll need helpers. Oh, and apparently, we have the wrong documents.

The litany of requirements grows absurd:

- "You need this."

- "You need that."

- "You will need $5,000."

The sum is laughable, and Steve pushes back, asserting repeatedly that the documents are valid. The issue is simply that the exit point was changed—a problem caused by their side, not ours.

But the officials remain steadfast, emphasizing the complexity of the situation. They explain how everyone's satisfaction must be guaranteed:

- Customs must be happy.

- The booking clerk must be happy.

- The Harbour Master must be happy.

- The Captain must be happy.

- Even the brother of the cleaner's nephew's next-door neighbour's cousin must be happy.

The only person who doesn't matter in this equation? Me. I'm the one paying, but happiness is not on my horizon.

The back-and-forth drags on for thirty minutes, with plenty of bluffing, dramatic sighs, and hand-waving frustration from their side. Finally, an agreement is reached: $500 in cash, and we're free to leave.

Naturally, I don't have $500 in cash. I'm promptly dispatched to the nearest bank, clinging to the back of a moped taxi as it weaves through the chaos of Batam Island.

By the time it's all said and done, I've spent over $1,500 just to leave Indonesia. Between the fiasco in Dumai, the nonexistent ferry, the unnecessary hotel stay, multiple ferry tickets, and the relentless bribery, the cost of this ordeal is staggering.

I hope reading this saga has been entertaining because living it has been nothing short of a nightmare.

NO ENTRY TO MALAYSIA

I can't believe it. For a brief, shining moment, everything seemed to fall into place. Batam Island and the misery of my Indonesian ordeal were finally retreating into the haze. I was Malaysia-bound, and for the first time in days, a glimmer of joy broke through the clouds of frustration.

The ferry ride was a stark contrast to everything that came before it: the captain, obliging and helpful, ensured the bike was professionally craned onto the bow and strapped down securely. The boat itself was compact, clean, and orderly, with a neatly dressed crew. Bottled water was handed out—for free! There were only a handful of other passengers, giving us the luxury of choosing our seats. It was as if I'd entered an alternate universe where things simply worked.

The crossing to Pasir Gudang took about an hour and a half. The exact location of this elusive jetty remained a mystery; it was nowhere to be found on my maps, save for a vague proximity to Johor at the southern tip of Malaysia. The moment we arrived, the stark reality hit: Pasir Gudang was, quite literally, just a concrete lump jutting into the water. No porters, no cranes, no equipment of any kind.

My heart sank.

How would we unload the bike? The bow of the ferry stood a meter above the dock, fenced by a wooden rail a meter high. To complicate matters further, the gap between the boat and the dock was six meters wide. Steve went off to deal with customs, leaving me to face this logistical nightmare alone.

We started by hauling the luggage off the ferry. Without porters, it took three grueling trips each under the relentless midday sun to carry everything ashore. By the end of it, I was drenched in sweat, utterly spent, and desperate for a drink. Inside the tiny customs building, a customs officer saw my state and, to my astonishment, offered to buy me a Coke. After the endless extortion and greed I'd endured in Indonesia, this simple act of kindness was almost surreal.

But the real challenge still loomed: unloading the bike. The captain, a jovial man reminiscent of a Humphrey Bogart film character, was incredibly accommodating. With his guidance and the help of a dozen bystanders, a plan began to take shape. Using a set of sturdy metal steps as a makeshift ramp and the boat's wooden rail as a fulcrum, we devised a way to shift the

400-kilogram beast from the ferry to solid ground.

The process was nerve-wracking. The rail creaked ominously under the weight of the bike, its paint peeling away as it bent under the strain. But there was no turning back. With everyone working in unison—pushing, pulling, and praying— we finally managed to lower the bike onto the steps, then onto the dock. Relief washed over me as the bike was finally safe on solid ground.

Unfortunately, my problems were far from over.

Steve returned with updates: the fixer arranged by Bagu was nowhere to be found. Harley-Davidson Kuala Lumpur, which was supposed to repair the bike, was delayed because their mechanic had been summoned to fix a bike for the Sultan of Johor. And then came the bombshell: the bike was prohibited from entering Malaysia.

Despite having all the correct paperwork—including an EU Transit Carnet accepted by Malaysian authorities—the customs officials declared that a non-working bike could not be classified as "transit." Instead, it was deemed "cargo," subject to entirely different regulations.

The customs officers were polite and sympathetic but firm: unless the bike could run, it would not be allowed to enter the country. The gate to freedom was no more than ten yards away, open and beckoning, yet utterly out of reach.

A customs officer, sensing my despair, offered a sliver of hope. He knew someone with a Harley who might be able to help fix the bike. While I waited for him to make the call, I reflected on the journey so far—a rollercoaster of challenges, setbacks, and fleeting moments of triumph.

The kindness of strangers like Smitty, who lent me his prized Fat Boy, and the customs officer offering a drink in my hour of need stood out amidst the chaos. There were moments of sheer awe, like witnessing the sunrise at Mount Bromo, the spiritual magnitude of Borobudur, and the surreal beauty of piloting the ferry past Krakatoa. But for every memory worth cherishing, there were countless frustrations, heartbreaks, and obstacles that threatened to overshadow it all.

This journey had tested me in ways I never imagined. And yet, despite it all, I clung to the faint hope that somehow, some way, I'd get through this latest trial and continue onward.

KERPOW!

I open the saddlebags and take out a Phillips screwdriver, an Allen key, and a small spanner—not because I know what to do, but because I need to do something. Sitting idly won't solve this. Once again, I remove the saddle and stare at the tangled mess of wires. Somewhere in there lies the cause of my frustration—and the key to my salvation.

For the umpteenth time, I reread the alarm manual, scouring it for a step I might have missed. I disconnect and reconnect the battery. I check the distilled water level; clean the terminals, tighten the connections, and replace the alarm fuse. I trace every wire for breaks or cuts, press the alarm button, and try the ignition. Nothing!

Start again.

This time, I completely disconnect the alarm. The installer had given me bypass instructions before I left England—just in case. I follow them precisely, press the button, and try the ignition. Still nothing!

Start again.

I rewire the alarm exactly as it was, triple-checking every step. I press the alarm button, try the ignition. Nothing!

Frustration grips me. The bike won't start with the immobilizer connected or disconnected. The lights and horn work fine, which suggests the battery is okay. The starter doesn't dim them, but I don't have the tools to check the circuits or battery charge. I suspect the alarm system is the culprit, but maybe the zapper itself is faulty. It doesn't feel right when I press it. A long shot, but it's a straw to cling to.

Somewhere in my gear, I have a spare zapper, tucked away with the spare key. Digging through the black holdall, my hand finds the familiar strap of the bum bag. With a few tugs, I retrieve it and hurry back to the bike.

One last time, I check the battery, connections, and wiring. One last time, I press the alarm button. Kerpow! The engine roars to life. Jubilation! Ecstasy! Relief crashes over me like a wave. A miracle! "Thank you, God!" I whisper, my voice cracking with emotion.

A crowd gathers to see what I've done, but all I want is to replace the seat and escape this customs yard. I need my carnet stamped before this fragile reprieve ends. But it's 5:30 p.m.—the main customs officer has gone home. He won't return until tomorrow.

The joy deflates instantly. After weeks of setbacks, this feels like another cruel twist. Steve and I talk quietly, deciding I should keep the engine running while he negotiates. I drive off to explore the industrial estate, pretending I'm free.

The area is a labyrinth of petrochemical plants—massive tanks and pipelines dwarfing the people working around them. I stick to a cautious route, always keeping my starting point in sight. Getting lost or labelled a customs absconder would be disastrous.

As I grow more confident, my circuits widen until I find myself on a dual carriageway. At its end, a security post marks the dockyard's boundary. Guards check every vehicle entering or leaving. This is my limit. I turn back, the engine's steady hum a small reassurance.

When I return, there's good news. The minibus from Kuala Lumpur has arrived—barely roadworthy, but here. More importantly, a senior customs officer has agreed to return from home to stamp my carnet. The Malaysian attitude is a refreshing contrast to the bureaucracy in Indonesia.

On my next loop to the security post, a glint of blue and chrome catches my eye. A Harley Softail Springer, slender and elegant, is being checked in. The rider waves and I follow him back to the customs yard.

We shake hands, and he introduces himself as Mohammed Nour Suleiman, Executive Chairman of S S Holidays in Pasir Gudang. Hearing about my predicament, he's come to help. His enthusiasm is infectious. "It's exciting to meet a Harley traveller," he says, beaming.

Mohammed examines my bike, appreciating the paintwork and the horse's head airbrushed on the front fender. He spots a few minor issues—blown bulbs for the brake light, indicators, and main beam—and offers to take me to a nearby shop.

To commemorate our meeting, Steve suggests filming some scenes. Mohammed and I ride into the sunset, the camera capturing us from a worm's-eye view. It feels exhilarating, a rare moment of joy amidst the chaos.

Dusk arrives as a car pulls into the yard. The senior customs officer has arrived. I practically prostrate myself before him, overwhelmed with gratitude. He signs the papers, and just like that, I'm free. No bribery, no corruption—just proper regulations followed.

The minibus and I follow Mohammed out of the customs yard. The Harley hums beneath me, and for the first time in days, I feel the intoxicating thrill of freedom.

Out from the dock area and onto a well maintained dual carriageway - as good as any found in Europe. There is an air of organised prosperity with obvious British influence. Mohammed knew I needed some fuel so our first stop, five minutes from the port, is a petrol station. A BP garage – the famous green and yellow canopy, four lines of pumps, paper towels, litter bins, the lot. It is a regular petrol station, identical to any found in Basingstoke or Birmingham. A couple of days ago I was buying petrol in plastic cans from a man stood next to a rickety old table in the jungle. Now I'm back in the land of the electronic displays and credit cards. Reverse culture shock or what?! I fill the tank and go to pay. Automatic glass doors open as I enter the shop. The others wait in the van. More surprises nearly make my eyes pop out of my head.

It was a fully-fledged air-conditioned BP shop, with a mini-supermarket, selling newspapers papers, magazines, drinks, cigarettes. All the usual stuff, albeit with a cosmopolitan, oriental bias. One special product caught my eye immediately.

I was drawn like a magnet. My mouth watered. I was ecstatic. I reach over and pick up - a bar of Cadbury's Whole Nut. I selfishly savour every bite. It melts in my mouth. It is absolutely delicious. Heavenly!

I snap back to reality. Businesses are closing and I have to get the lights fixed. Mohammed knows someone just up the road but we need to hurry.

We approach a series of scruffy shops-cum-workshops that are in a slip road that runs parallel to the main drag. We are now in a slightly less salubrious part of town. Most of the signs are now in Chinese. They make up around 35% of the population here in Malaysia and an even greater proportion of the business community. Stopping outside a dusty, grimy unit, littered with empty oil drums and bits of old motorcycles, Mohammed dismounts and disappears inside, reappearing a couple of minutes later with a Chinese man dressed to match his surroundings. Wiping his hands on his overalls, he reaches into his pockets and brings out a couple of screwdrivers.

He carefully removes the chrome surround and gently pulls the headlamp unit, allowing access to the bulb at the back. He twists it out and slips it into his pocket. Moving round the bike he checks all the bulbs, removing all those that need replacing. A few minutes later his task is complete; all up and running apart from main beam, which appears to have a slightly more serious problem. I can live with that - I still have the dip and two driving lamps.

It has become apparent that the garage man speaks no English so I ask Mohammed to find out how much I owe him. Mohammed will have none of it. A guest of his in trouble need not worry. He had sorted it already. Wow - my second experience of Malaysian generosity and hospitality.

I tell you, after all the crap in Indonesia my heart has been lifted by these people. My spirits are in good form as we follow Mohammed back onto the main road. He points us in the right direction, raises his arm in farewell and leaves, speeding off left at the next intersection.

INTO THE DARK

We trundle along at a steady sixty miles an hour, the bike running smoothly. The road is a modern, European-style highway, complete with cat's eyes and a hard shoulder. But it's very dark. The only things visible are the headlights of oncoming cars and the taillights of those ahead.

Hours pass, the monotony broken only by occasional signposts: Ayer Hitam, Yong Peng, Melaka—places vaguely familiar from the map I studied back in Batam.

I can't help but feel disappointed. This is meant to be an adventure, a chance to experience a new country. But in the darkness, Malaysia is reduced to headlights, asphalt, and shadows. Still, I remind myself that riding my bike—finally—beats being stuck on a truck.

As the hours crawl by, I replay the day's positive moments in my mind. I think about calling friends and family back home, eager to share some good news for once. I've avoided contacting them until now, not wanting to worry anyone. But tonight, I feel ready.

Finally, the van turns off the motorway and into a small town. The black void gives way to neon signs and garish lights strung across the streets, their cheap glow lending the place a tacky, carnival-like atmosphere.

We pull into a roadside truck stop, its garishness matching the rest of the town. "The driver hasn't eaten all day and needs a break," someone explains. I take one look and shake my head. "Not here," I insist. "It's awful. Let's find somewhere else."

After some grumbling, I spot another place just up the road. Without waiting for a reply, I go to investigate.

It's a simple, clean, bustling eatery. It is the kind of place where you can see the food being cooked—usually a good sign. Relieved, I report back. We drag a few red Formica-topped tables together and sit down.

I order a Fanta from a cheerful, fresh-faced Chinese woman. The others, as usual, attempt to drain the place of its beer supply. The van drivers sit apart, devouring enormous plates of steaming rice and chicken. I can't tell if they're being respectful or just antisocial, but it's clear the camaraderie in the van has been less than stellar. Judging by the muttered curses about "wankers," I'm glad to have stayed on the bike.

BEYOND EXHAUSTED

Exhausted, I sip my drink and try to ignore the chatter around me. Sleep is all I want now; though I know it's still far off. For the moment, I cling to the positives—the kindness of strangers, the satisfaction of a running bike, and the simple pleasure of being on the road again.

The remainder of the night's journey blurs into a monotonous slog. The pod of light cast by my dipped beam illuminates only a few meters ahead, leaving the world beyond shrouded in darkness. To my left and right, there is nothing—only the occasional glint of distant headlights across the central reservation.

Matching the van's steady but sluggish pace, I rarely overtake anyone, and only a few vehicles pass me. It's a tiresome, dull, and seemingly endless drag through the black void.

A GLIMPSE OF SPLENDOUR

By the time we reach Kuala Lumpur, exhaustion has dulled my senses to the point where the city registers as little more than a blur of lights and shadows. It's just another urban sprawl to me, indistinguishable from any other, with one notable exception.

Amidst the glass-and-steel anonymity of modern Kuala Lumpur, a single building rises in luminous grandeur. I don't know what it is, but it's enormous, stunning, and magnificently lit. Its dome-topped towers and intricate arches in two-tone white and caramel seem to belong to another era, evoking an air of Arabian Nights' mystique.

The tallest tower features a clock on each face, reminiscent of Big Ben, while the rest of the structure stands alone, a jewel of architectural beauty.

Later, I learned this was the Sultan Abdul Samad Building, the most photographed landmark in Malaysia. Today, it houses the Malaysian Supreme Court, but its history is rooted in the colonial era. Originally the secretariat headquarters, it was the first building in Malaysia to feature a North Indian/Moorish architectural style. This trend was introduced by 19th-century architects A.C. Norman and A.B. Hubbock, who believed buildings in predominantly Muslim countries should embody Arabic, Indian, and Moorish motifs.

Ironically, their designs overlooked the practicality and charm of traditional Malayan architecture. Even then, the governor, Sir Charles Mitchell, dismissed the building as a costly extravagance. Yet, despite its controversial origins, I have to admit—it's truly fabulous, an incongruous masterpiece amidst the modern skyline and well worth a visit.

RAGGED AND FILTHY

Ragged, filthy, and desperate for a bath and sleep, I finally roll into the Holiday Inn, City Centre, at around one in the morning. The bright, elegant facade feels surreal after hours of darkness and fatigue.

I shuffle up the grand entrance steps and through the luxurious lobby - a scruffy, smelly biker entering a fragrant palace. My helmet drops onto the reception desk with an audible clunk as I lean heavily against the counter.

Around me, fellow guests glance up, eyebrows raised, as my

equally dishevelled crew piles in behind me, depositing a mountain of battered luggage onto the polished floor. We're a ragtag band of road-weary travellers, completely out of place amidst the hotel's plush surroundings.

I manage to ask for the manager, slouching over the counter, my voice thick with fatigue. A slim, attractive Chinese woman emerges from behind the desk, her radiant smile cutting through my haze of exhaustion.

"Hello," she says softly, her tone warm and welcoming. "You must be Mr. Mike Orr."

Her words are a balm to my frayed nerves. Finally, I've made it.

SATURDAY 25 JUNE

KUALA LUMPUR

Saturday morning arrives with a sense of anticipation as I prepare to visit the only official Harley-Davidson dealership in Southeast Asia. After days of weariness and stress, I feel rejuvenated—almost like a new man.

I book a taxi for ten o'clock. The dealership, located in P.J. Industrial Park, Petaling Jaya, is supposedly about 30 minutes away. Factoring in Kuala Lumpur's notorious traffic and the possibility of my driver getting lost, I estimate I'll arrive by eleven.

Petaling Jaya, once a quiet dormitory town for Kuala Lumpur, has evolved into a bustling suburb and major industrial hub with a population of 250,000. It's also among the city's wealthier areas, which explains why Harley-Davidson chose to set up shop there.

The ride is predictably delayed—my taxi arrives late, and the driver initially takes me to the wrong industrial park. Thankfully, the traffic isn't as bad as expected, and I pull up to the dealership at 11:15.

Nestled in a modest terrace of shops and offices, the showroom is unassuming by Harley-Davidson standards. Small but stylishly decorated, it exudes the iconic brand's character. However, the inventory is sparse—just five bikes. Three of the big models are already sold, leaving only two 883s.

Despite Malaysia's exorbitant import tax of 120%, demand far outstrips supply. An Evo costs around $50,000 USD, a price only the mega-rich can afford. During my visit, the Sultan of Johor orders two more.

I'm greeted by a stocky, affable man in his thirties, dressed predictably in jeans, a white T-shirt, and a black leather waistcoat. He introduces himself as Ani Yahaya, explaining his nickname, "Animal," which he earned while living in Holland. It's a playful blend of his name and his Malaysian roots: ANI from MALaysia. Now, it's his street name, a tradition among the Harley-Davidson community here.

Ani explains that Nazary Ahmad, the Sales and Marketing Manager I've come to meet, is tied up in a sales meeting and will arrive shortly. In the meantime, he offers me a Coke. As I sip my drink, I strike up a conversation with an elegant woman clad in designer biker gear, complete with a bandanna and gold Rolex.

I share my reason for being in Kuala Lumpur, inviting her and as many friends as possible to join us at a Harley party at the Hard Rock Café that night. She promises to spread the word, though she reminds me that Friday is Harley night at the Hard Rock, not Saturday. Undeterred, I cheekily ask if she knows anyone famous or influential who'd be willing to appear in my film and, if so, whether she'd be willing to make a few calls.

MAO AND THE GRAPEVINE

Just then, Nazary Ahmad arrives. Clad in Harley-standard

attire—jeans, cowboy boots, a branded T-shirt, and a baseball cap—he apologizes for the delay. With a friendly smile, he introduces himself by his street name, Mao. I suspect the moniker comes from his tendency to take charge.

Mao listens attentively as I explain my goals. Rallying Kuala Lumpur's Harley-Davidson community for a party with less than nine hours' notice is no small feat, especially since Friday is the designated Harley night. Nevertheless, he promises to try. He immediately begins making calls, urging everyone he contacts to spread the word further.

While Mao works the phone, his friend Hussein arrives on a gleaming Evo. By now, it's noon, and Mao suggests we head to the Chinese restaurant next door for lunch and a strategy session. Over plates of chicken, fish, and rice, I start to grasp the scale of the Harley scene I've stumbled into.

Hussein isn't just a biker—he's an iron mine owner. Not a miner who works the land, but someone whose family owns the land. Another supporter, Alvin, soon joins us, eager to help with the film. Refusing any cash for lunch, Mao insists on covering the bill before we return to the dealership to make more calls.

The next suggestion is to take a ride through town to see if we can connect with other bikers. Hussein, Alvin, and I mount up and cruise to a nearby open-sided Chinese eatery, a common meeting spot.

This "restaurant" is a collection of mismatched tables and chairs beneath a plaza roof, served by several independent food stalls. Despite its ramshackle appearance, the place is packed—always a good sign. Though I'm not hungry, I order a beer and soak in the atmosphere.

Looking out at the street, I'm struck by Kuala Lumpur's blend of old and new. It's far removed from the third-world image often portrayed in the West. Across from us, a shop advertises top-tier Alpine and Kenwood stereo systems, luxuries even in the UK. Meanwhile, new Toyotas, Nissans, Mercedes, and Jaguars share the roads with older vehicles, a mix reminiscent of Britain.

Kuala Lumpur feels strangely familiar. Unlike much of Asia, the city's standards are high, with many remnants of British influence—three-pin plugs, rigorous safety measures, and overall quality that wouldn't feel out of place back home.

We're soon joined by Yeam, an electrical engineer, and his girlfriend. Like about half of Malaysia's population, Yeam is of Chinese descent.

As I chat with this eclectic group, I feel more connected to the city and its people. The Harley community here isn't just about bikes—it's a network of individuals who span industries, backgrounds, and lifestyles, united by their love for the ride.

A LITTLE BIT OF HISTORY

The story of Malaysia is as complex as its diverse people. During the 19th century, British rulers in Malaya—now Peninsula Malaysia—sought to expand the lucrative tin and rubber industries. However, the local Malay population wasn't large enough to meet the growing demand for labour. To address this, thousands of immigrants from India and China were brought in to work the plantations and mines. Over time, these immigrant communities outnumbered the indigenous Malays, creating a unique but sometimes fragile societal balance.

After Malaysia gained independence, the newly formed nation had to find its footing. Peninsula Malaysia was joined by Sarawak and Sabah to form East Malaysia, and for a brief period (1963–1965), Singapore was also part of the federation. Politically, the Malays held power, while the Chinese community dominated commerce, creating a significant economic disparity.

By 1969, a survey revealed that the average Malay earned less than half of what non-Malays earned. In response, the government introduced policies granting Malays significant privileges in areas like land ownership and business licenses. While these measures were intended to address inequality, they stirred resentment among the Chinese community. Tensions boiled over into violent riots that claimed hundreds of lives.

Eventually, the Chinese recognized the need for economic stability, and wealth distribution began to even out. Malaysia's abundant natural resources also helped bridge some of the gaps. Today, while Malays still enjoy certain privileges and the Chinese community remains economically influential, open conflict has largely subsided. According to Yeam, Hussein, and others I've spoken to, Malaysia is now focused on its thriving economy rather than its past divisions. I hope their optimism holds true.

BACK AT THE DEALERSHIP

Sitting around the table with Yeam and the others, I find myself fully engrossed in their stories. Yeam, in particular, is a natural entertainer—a joker with an infectious laugh. I like him immediately. His English, like everyone else's at the table, is impeccable. As we chat, I learn that he spent five years studying in Brighton and knows England almost as well as I do.

Curious, I ask why he's speaking English not just to me but also to his friends. He explains that Malaysia's multilingual landscape includes dozens, if not hundreds, of dialects across the Chinese and Malay communities. For many of them, English is far more practical—comprehensive, neutral, and less of a hassle than guessing another's dialect.

We linger at the eatery for about an hour, sharing laughs and anecdotes. Watching the eclectic street life of Kuala Lumpur pass by, I feel a growing affection for this city and its people.

Eventually, someone suggests heading back to the Harley dealership to check on Mao's progress. By a happy coincidence, we arrive just as Steve, Paul, Sean, and Chris pull up. Together, we spend about half an hour filming, trying to make the compact showroom appear dynamic and engaging on camera.

Despite the vibrant energy of the group, a nagging concern occupies my mind: the reliability of my bike. After the punishing ride through Sumatra, the machine is barely holding itself together. I ask if someone could take a look at it. Unfortunately, their chief mechanic, Harris, is still tending to the Sultan of Johor's bikes down south. Mao assures me Harris would be happy to do a full check-up and service—for free—but the earliest he could return would be noon on Monday.

This poses a dilemma. I'd planned to leave Kuala Lumpur early Monday to keep our tight schedule, with plans to film in the Malaysian highlands. The Cameron Highlands are renowned for their breathtaking scenery: vast tea and rubber plantations, sprawling forests, and jungle vistas that seem to stretch into eternity. However, my bike desperately needs attention. The miracle fix that got it running might not hold much longer.

I sit for a moment, weighing the options. Do I delay and risk derailing the schedule, or press on and risk the bike falling apart in the middle of nowhere?

DILEMMA

I find myself in a classic dilemma. If I wait until Harris can service the bike, we'll fall behind schedule—again—and risk missing the climactic Hard Rock party in Bangkok, a crucial part of our film. On the other hand, if I push on without a proper check-up, there's a very real chance the bike might not make it to Bangkok at all.

Sitting there, I can't help but reflect on how naive I'd been when this whole plan was hatched. The idea of simply riding a Harley from Bali to Bangkok sounded so romantic back home, staring at the map with a drink in hand. I couldn't have imagined the chaos I'd encounter: political unrest in Java, the wild ride-outs in Bali, the mechanical catastrophes of Sumatra, and the logistical nightmares in Malaysia. And I'm only halfway through. What else could possibly go wrong?

I decide to shelve the decision for a day or two. For now, I'll ride with Yeam, Hussein, and Alvin around Kuala Lumpur, with Steve hopping on the back of my bike. Mao peels off to drum up last-minute support for the Hard Rock party.

The warm, balmy air rushes past as we weave through KL's afternoon traffic. Alvin, as usual, is the star performer. Despite his intimidating appearance—decked out in a German army helmet and goggles—he's a big teddy bear at heart, albeit a crazy one. He reclines deep in the saddle of his red low rider, steering with his legs, hands-free, on quieter roads. It's both ridiculous and impressive.

The ride takes us from sweeping highways lined with palm trees and stunning views of the KL skyline to the congested alleys of a Chinese neighbourhood. Traffic jams are no match for motorcycles, and we slide through the gridlock with ease. Eventually, we pull into a cozy café, but as we're about to sit down, the first few drops of rain start to fall. It's monsoon season, and those drops are a warning of what's to come.

Alvin wastes no time. "Follow me," he shouts, "I know another spot—it's only two minutes away!"

A few turns later, we arrive at our "alternative venue." I can hardly believe my eyes. McDonald's. Really? The supposed meeting place of rebellious bikers from hell is a fluorescent haven of Happy Meals and free toys. Steve and I exchange incredulous looks, but the others seem unfazed. Hussein kindly offers to buy drinks, so Steve and I settle for orange juice while they grab Cokes.

Inside, the air-conditioning is cranked up to an arctic level. My nose might as well have icicles hanging from it. Shivering and annoyed, I suggest we leave. Thankfully, everyone agrees.

LOST AND FOUND

Back on the road, Hussein and Alvin offer to guide us back to the hotel. "It's only twenty minutes," Hussein promises, "but hard to explain."

Alvin, true to form, rockets ahead, leaving me to stick close to Hussein. For ten minutes, it's smooth sailing through traffic. But then, as the lights turn red, a bus traps me behind, separating me from Hussein.

"Did you see which way they went?" I ask Steve.

"Yeah, up the ring road ahead," he replies.

We take the slip road, but the signs quickly become unfamiliar. Rain starts falling—lightly at first, then with monsoon-level intensity. We're cold, drenched, and, worst of all, lost.

For miles, we follow exits leading to nowhere. Every new turn deepens the confusion. I feel helpless, wet, and stupid. Kuala Lumpur's labyrinthine road system has trapped us in an endless loop of highways, flyovers, and meaningless signs.

Two hours. That's how long it takes us to stumble our way back to the hotel. It's a relentless slog of trial, error, and increasingly soaked misery. Finally, a familiar landmark—a massive courthouse—appears like a beacon of hope. From there, we spot the green lettering of the Holiday Inn atop a skyscraper. Eureka!

As we pull under the hotel's protective canopy, Steve and I are two drowned rats, dripping and exhausted. And there, casually sitting on the steps, are Alvin and Hussein, grinning ear to ear.

"Where have you been?" Alvin laughs.

"You bastards!" I snap, half-joking. "You left us behind, and we got totally lost!"

"We thought you were with us," Hussein chuckles. "You do look a bit wet."

"A bit wet?" I mutter, shivering. "I'm going for a shower. See you at the Hard Rock at nine."

As I trudge up the steps, Alvin steps into the rain, smiling. "Looks like it's stopping," he says cheerfully. "See you later."

Typical Alvin - always the optimist!

HARD ROCK NIGHT

The night at the Hard Rock Café in Kuala Lumpur was nothing short of extraordinary. With Mao rallying the local Harley Owners Group (H.O.G.) chapter in just hours, the evening turned into a festival of roaring bikes, gleaming chrome, and shared passion for the open road. From the reserved Harley parking spaces to the constant flow of introductions and camaraderie inside, it was a celebration that only grew larger as the hours passed.

Then came Jo-Jo; unassuming in a brown suit at first glance, the owner of the Hard Rock Café quickly revealed his larger-than-life personality. He transformed into a rock-and-roll icon with the simple addition of a leather jacket and dark glasses, becoming the embodiment of cool—a mix of Roy Orbison and Johnny Cash.

MICHAEL JACKSON AND LISA MARIE

Off-camera, Jo-Jo revealed an unexpected twist: he had just returned from a three-week stay at Michael Jackson's Neverland Ranch. As if that weren't enough, Lisa Marie Presley had been there too. Jo-Jo casually shared a stack of photos featuring himself with the King of Pop and the King of Rock's daughter, their camaraderie unmistakable. Two months later, when the shocking news of Michael and Lisa Marie's marriage broke, the world reeled in disbelief, and Michael publicly denied they had been close. But I knew better—those photos were proof of a reality few could imagine. If only I'd kept one; it could have been my ticket to a headline-grabbing scoop.

As we talked more, Jo-Jo's Harley passion emerged. An experienced rider with a Springer in his garage and a wealth of tales from his travels across the U.S., he mentioned a close friend who shared his enthusiasm. "Would you like to meet him?" Jo-Jo asked casually. "He's a big fan of long rides and took part in the Ninetieth Anniversary Run from San Francisco to Milwaukee."

"Who's your friend?" I asked.

"Prince Idris, the Crown Prince of Malaysia," Jo-Jo replied, as if discussing a neighbour down the road. He offered to call the palace and confirm that I'd meet the future king the next evening. Would I be there? Of course! This was the stuff of dreams.

The night continued with more socializing, a flurry of conversations, and endless offers of drinks—most of which I declined in favour of diet Coke, knowing I still had to navigate my way back to the hotel on my less-than-reliable bike. Mao, the real hero of the evening, was my last farewell before I stepped outside. In less than a day, he had mobilized an entire chapter of Harley riders, orchestrated an unforgettable party, and charmed a café owner into footing the bill. His response to my thanks? - a humble, "No trouble, man. See you tomorrow at ten."

As the night wound down, reality reared its head. The bike wouldn't start, and with the battery barely holding a charge, I found myself relying on a push from the remaining crowd. Hardly the smooth exit I'd envisioned.

To top it off, navigating Kuala Lumpur's maze of one-way streets proved disastrous. What should have been a quick five-minute ride back to the Holiday Inn turned into a 30-minute fiasco, complete with missed turns, a confusing ring road, and, inevitably, rain. By the time I stumbled into the hotel at 2 a.m., the euphoria of the evening had faded, replaced by exhaustion and a reminder that even the grandest nights have their humbling moments.

But even as I collapsed into bed, I couldn't shake the amazement of the day: from Jo-Jo's celebrity anecdotes to the promise of meeting a prince, this journey had taken me far beyond the open road, offering glimpses into lives and stories I could never have imagined.

 # SUNDAY 26 JUNE

RIVER RIDE-OUT

The morning began with nervous anticipation. At five minutes to ten, Jeannie, the poised yet frazzled PR lady from the Holiday Inn, was pacing anxiously. The press had arrived promptly, but the riders were nowhere to be seen. "Don't worry," I reassured her, though my own confidence wavered. The coordination for this event had been solid—albeit planned amidst the haze of last night's festivities. Surely Mao, the mastermind of yesterday's success, wouldn't drop the ball now.

Ten minutes passed, then twenty. Jeannie's flustered questioning only added to my unease. Where were they? The Malaysian segment of my film desperately needed the energy of roaring bikes and scenic roads. Just as the situation seemed dire, an unmistakable sound filled the air: the thunderous rumble of Harley engines.

Like a cavalry charge, they appeared over the horizon—thirty gleaming Harleys, led by Hussein, roaring down the road in perfect formation. It was a cinematic entrance that not only salvaged the day but also sent a wave of relief through Jeannie. The riders parked in a neat line before the hotel, banners unfurled, ready for the press photo op.

As cameras clicked, there was one glaring absence: Randy, the mechanic who'd promised to deliver a new battery for my bike. Calls were made, and it turned out he'd overslept, still nursing a hangover from the night before. With some nudging, he arrived, battery in hand, and after a brief apology, we were finally ready to roll.

The ride-out itself was nothing short of exhilarating. Though modest by American standards, with its massive rallies, this thirty-strong group represented the heartbeat of Malaysia's Harley scene. Together, we roared out of Kuala Lumpur and into the lush, green expanse of rural Selangor.

The contrast was striking. The jungle canopy above framed the road, sunlight filtering through the leaves and dancing on the chrome of the bikes. The midday sun was warm, and the air was filled with the scents of tropical vegetation. Coconut palms and banana trees lined the route, giving way to small roadside stalls where farmers sold fruit and vegetables under makeshift shelters.

After an hour of riding, we turned off the main road and followed a winding path that led us to a palm-fringed beach. The scene was postcard-perfect, straight out of a travel ad. The group introduced me to their weekend retreat, a quiet spot to relax and enjoy local delicacies. From spicy satay chicken to fresh coconuts, the flavours of Malaysia were as vibrant as the scenery.

Then it was back on the road, heading for Yeam's favourite riverside restaurant. The ride took us through peaceful countryside—straight roads stretching endlessly ahead, dotted with small wooden farmhouses. Occasionally, an elderly man could be seen sitting on his porch, daydreaming in the shade of a banana palm. The simplicity and serenity of life here were striking, though the reality of subsistence living likely told a different story.

As we rode, the horizon revealed a breathtaking sight: a grand mosque, its pale blue and gold façade glowing against the verdant backdrop of jungle-clad mountains. The scene was surreal—like an otherworldly painting. The line of Harleys heading toward the mosque's open doors only added to the magic, creating an unforgettable moment of cultural and visual harmony.

A sharp left turn brought us to our destination: a humble yet charming riverside restaurant. The peace of the setting was shattered by the arrival of thirty roaring bikes and their lively riders, but the owners didn't mind. This group would leave their tills ringing with a week's worth of revenue in a single afternoon.

This segment of the journey, with its vivid contrasts and unique experiences, felt like a microcosm of my adventure: the blend of camaraderie, exploration, and unexpected beauty. It was a day that would stay etched in my memory and, more importantly, in the footage we captured.

Paul and Sean are filming. Following me wherever I go, they record me looking at the bikes, the scenery, and the river; talking to Yeam, Mao and some of the others. Yeam wants to show me the kitchens. The fish is as fresh as can be. It was literally pulled out of the river a few minutes ago and cooked. The whole family were there, possibly twelve of them, beavering away in the heat, preparing the feast. Huge, razor sharp cleavers glint as they flash through the air, maniacally wielded by the wild looking Chinese chef you wouldn't want to upset on a dark night – or any night for that reason. Apparently he is dad. Granny is washing vegetables; the kids are clearing up. Dozens of pots, pans, knives and other utensils hang from the ceiling. Up against every wall, there are stainless steel fridges, hobs, sinks and cupboards. Remarkably sophisticated equipment considering we are in the middle of the jungle with no mains services. Everything is running off generators and bottled gas. So busy is the kitchen, so much going, on the din is deafening. So many dishes being cooked all at once, so much steam is rising. Yeam has to shout to let me know what is going on. There is so much moisture in the air that, at one point, my glasses mist over and I can't see anything. It is frantic in here; very well organised chaos.

We walk from the kitchen and out the back. It is somewhat more primitive here. Apparently the dustmen don't call very often - in fact, never. Rubbish is simply thrown behind the building and burnt every few days. Until then, flocks of birds hang around scavenging what they can. The toilet is the most interesting. It reminds me of what you may find in a medieval castle, or if I was being kind, perhaps a train or plane. Basically the porcelain section was much like a suburban semi. A bit scruffier perhaps, not as well maintained with no seat or lid. The walls and ceiling of the structure are made from gappy wooden planks, but nevertheless, to be fair, all the elements are here for comfortable relief. At least there is a sit down, rather than a squat down Asian, affair. Then there is the ablution exit.

The waste pipe simply goes down out of the floor and stops in mid-air. The waste disposal system consists of what the river washes away - an interesting natural system that would possibly cause the health inspector a modicum of heart failure back home in Milton Keynes.

We go back in and sit down. The first course of this great
feast is on its way. At the table, the meal is great fun, laughing
and joking with all those sat around me. Opposite turns out
to be a guy called Nazarradin Sharrudin and his wife. It was
Naza whom I had faxed initially from England and who had
started the ball rolling for me here. He is a director of Harley
Malaysia and Mao's boss. Food keeps coming and coming.
Prawns, chicken, a whole river fish.... and just when I thought
I could eat no more, another course comes. I am bloated.
Eventually I can take no more. I can't even bear to look at the
last course, let alone eat it. I slink back in my chair, chin on
my chest, arms dangling by my side. In the balmy atmosphere
of early afternoon I want to go to sleep. I am very content,
thank you very much.

As with all functions, however, now is speech time. I am
welcomed to their club and I take great pleasure in thanking
Mao and Yeam and everyone for making my visit to
Kuala Lumpur so special. They could not have been more
hospitable. And it isn't over yet. The Crown Prince has kindly
organised a reception for us at six o'clock. We are all due at
the Palace for a Royal Harley party, hosted by Asia's number
one Harley fan.

We leave the riverside restaurant at four o'clock, which gives us
two hours to get to the Palace. Most have been there before;
the Prince is a friend and likes to be involved in the Harley
scene in general. I have never met a prince before but, on the
other hand, a prince has never met me.   So it will be special
moment for both of us. It would be yet another unique and
special element of my journey; yet another significant event to
be recorded.

Steve left ahead of the rest of us. He has taken the crew and the van to set up some special shots of the gang leaving. With the camera running, Paul stays with me so that he can ride on the back of someone's bike to get another perspective of the moment.

For about ten minutes we are filmed from the front, from the back, from the side. Some low shots were taken at road level. From the top, we fixed the Handy-cam on a pole. Some close by, some far away. All angles exhausted, they stop. Great, I can relax again and continue on to the palace. Then, up ahead I see two bikes have stopped at the side of the road. A hundred metres further on, the main pack has also stopped and many were removing their helmets. I pull off the road onto the verge, stop my bike, get off and wander over to a middle aged chap sat on his Ultra Glide, listening to the radio. He looks as if he is planning to be here for the duration. He looks a bit like Charlie Chan, a grey haired version with straggly goatee beard and glasses. He is wearing a green polo neck shirt with a black, badge encrusted, leather waistcoat.

"What's up?" I ask.

"One of the older bikes has broken down." he replies, "I'm not sure what has happened. I think the belt or chain has broken."

A rescue party has by this time returned to see what could be done. The rest of us settle down to relax while we wait for the outcome. Spotting a group of visitors at the end of his drive, the farmer walks out to see who we are. So as not to miss an opportunity, he has come to see what he can sell us. After a chat, he disappears and returns a few minutes later with half a dozen coconuts and some rambutans, each cut from his trees only moments before. Machete in hand, he crouches down, sharpening the coconuts to a point and then slicing the

259

tops off to gain access to the milk and flesh. I think that fresh coconut milk is one of life's greatest pleasures. It is delicious. The rambutans are left in a pile for us to help ourselves.

As I drink from my coconut I start chatting to my Charlie Chan friend, asking what he does and how long had he been into bikes. He tells he had taken up riding on his retirement. Funnily enough, he continues, he knows this area very well. Behind those trees, he raises his arm to point behind the farmer's house, are what used to be his quarries.

"What did you do?" I enquire.

"Concrete."

From what I could make out, he was concrete. Mr. Concrete. You wanted concrete, you bought it from him. That's a good job, isn't it, in a country full of skyscrapers and bridges. I believe his son has taken over as Mister Concrete now.

The broken down bike turns out to be irreparable - at least until tomorrow. It will have to be left here and collected on a pickup in the morning. The farmer on the opposite side of the road offers to look after it.

We are now running late. To get from here to the Palace in an hour is just about impossible. The plan was to meet at the Hard Rock at five thirty and go from there. Kuala Lumpur is forty miles away and it is almost five o'clock.

And it is starting to rain.

In fact it is starting to rain very hard. Very, very, hard!

Believe me, travelling forty miles in a Malaysian monsoon makes you very wet. In fact it would be difficult to get wetter.

Even my bones are wet. Water travels down my neck, down my back, through the crack in my bum onto my legs and meets up with the water that had already seeped through my jeans and flowed down into my boots so that when I wriggle my toes it feels all squishy. It is not a delightful feeling. It isn't cold, it is still ninety degrees. It was uncomfortable, though, really, really uncomfortable.

It isn't that that concerns me, though. It is the meeting with the Prince. By the time I get back to the Hard Rock, it is about a quarter to seven. Only Naza and Mao are still there; kindly waiting for me. The others had decided it was too wet, too far and too late. They had gone home for a shower and change - understandably, of course. They had been to the Palace before, and what sort of party could we have in the rain anyway?

I ask Mao to ring the palace and find out the story - should I still go or not? Mao said unfortunately, owing to the bad weather the party has been postponed. The Palace is thirty five kilometres from where we are. It is impossible. It is still raining. We are soaked. We are late.

I am devastated. To meet the Crown Prince would have been such an incredible highlight of my visit to Malaysia. Indeed, it would have been such a coup, such a wonderful element in my film. Mao was immovable. Sorry, he reaffirms, it is impossible. There is nothing I can do. It is a grave disappointment.

I return to the hotel with a heavy heart but with my brain in overdrive. I am determined to meet the Prince if it is the last thing I do. Aside from the personal honour I would receive being presented at the Palace, the event would give such an added dimension to my film. Circumstances have so far taken my journey from a simple ride from A to B into the realms of serious adventure. The difficulties, the worries, the trials and tribulations need a brighter side to balance the programme. Thus far, the aggravation has only been tempered by bike oriented pleasures - the ride-out yesterday and on Bali, the Hard Rock party and so on. A visit to meet the Prince in his palace would give a much needed uplift to me and the film.

The best thing to do is to see Jo-Jo. The whole thing was his idea, the Prince is his friend. I decide to return to the Hard Rock later in the evening and see if I can find him.

I tell Steve and the others my plan and we agree to go there around nine. We need to eat anyway and that is as good a place as any. So we do. After a shower, shit and shave and go down and meet the crew in the foyer of the hotel. I will ride my bike and they will go by taxi. Fortunately it has stopped raining. The air is still damp with a threat of further rain, the roads are still wet, but at least I can get there without getting soaked again. I don't care what happens on the way back.

THE CROWN PRINCE IS DISAPPOINTED

The hours leading up to midnight are a whirlwind of agitation, hope, and frustration. Miscommunication had turned what should have been a seamless meeting with Prince Idris into a nerve-wracking ordeal. After being assured earlier that Jo-Jo would help set things right, I'd clung to the hope that we could salvage this opportunity.

Jo-Jo is true to his word, trying tirelessly to contact the Prince. But the man is elusive, his whereabouts uncertain. Each failed attempt chips away at my optimism. Despite the lively atmosphere at the Hard Rock Café—where the crew drinks, laughs, and enjoys the evening—I remain tense and distracted.

At midnight, with no resolution in sight, I decide to make one final push. Jo-Jo, ever patient and kind, dials the Prince's mobile yet again. It's engaged. My heart sinks momentarily, but I cling to the fact that the phone is on—there's still a chance.

The next call connects. Jo-Jo explains the situation, apologizes for the late hour, and makes the request on my behalf. I hold my breath, every second stretching into eternity. Then Jo-Jo turns to me with a grin. "The Prince is delighted," he says. "He was disappointed about today but would love to meet you. Seven-thirty tomorrow morning."

The relief is immense. After hours of uncertainty, it feels as though a massive weight has been lifted. The meeting is back on!

As I ride back to the hotel after confirming my meeting with the Crown Prince, the rain gently falls, but it doesn't dampen my spirits. I'm elated, the challenges of the past few days momentarily forgotten. The road is familiar now, and I make it back without getting lost—a small but satisfying victory.

The friendly smiles of the security guard at the hotel are reassuring. I park the bike and head up the steps into the lobby, where I'm immediately met by Steve. His expression is serious, a stark contrast to my cheerful demeanour. Pulling me aside, he quietly says, "We've had a fax from Steve Bradley."

BAD NEWS FROM LONDON

The message from Steve Bradley was succinct and cryptic, carefully worded to avoid alarming any hotel staff who might read it; this is the translation:

"Get out now. Your visas were turned down; you're there illegally; if they find you, you're in deep trouble!"

Steve Bradley, our shipping agent and ally back in London, had been instrumental in coordinating logistics for our journey. He'd helped with everything from arranging shipping for the bikes to navigating the labyrinth of permits and visas required for our documentary. His message, however, is anything but good news.

As Steve hands me the fax, I recall the hoops we'd jumped through to secure permits for filming in Indonesia and Thailand. Malaysia, however, had been a different beast altogether.

POLITICS AND PERMITS

The timing of our permit application couldn't have been worse. In the spring of 1994, as we planned our journey, a major political scandal was dominating headlines: the Pergau Dam affair. Allegations surfaced that Malaysia's Premier, Dr. Mahathir Mohamad, had accepted substantial bribes in awarding a lucrative construction contract to a British company. The scandal triggered a diplomatic row, with Malaysia banning trade with British firms.

The fallout was immense, impacting billions of pounds in trade and souring relations between the two countries. In Malaysia, British media were persona non grata, viewed as hostile agents bent on discrediting the government.

Despite this tense backdrop, we'd applied for permission to film, emphasizing that our project was a benign travel documentary. We wanted to showcase Malaysia's beauty, its culture, and its appeal as a tourist destination. But our assurances fell on deaf ears. The Malaysian authorities, suspicious of all British media, ignored our requests.

When it became clear that no permits or visas would be issued, Steve and I decided to take our chances. We convinced ourselves that Malaysia, as a Commonwealth member and former British colony, would ultimately prove fair and reasonable. After all, what harm could a group of motorbike enthusiasts and filmmakers possibly cause?

Entering the country through an obscure port, we began filming clandestinely. For three days, we captured the splendour of Malaysia without a government minder, travelling over 700 miles and documenting every moment.

We knew the risks. Officially, we had no right to be here, let alone film. But we were operating under the assumption that, in the grand scheme of things, our presence would go unnoticed. Who would bother with a scruffy biker?

Apparently, someone did.

The reality hits me like a freight train. We are illegal aliens in Malaysia. Worse still, I'm scheduled to meet the Crown Prince tomorrow morning. If anyone connects the dots, it could lead to a diplomatic incident of epic proportions.

A TENSE NIGHT AHEAD

The irony of the situation is almost laughable. Here I am, about to shake hands with royalty while technically on the wrong side of Malaysian law. The Crown Prince meeting an illegal foreigner—a British one, no less—could spark a scandal neither of us wants.

Despite the gravity of the situation, I resolve to press forward.

The meeting with Prince Idris is a once-in-a-lifetime opportunity, and backing out now would only draw more attention. I'll face whatever comes after that, but first, I need to see this through.

As I return to my room, the elation I'd felt earlier has been replaced by a simmering unease. The rain outside has turned into a steady downpour, mirroring my mood. I double-check my belongings, ensuring I'm ready to leave at a moment's notice. Tomorrow's meeting looms large, both a source of excitement and potential peril.

One way or another, the next 24 hours will be unforgettable.

MONDAY 27 JUNE

The day began with a mixture of anticipation and anxiety. A taxi was scheduled for 6:15 a.m., and I made it clear to the reception staff that punctuality and the driver's familiarity with the route were essential. In my experience, taxi drivers outside of London often operate on a wing and a prayer. This morning could not afford such a gamble.

At 6:15, of course, no taxi. I instructed the reception staff to call and give the company a piece of my mind. They assured me the driver was en route and apologized for the inconvenience, but I was livid. The Prince had a flight to catch, and I couldn't risk being late.

The taxi finally arrived at 6:30. The crew piled in with their equipment, and we set off for Jo-Jo's house. I followed on the bike, grateful for clear skies.

FINDING JO-JO'S CASTLE

Jo-Jo, a friend and close associate of the Crown Prince, had invited us to his home for breakfast before the big meeting. Located in Shah Alam, about 35 kilometres from the city centre, his house was supposedly near the Prince's residence. With traffic mercifully light at this hour, we reached Shah Alam without issue.

However, locating Jo-Jo's house was another matter. He had

provided us with a hand-drawn map scrawled on the back of a coffee shop place mat, a guide that proved incomprehensible to our taxi driver. After driving aimlessly through Shah Alam's leafy avenues, we spotted a golf course with an armed guard at the entrance. I suggested the driver seek help.

Fortunately, the guard deciphered our crude map, and we soon arrived in a posh residential area filled with elegant homes. This was the sort of neighbourhood where pristine lawns and gleaming luxury cars were the norm. After a few wrong turns, we finally found Jalan Cekak and Jo-Jo's castle-like home.

Jo-Jo's house took my breath away. A brilliant white mansion with battlements, it stood behind tall wrought-iron gates. The expansive driveway was paved in pale grey marble, polished to perfection. Not a single speck of dirt or stray leaf marred its surface.

The mansion's architecture was a mix of Southern plantation grandeur and Romanesque opulence. Its overhanging first floor was supported by classical pillars, forming a carport beneath which sat an enviable collection of vehicles: a Ferrari 328 GTS, a Harley-Davidson Springer Softail, a Buick convertible, a Range Rover, and a Mercedes 560 SEL, among others.

A servant greeted us at the gate, unlocked it, and beckoned us inside. As we passed through the carport and entered via patio doors, the interior revealed an entirely different world. The sitting room was like a marble stage, with an enormous Persian rug at its centre and gilded plasterwork framing twinkling chandeliers above. It felt more like a museum than a home—immaculate, precise, and devoid of clutter.

BREAKFAST AND BUSINESS

Jo-Jo appeared, still in his pyjamas and slippers, and greeted us warmly. Apologizing for not being ready, he instructed his staff to prepare breakfast and gave us a quick tour of the house. He led us upstairs, where the balcony offered a stunning panoramic view of Shah Alam. The city stretched out below, with the magnificent blue-domed state mosque catching the first light of dawn.

When Jo-Jo returned, now dressed in a pale blue shirt, a stars-and-stripes tie, and tinted glasses, he invited us to the dining room. The table was set with fine bone china trimmed with gold, contrasting starkly with a collection of plastic biscuit jars and condiment jars.

As breakfast was served, I nibbled at a few biscuits and sipped coffee, chatting with Jo-Jo about his plans with the Prince. He explained they were heading to Singapore to finalize a business deal involving none other than Michael Jackson. The project? They plan to build a replica of Neverland on 3,000 acres of beachfront property in Johor.

Despite the morning's hiccups, everything seemed to be falling into place. As I listened to Jo-Jo's tales of grandeur and ambition, I couldn't help but feel a mix of awe and disbelief. Here I am, an anonymous sign-maker experiencing a world of unimaginable luxury and influence.

But the clock was ticking. The Prince awaited, and with him, the next leg of this incredible journey.

At 7:45 a.m., we left Jo-Jo's house for the palace. Steve, Paul, Sean, and Chris piled into Jo-Jo's gleaming white Mercedes while I followed closely on my bike. Jo-Jo dismissed his chauffeur, choosing to drive himself, which only added to his enigmatic charm.

The palace was mere minutes away, and the drive was a serene journey through tree-lined streets and immaculately tended flowerbeds. Arriving at the palace gates, the guard instantly recognized Jo-Jo's car. Without questioning, he saluted sharply and opened the gates, allowing us to proceed up a grand tarmac driveway. Passing a sign for the "Peacock Garden," I scanned for any actual peacocks but saw none—perhaps they were sleeping somewhere.

A SURPRISING FIRST IMPRESSION

The palace was not what I had imagined. Where I had expected golden domes and marble grandeur, the exterior was a modest red brick structure. It resembled a high-end corporate headquarters more than a royal residence. However, once inside, the contrast was stark.

As we entered, a servant in traditional Malay attire—complete with a sarong and songkok—met us at the entrance. Jo-Jo explained our purpose, and the servant promptly disappeared to inform the Prince.

The entrance hall was lined with portraits of royal ancestors, each dressed in splendid regalia. The understated exterior gave way to an interior of unexpected opulence. A massive model galleon stood proudly in the hall, an exquisite replica of a 17th-century trading ship. The palace itself seemed to be built around a central swimming pool, its design blending leisure and luxury effortlessly.

THE HARLEY COLLECTION

As we waited for Prince Idris Shah, Jo-Jo suggested we explore the Harley-Davidson collection, the main purpose of our visit. The courtyard to the left of the pool housed an incredible display.

On one side was a garage for cars—though "garage" felt like an understatement. The glass-fronted structure stretched 30 meters and housed an enviable fleet, including a Porsche 911 Turbo with the coveted registration "A1," a future gift for the Prince's young son.

On the opposite side was the Harley collection. Sliding open the glass doors revealed a marvel of design and passion: a marble-floored, air-conditioned room dedicated to Harley-Davidson memorabilia.

The collection was staggering. Walls were adorned with caps, flags, and airbrushed fuel tanks, including a stunning set featuring a tiger motif. Cabinets displayed everything from Harley-branded Zippo lighters to rare badges and belts. Photographs commemorated the Prince's visits to Harley factories, ride-outs, and the opening of Southeast Asia's only Harley-Davidson dealership—a milestone he was particularly proud of.

The centrepiece of the room, however, was the bikes. Three magnificent Harleys were displayed:

- A red flame-painted Heritage Softail.

- A blue and white Springer.

- A black and white custom masterpiece.

These were flanked by two classic cars: a pristine yellow Jaguar XK 140 and a pre-war American Buick, each shining as if just rolled off the showroom floor.

MEETING THE CROWN PRINCE

As we admired the collection, Prince Idris Shah arrived. He greeted us warmly, his genuine excitement mirroring my own. A true Harley enthusiast, he was eager to share stories of his epic rides, including a legendary journey from San Francisco to Milwaukee for Harley-Davidson's 90th anniversary.

He listened intently as I recounted my adventures, nodding with appreciation. Before we parted, he extended an extraordinary invitation: to join him on his next ride, a monumental journey from South to North Vietnam. It was a thrilling prospect, though one I knew was beyond my means.

Walking through the palace and witnessing the Prince's collection was an experience of rare privilege. It was not just the luxury or the exclusivity that struck me but the shared passion for the open road and the machines that make it possible.

The Prince was not only a royal figure but a kindred spirit, a fellow biker whose love for Harley-Davidson had brought him closer to strangers from across the globe. This brief meeting, filled with stories and shared admiration, would stay with me for a long time.

He now wants to see my bike. We chat as we walk back past the pool and out towards where we had parked. There is no ceremony or protocol here, just two bikers reminiscing about their exploits. The Prince himself is very natural. There is no royal 'attitude' that we traditionally associate with British monarchy. A servant approaches with some drinks. I thank him, take a coke and point to where my bike is. Jo-Jo comes up and reminds the prince that they should be leaving very soon or they may miss their plane.

Prince Idris tells him not to worry, they have a few minutes.

By this time I have had enough of my coke and am looking for somewhere to put my glass. I can't see anyone to give it to, nor anywhere to put it. Finally, I spot the man with the silver tray at the far end of the swimming pool. More as a question than anything else I hold up my glass and point to it. Never have I seen anyone move so fast. He literally sprints to my aid. What service. I can't believe it. I have never experienced such dedication to duty. Certainly not the 'I'll be there when I'm good and ready' British attitude I am used to. But then I have never been attended to by a Royal servant before. As he arrives at a reasonable distance from me, he stops running and slows to a respectful march. He graciously takes my glass, bows and disappears. I am very impressed.

The Prince wants to know all about my bike. Who had designed it, who had painted it and so on. When I told him that I had done it all myself with a friend at work, it is his turn to be impressed.

Time was pressing by now, so after a few souvenir photographs of Prince Idris sat on my machine and with lots of smiles and arms round each other in a Harley brotherhood sort of way, it is time to leave.

We all leave together. Prince Idris and Jo-Jo climb into the Range Rover ready for their dash to the airport; the Prince's chauffeur is ordered to drive the crew back to the hotel in Jo-Jo's Mercedes and I follow close behind.

It is still only ten o'clock when we return to the hotel. This full and no doubt eventful day has started in the best possible way, now the work has to be done. Mao has arranged for the bike to be serviced at twelve o'clock. If all goes well the plan is to leave K.L. around three. I have a long ride ahead to the Thai border - Steve Bradley's fax from England has made it very plain we should not caught in this country, so the clever money says leave before anyone untoward finds out we are here.

The visit to the Palace, as unmissable as it was, put us a day behind schedule. We have to meet E.D. (our Thai fixer), at the border tomorrow morning, so if we are to film any of the fabulous Malaysia scenery as early a start as possible is necessary. I have considered foregoing the service, but that may be foolish given my experiences so far. There are no other Harley dealerships between here and London so, as far as I am concerned, a sacrifice needs to be made. Plus, to be caught filming in Northern Malaysia without the protection of our K.L. friends may have severe consequences. It may make good T.V., but I don't fancy becoming an international incident or spending a few days (or longer) in some dodgy Malay jail. Even worse, they may confiscate my bike. Sod that!

MEGA-DECIBELS

As requested I arrive at the Harley dealership in Pataling Jaya just after noon. 'Animal' takes me round into the workshop where Harris (their top mechanic and the man diverted off to tend to the Sultan of Jahore) and his assistant Amin immediately get to work on my bike.

They are very thorough, checking everything, replacing all my bodge up nuts and bolts with the proper parts, tightening everything that is loose and lubricating all the bits that need lubricating. The only thing he can't fix is the headlight main beam. That is part of a sealed beam unit and the cost of replacing that in Malaysia is ludicrously high. Because of the expense they can't give me that for free, so recommend I wait until I return to England. No main beam is no big deal so I agree.

Due to the ardours of my journey my gloves have definitely seen better days. In fact they are totally knackered. The palms of both hands are split and one of the thumbs is all but falling off. I decide to splash out on a new pair, so while Harris and Amin are finishing off I wander off into the shop to pick a new pair.

The total bill for the gloves and the service comes to the equivalent of twenty five pounds. That is a very good deal indeed. All in all the Harley boys in Kuala Lumpur have been very good to me. If only I could stay longer. It is with a great deal of sadness that I wave them good-bye and head off back through the confusion of the K.L road network to the Holiday Inn.

As I reach the hotel it is once again starting to rain. This time, fortunately, I miss the deluge, but as I pack ready for the run to the Thai border the prospect of a few hundred miles in the pissing rain does not enthral me.

With all the luggage piled in the foyer I go out to check the bike. Even after its service I have a funny feeling that all is not well. Luck has not always been with me on this trip and I feel that it is better to be safe than sorry.

Just as well I did! Would the bastard start? Would it hell! Dead as a bloody dodo! Poxy thing! I can't believe it. Two hours ago it was running as sweet as a nut; now nothing. It has to be the alarm. I wish I had asked Amin to disconnect, rather than fix it.

I hope he is still there and can help me. I immediately ring him at the dealership and explain my dilemma. Needless to say he is devastated. Obviously it makes him look a right Charlie having a bike breakdown minutes after he has supposedly serviced it. He promises to be there as soon as possible, but with the K.L. rush hour looming he can't say how long that will be. He tells me not to worry - whatever it takes he will help me. He will not let me down. I am sure he won't.

While all this is going on, Steve is having serious aggravation with Oddbod, the dopey driver of our mini-bus. He is a total wanker, letting us down on so many occasions. Even when he does turn up in his clapped out wagon, he is moaning endlessly about how his eyesight is bad and how he shouldn't be driving and how we are not paying him enough and that we should give him more money and countless other whinges. Steve has sacked him. There is no way we can rely on him to get us to the border on time. Apart from the fact he is insufferable, to spend one moment longer in his shagged out van is totally unacceptable. For all that, when Steve phoned him and told him his services were no longer required, he did it very courteously and in an even business-like manner. In response, Oddbod freaked out. Screaming down the phone at

Steve, threatening to sue us, to have the border posts notified that undesirable aliens were approaching. To generally have us hung, drawn and quartered and have our bits nailed up for the vultures to pick at.

Unbeknown to Oddbod, of course, some of those threats were achievable. The immigration authorities were one body we did not want informed of our situation in the country. Empty threats they may have been, but we nevertheless thought it sensible to buy him off; for as little as possible of course. One thing in our favour is that as a total tosser his buy off price was fairly cheap - something around a hundred dollars in the end. To get rid of that obnoxious little shit it was well worth it.

That left us, of course, with no transport to the border. However, with no vehicle and about four hundred miles to do by the morning, this is not actually as major a problem as you may think. Kuala Lumpur is a very organised place. To get transport would be easy; to get it at a reasonable price, though, not quite so.

With the help of Jeannie, our helpful Holiday Inn PR person, Steve let his fingers do the walking and after relatively few strides, Yellow Pages had found us a new minibus, two drivers, an overnight ride to the Thai border and our transport problems solved for the very reasonable cost of one hundred and fifty US dollars.

Steve arranged for them to pick up the crew and equipment from the Holiday Inn at seven o'clock.

Meanwhile it is pissing down. A serious Malaysian monsoon will make my twelve hour motorcycle ride, in the dark, unimaginable torture. Assuming, of course, we get the bloody thing working.

At five o'clock two guys turn up in the Harley dealership van and park it under the hotel canopy, so at least we can load the bike into it in the dry.

As they prepare, I find Jeannie Tan and thank her for her help and hospitality. As usual on my journey the Holiday Inn people have been excellent. To commemorate my stay she kindly presents me with a book - The Insight Guide to Malaysia - inscribed with her best wishes. After a friendly peck on the cheek she waves me good-bye as I walk down the steps of the Holiday Inn City Centre for the last time. The bike is by now firmly secured in the Harley van and we are ready to leave. I agree to ring Steve with regular progress reports, the plan being for the crew to meet me in Pataling Jaya, from where we will depart to the Thai border. E.D., our Thai film production manager has, by now, left Bangkok and is expecting us at the Hat Yai checkpoint at nine o'clock tomorrow morning. We have no way of informing her of our problems, so we just have to make it happen. Fingers crossed.

The drive to Pataling Jaya was interesting. The electrical problem has rendered the alarm totally uncontrollable. Consequently, the constant movement repeatedly activated the audible alarm. What a pain in the arse. Mega-decibels echoing round the confined space of this empty tin can of a van. How the bloody hell our eardrums will survive I don't know. We can't even open the windows to let some of the terrible noise escape because of the torrential rain. If it wasn't so horrible it would be funny. Soaking wet or deafened, there's a choice. We couldn't even dampen the noise because the speaker was hidden deep in the bike to prevent potential thieves doing exactly what we wanted to do. Fortunately for us, the battery was dead due to my numerous attempts to get the bike started, so the alarm was now running on its own reserve supply. Theoretically, it should wear itself out soon.

About fifteen minutes it took. Five minutes of hell, five minutes of pain and five minutes of nuisance; the noise level slowly decreasing as the power faded.

Travelling through Kuala Lumpur in the rush hour in the rain is excruciatingly slow. Even though the roads are by far the best in South East Asia, there is so much traffic they become totally clogged. Had there been any cones it would be almost as bad as the M25.

It is certainly a relief when the alarm finally stops; and with it, believe it or not, the rain. Please God, no more rain, until tomorrow at least. I've got enough worries without the additional burden of coping with marble-sized lumps of rain hitting me in the face at sixty miles an hour on some pitch black Malaysian motorway.

The bike is wheeled straight into the workshop where Harris is waiting, screwdriver at the ready. It is now about quarter past six and everyone apart from Harris and his trusty assistant Amin have gone home. The battery is immediately put on charge while my two saviours set about the task of totally disconnecting the alarm, and reverting the electrical circuit back to standard Harley-Davidson.

By seven, the job was complete. The bike fires first time, and, for the first time in ages, I actually felt confident that I could reach Bangkok. I ring Steve with the good news and he says that the mini-bus has arrived and they are all set to leave. They expect to be with me around eight.

I gave Harris three bottles of Jim Beam whisky for his staff and thanked him very much for staying behind to help me. The thanks are appreciated, the whiskey less so - most of his staff were Moslem and didn't drink. Nevertheless, the gesture is well received and he feels sure he will find a home for it.

Amin, by this time, has gone home. I have an hour to kill and offer to buy Harris dinner in the Chinese restaurant next door, the one where I had had such a delicious lunch a few days previous.

He locks the workshop and we cross the yard and enter the restaurant by the back door. Although quite busy, we explain that some people are on their way to meet us at the Harley place next door and could we therefore be served fairly promptly. I leave Amin to order what he considers to be the house specialities while I ask for one of my favourites - fresh coconut milk. I have grown to absolutely love the milk and it compliments Chinese food perfectly.

We finish our superb meal of fish and chicken just as the crew arrive. Perfect timing! To cap the most incredible hospitality I have received in this country, Amin absolutely refuses to let me get the bill. He says what an honour and pleasure it has been to meet me and there is no way he could allow me to pay.

He then gives me his personal telephone number should I break down while I was still in his country.

How lucky I am to have met such wonderful people on my journey. I hope I can repay them some day.

I AM ON THE RUN NOW

Having had the visa rejected, we are here illegally and need to head for Thailand as soon as possible.

I can finally leave Kuala Lumpur at nine o'clock. The roads are still very wet, but at least it isn't raining.

I try not to think about the journey in front of me. The hectic, non-stop, ride, in the dark, of over four hundred miles is very daunting. To start fresh after a good sleep would be bad enough, but I have been up since five o´clock, visited the Palace, had the bike serviced, coped with the trauma of the bike breaking down again, got it repaired again, listened to threats by Oddbod of exposing us to immigration and so on and so on. This has been a heavy fourteen hour day even before I start.

In case it rains unexpectedly I have donned all my protective clothing. It was still warm; in the tropics it is never really cold, but much fresher after the storms. Looking at the map the motorway north seems to skirt the high ground, avoiding both the Genting and Cameron highlands, so hopefully the temperature will not drop too much, even in the middle of the night. So, although I reckon only a T-shirt and jeans would be sufficient for warmth, I decide to put the removable sleeves back on my leather jacket and wear my chaps for protection. Helmet, glasses, a leather bandanna, fingerless gloves and cowboy boots completed the ensemble. I may look good; I feel crap.

So it's on the motorway and away; on and on and on, seemingly forever. The one consolation is the quality of road. It is excellent - wide, smooth, well sign-posted; but very dark and very endless. Fortunately, I don't know any of the place names, so time and distance become meaningless. I never really know how far we have come, nor how far we have to go; probably the best way. I sing to keep myself awake. Trouble is, I can never remember the words to any songs when I'm really tired, so I end up singing the same one over and over. This time the one that sticks in my head was 'I saw her standing there,' by the Beatles. This was frustrating, because normally I know the words to dozens of songs. There you go - my own personal stress phenomenon.

For once I wish I was in the van, asleep with the rest of them. Boring and moaning sods they might be, but at least they are tucked up comfy.

Generally, I follow close behind them for security reasons. To fall back or be too far in front would be foolish. If they, or I, break down the other wouldn't know and continue, oblivious to the problem. A disaster best avoided. Now and again, though, I need to have a little burst and throw caution to the wind. Just to break the mindless monotony. In the blackness, with nothing to look at except countless little posts with reflectors I seriously need the occasional diversion. I try counting the white lines as I speed by, but get fed up after about two hundred. I get lost in little fantasies about what will happen in Thailand or where my next epic trip will be or what could have happened if only I had had more time to explore Malaysia.

I am desperately tired; desperately, desperately tired. I cannot go any further. I speed up slightly and overtake the van. I keep telling myself that I must go on, we must get to the border on time. On the road north there is nothing. I would give my left bollock right now for a service station and a cup of coffee. Not one Little Chef, no transport cafes, nothing.

I must stop. I must stop. I indicate and pull onto the hard shoulder. The van pulls in close behind. I climb off the bike to find all my limbs have seized up. My legs won't work properly; my back aches and my arms have all but dropped off. Painfully, and with great effort, I try to stretch myself back into normality. Under the van's headlight I pull back my jacket sleeve to see the time is just past midnight. I guess we must have travelled around a hundred and fifty to two hundred miles - a third of the way perhaps.

The side door of the van opens and Steve gets out, enquiring if anything is wrong. I can't believe it, he is totally pissed. They all are. They haven't been asleep; they have been quaffing vast quantities of Jim Beam. Here I am, desperate for someone to take over for a while and they can't stand up, let alone ride a bike.

I want to scream, but I have no voice left after all the "I Saw Her Standing There" business! What can I do? I have had it. I must sleep. Now! I have no alternative but to lie down on the hard shoulder and sleep. I don't care about the border, or meeting E.D., or Steve Bradley's fax, or anything except sleep.

For five minutes they all look at me incredulously. Helmet off, flat out on the tarmac, arms splayed, legs akimbo, I pray for sleep.

This was a bad move. Never have I suffered so many mosquitoes. It makes me itch just to think about it. It is dreadful. Over the last few seconds, I have had more dangerous flying objects land on me than the Ark Royal. How such a shit analogy popped into my head, I don't know! But it did, so there you are! Anyway, there are bloody thousands of them. Bloody tropics!

These terrible mosquitoes have certainly woken me up. Tired as I am I can't wait to get going again. I can't understand it. On a motorcycle in England there is always the constant threat of a bluebottle splattering on your glasses or a bumble bee impaling itself in your forehead. In the jungle I had experienced none of that. At speed my body has remained totally insect-free. Stop and the whole bloodsucking world comes down to take a bite.

So, resigned to purgatory, it is back on with the helmet and away, with more singing 'I saw her standing there', more fantasies; more black, endless road.

To be honest the rest of the journey is more or less total blank. The only thing I can remember is passing a sign to Georgetown and thinking how much I would have liked to visit Penang; it was so close and yet so far.

NO PAPERS TO ENTER THAILAND

We finally reach the Malaysia/Thailand border just before 6am. I am so knackered my brain feels inside out. All I can do is squeeze in the van and collapse. I just about manage to take my helmet off before I am asleep. Once again, the crew had spent most of the journey drinking Jim Beam so are comatose. There is a distinctly horrible, boozy, farty aroma to cope with. I wake up a couple of hours later feeling shit - with cramp in more places than most people have places. And, also as usual, we find ourselves in the middle of nowhere with no paperwork to get through the border.

TUESDAY 28 JUNE

THE BORDER

The Malaysia/Thailand crossing point really is in the middle of nowhere. Situated a few miles north of Changlun, the exit border post reminds me of a small picnic stop on a German autobahn. There is nothing except a lay-by and some toilets situated next to the customs point. Dead quiet. No one about at all that I can see. Even the officials are cosseted away in their office away from the early morning chill.

There is something very romantic though about this place; deep in the jungle at daybreak. Little hints of light peeking through the mist, forming strange shapes that appear and disappear past the first batch of palm trees, as their large leaves sway in the gentle breeze. A large unmarked truck and trailer pulls into a bay and stopped. The invisible driver turns off his lights and settles down for a rest.

I wander past the buildings to a series of shacks built in the dust alongside the road. Shack is probably too harsh a word. More a row of economically-built shops constructed from locally available materials. Each has a canvas awning to protect customers from the rain or powerful midday sun. One or two sell snacks, groceries and drinks, three more are cafes preparing to serve breakfast. None is particularly inviting. Beggars can't be choosers, however, so I sit down on one of the white plastic garden furniture chairs and wait the few remaining minutes for the place to open. As I sit here, idly shuffling my foot in the dust, I marvel at how such a small space could sell so much stuff. Things are piled on things on top of every flat surface. Strange looking pieces of chicken in a glass fronted rotisserie are flattened and skewered in lines of six or so; packets of dried strange shapes, with no labels to tell you what they are, perhaps something fishy, no pun intended. There are boxes and boxes of chewing gum in a great variety of flavours, some unhealthy-looking sweets, packets of biscuits and lots of other stuff that a cross-border trucker may find useful. A portly Chinese lady, dressed in white, is rearranging things, preparing for the day's onslaught. Other invisible people clutter about out back. I wonder what the kitchen is like. From the tangle of wires above, they may have electricity, but I doubt if some of the other services are quite as efficient. I am dying for a coffee, but as yet my hostess takes no notice, her face blank as she continues her preparations.

A chair scuffs up next to me. A bleary-eyed Steve has arrived, the effects of a bottle of Jim Bean still very apparent. Soon followed by Sean, his beaming chubby face never affected no matter how much alcohol he consumes. To be fair, we must look a pretty grim bunch. Me in a black T-shirt – with matching face and hands - grubby jeans, leather jacket, chaps and knackered cowboy boots; Steve was in a crumpled black Fat Boy T-shirt, dirty black shorts and Doc Martin boots. Sean is slightly better dressed in a white(ish) T-shirt with safari shorts and walking boots. Mind you, he is one of those people who always looks respectable no matter what state he is in. I am absolutely filthy - I have just ridden the bike for a few hundred miles through rain and dust and look like it. My two companions, although protected from the elements in the comfort of the van, still look like they need ironing.

Sean raises his hand to beckon the Chinese lady who comes over with absolutely no enthusiasm whatsoever. It's just as well she relies on passing trade, I thought, no one would return here out of choice! The best we can get is weak tea. After a few minutes, she brings us a glass of hot water with a tea bag on a piece of string in it. We are offered milk, but to be honest I don't like the look of it; it is a sort of brownish grey and not very fresh milk-like. Wet and warm is the best on offer. Still, in our condition, it is a thousand times better than nothing, I suppose.

We sit in exhausted silence for a while but, as it is approaching eight o'clock we need to discuss the day's plans. We are to meet E.D., our Thai fixer, at ten o'clock, somewhere on the other side of the border; the border we have no papers to cross. We have been assured however, that she will sort that problem. When I'm actually in Thailand, however, I'll believe it, and not before. So many people on this trip have been all talk and no action. Needless to say I am the most concerned as I have the most to lose. At the end of the day the others can just fly home. I'm trapped with a very valuable motorcycle in a country where I should not be, making a film I should not be making, with no visa, no documents, no permission. I wish to enter another country for which I also have no visa, no documents and no permission. I must be mad.

As I sit here, a feeling of extreme loneliness engulfs me. I feel naïve and stupid. Sitting in Steve's lounge, all those months ago, I really believed in his organisational ability. With the benefit of experience, I now feel Steve's idea of organisation is to cross that bridge when we come to it. In England, that works. When you know the system, you can work around it.

288

Out here, it's a little different. Out here, we need other people to fiddle the system for us. And the people Steve has chosen appear to be robbing me blind. I just hope E.D. is reliable. He assures me she is. His confidence, however, does not stop my sphincter twitching.

Eight thirty and it's shit or bust time. They decide we may stand a better chance of blazing our way through, should we have to, if there are few people about to witness it. What sort of decision is that, to rush a frontier? How can I disappear over the border with an extremely obvious huge Harley-Davidson with an English registration? I am the one that will end up in prison with the key thrown away.

Leaving Malaysia is easy. They just check our passports and wave us through. They don't care, of course, they are happy to see the back of us – getting into the next country is the problem. After about a kilometre of no-man's land, it opens up into a huge duty free zone. The large concrete and glass supermarket, although still closed at this time of the morning, comes as a complete surprise. Given the huge import taxes imposed when taking goods into either country I can't see the point. As we pull in, the car park is deserted. This is to be the changeover point. E.D. had promised her van would meet us and carry us through to the other side. I quietly pray someone will actually turn up.

A few minutes later, someone does turn up - in a nice new van, and on time. It certainly lifts my spirits - for just a moment, anyway. There was no E.D., just a driver who knows very little about what is going on except to say E.D. would meet us about ten o'clock. We can't ask him too many questions, however, because his English is almost as good as my Thai. I am just as confused and worried as before. We transfer all the kit over to the new vehicle and bade farewell to our two Malay drivers. On the bike I have had very little to do with them since leaving Kuala Lumpur, but the others are all hugs and fond farewells, saying how much better the trip would have been had they been with us all the time. Umm… seems like backslapping, drunken bonhomie to me.

Anyway, our Thai driver is polite and respectful - it remains to be seen how efficient he will be. Let's see if he gets us through the border first.

I follow the van back on to the road and then on a few hundred metres more into the covered customs area. It resembles a garage forecourt without the pumps. I park the bike alongside the van and dismount. Somehow, I feel we are in for a long wait. A uniformed officer, small but intimidating in his bemedalled, crisp khaki uniform, confronts us. He is wearing a small leather holster which holds what looks like a very dangerous weapon. He collects our passports and disappears into the office building to our left. The most frustrating thing to me is that I can see Thailand. I can see the small bustling border town literally a few metres from where I stand. Frustratingly, because the gate is open, I could actually touch Thailand if I want, but I am not allowed to be there.

This dusty frontier town has everything I want - the road north.

We wait……and wait. Five minutes, ten minutes, half an hour. I sense all is not well. But I did not know what or why. Had E.D. failed? Or been caught? Or lied? Not knowing is the worst. We can't go back and we can't go forward. Shit. It is almost nine thirty now. I wish E.D. was here. She's the one with connections. Fluent in English and Thai, I am told. A million disasters race through my mind. Roll on ten o'clock; I pray she is punctual.

I am summoned into a small office next to where the bike is parked. A document is thrust at me for me to sign. Totally incomprehensible in Thai script, all I can make out is 1,100,000 baht. God, what is that? I can't pay that much. At 35 baht to the pound that is Sultan of Brunei money. Shit. What does it mean? I can't understand and the man holding the document can't explain. Frustrated at my lack of co-operation he leaves, shaking his head. My heart is pounding. I am scared. Very scared...and more waiting!

He returns with someone who appears to be his superior. And who speaks English - limited English anyway. I do not have to pay. I only have to guarantee I would pay, and only if the bike is in the country more than 28 days. Whereas, officially, I should pay a returnable bond to enter the country, they were, in these exceptional circumstances, waiving that, on trust I would leave as promised. A higher authority had given me permission to enter Thailand in transit. Fuck me, am I relieved. She has done it. Well done E.D. The only thing I have to do is register at the office through the gate (through the gate, mind, in Thailand!) and buy special transit motor insurance.

In seconds, before he can change his mind, I am gone. We are through. No checking what is in our van. Nothing! No worries about thousands of pounds worth of camera gear. No worries about four crates of Jim Beam whiskey. Nothing! It was all I could do not to cheer. I am totally overwhelmed. It is fabulous. I virtually skip into the insurance office. Even that is pretty good. What am I talking about – it is incredible. Two hundred and thirty five baht for one month's insurance with the Liberty Company. Less than ten dollars - sorted!

E.D. and Nong, her young assistant turn up, as arranged, spot on ten o'clock, at a roadside restaurant about two miles up the road into Thailand proper. E.D. I had met before at a planning meeting at her house in Holland Park, London. Although only 5'2" (that is about 152cm in new money)or so, she had an 'in-control' presence about her. Not an endearing quality, mind you. More "do-as-I-say or else" arrogance. Nevertheless, I have no doubts that she can get the job done. She is an elegant woman in her mid-thirties, well dressed today in designer shorts, neatly pressed with creases down the front, an expensive t-shirt and a gold Rolex watch. Her long hair is neatly tied in a ponytail. She is almost pretty, but not quite. When she spoke she had the unfortunate habit of blinking her eyes rapidly in a twitching movement. I suppose you'd call it a nervous tick. Nong, her long-serving (and suffering) colleague is slim, slightly taller, late twenties and again, almost pretty in a librarian kind of way. She is wearing jeans and a simple white t-shirt.

Before leaving we have to wait for E.D's contact from the customs to join us. There are two reasons for this: firstly, she wants to thank him for smoothing our entry - he is a good friend of her brother's and she needs to keep him sweet for the future; and secondly, he probably wants his bung. Away from the rest of us, she passes him an envelope - I'm not told what was in it; plus we give him a crate of Jim Beam. Cheap at the price, whatever it was.

We have also been told that the van that carried us through the border is not the one that will be used on the journey. That is on its way from Bangkok and would meet us in Hat Yai, the closest major town, around fifty kilometres away from here. Seeing we are knackered, the suggestion is that we stay there the night and move on in the morning.

Thank God for that. I am exhausted beyond belief. A lovely hot shower, a sleep, a nice meal and some clean clothes - wonderful. I can't wait.

We arrive in Hat Yai around one o'clock. It is the principal city in southern Thailand and a bustling metropolis. Crowds of people jostle their way through a myriad of tiny streets, risking life and limb as they attempted to avoid the never ending stream of foul smelling, diesel pumping lorries and busses, crazy taxi drivers and lunatic kids on clapped out mopeds. Small tired looking shops, selling tired looking, fashionless, clothes are squeezed between larger tired looking shops, garish with neon and bright lights, selling just about everything that can be counterfeited and sold on the cheap. Desperately unsafe looking wiring dangles from lampposts - compulsory, it seems, in South-east Asia, where just about every builder must have served his apprenticeship under Heath Robinson. My first impression is, I'm afraid, what a scruffy dump! I wish I could think of something positive, but I can't.

The Diamond Hotel is equally soulless. It is an early seventies, anonymous, block-of-flats looking place, squeezed into what would be the equivalent of Hat Yai high Street. Three stars, allegedly, although I'm sure it must have been the owner's brother who did the evaluation. It is tired like the town, with its cheap veneered furniture and shabby fittings that had all seen better days. Still, the beds are clean, the showers hot and I am exhausted, the latter no doubt having some negative and perhaps unfair influence on my feelings toward the town. I've no reason to complain, I would have given my right arm for this luxury not so many hours ago.

After some desperately needed sleep, I ring Steve and agree to meet the crew at eight o'clock in the hotel foyer.

E.D. recommends a restaurant a couple of blocks away. We nod acceptance, so she leads and we follow in a line, snaking our way through the early evening throng. The restaurant is red. All red! Red table cloths, red carpet, red lamps peering through red glass lampshades similar to those found in TGI Fridays. It does have a few bits of white, here and there, but the owner must have a particular fondness for red. We have a simple chicken meal and, as usual, Sean drinks his own, not inconsiderable, weight in beer. E.D. discusses her recommended plan of action with Steve and I chat with Paul and Chris. A bit of ear-wigging gives me the distinct impression that Sean is being extremely smarmy with ED´s assistant Nong.

Around ten we all troop back to the hotel. E.D. says Nong and her are going to bed. The rest of us have been asleep all afternoon, so are still raring to go. We wish the girls goodnight and wander off in search of some fun.

We very soon find that that is not an easy task in Hat Yai. For a border town with reputation for cheap sex and easy action, all I can say is, they keep it well hidden. Half an hour of up and down, round and round gets us nowhere. The best we manage is a dingy looking disco, built in the style of a John Travolta nightmare. We do go in for a moment, find we are the only revellers, shrugged our shoulders and leave. We agree it looks like a quick beer and back to bed. A couple of dodgy looking hookers, no doubt somewhat grateful that it was dark in there, make a half-hearted attempt to interest us. We politely decline their offer. Expressionless, they turn around and disappear into the gloom of the corner opposite.

By twelve, I am cleaning my teeth ready for bed.

WEDNESDAY 29 JUNE

RIDERS IN THE STORM

Up early because we to get a few things organised. E.D. needs a float, so Nong and I are despatched off to the bank to change £500. While out and about I buy some new Ray-Bans to replace those pilfered in Dumai. I get some real groovy gold framed jobs for less than £40 in a sale. That is about a third of the price in England. And genuine too, not Thai counterfeit; a bargain too good to resist. Next off, we went to the market. I desperately need my boots repaired; three weeks of jungle had worn them to the point where cardboard was needed to stop my feet touching the street. I find a great cobbler sat in the street surrounded by a mountain of shoes for sale or repair, he very quickly does an excellent sole and heel job for a couple of dollars. Marvellous value!

My good fortune in the purchasing department was tempered a little by the fact it had started raining. Not a very welcoming prospect for the forthcoming three hundred mile ride to Phuket.

And boy, as we leave Hat Yai, does it rain!. Never in my whole life have I been so wet. Mega-rain! Even my bones are wet. I am even wetter than I had been, when lost in Kuala Lumpur with Steve. But somehow it isn't horrible wet, it is warm wet; even exciting wet. God knows why, but I am enjoying it.

The road often disappears into a stretch of construction; a few minutes plodding along on wonderful tarmac, then nothing. Straight into mud and gravel and bomb crater potholes. Blimey, this is an exciting ride -motocross slipping and sliding, for hours on end. All filmed, of course, from the comfort and dryness of the van. They have to just record the soggy state I am in - a brown slime ball, wringing from top to toe. A Rider in the Storm!

KRABI

We stop briefly in Krabi, about two thirds along the route to our next overnight stop on Phuket Island for something to eat. What a sight I must be to the perplexed locals as they watch me park my huge motorcycle in the middle of town. I am so wet. Riding my motorcycle I wear fingerless gloves and, looking down, I see my fingers are all wrinkled like I have been in the bath for an hour. It has been a beautifully scenic journey from Hat Yai. It occurs to me that it would be wonderful to live in the rain forest – if it wasn't for the rain! With legs akimbo, I splish-splosh into the restaurant. What a strange looking place this restaurant is. In the midst of all the traditional Thai concrete block shop houses and corrugated iron makeshift shopettes, is this amazing building. A three storey Georgian replica, pastel emulsioned, lifted straight out of Regency Cheltenham or Bath. Incongruous to say the least! All on its own, but built in the middle of a terrace of ordinary concrete places, with a tiny gap in between to make it 'detached'. The ground floor is open-fronted like everywhere else. Although obviously established for many years, it has a kind of work-in-progress look about it with piles of bricks and buckets and crates stacked alongside the fridges and freezers in the entrance. Inside are a number of simple ancient tubular tables and white plastic chairs; a Somerset Maugham, slowly revolving, ceiling fan; a glass fronted cabinet with very little in it and the obligatory Coca-Cola chest fridge. That is it. On the floors above, was this strange, elaborate and expensive facade. I wonder why!

Half hour break for something to eat and a look at the map and it's on the road again - in brilliant sunshine this time; hot and dry and much, much better. Fantastic! It's amazing how soon you forget the discomfort as the sun and wind get to work. A fifty miles an hour hair dryer, with lovely countryside, lush and green. On and on through miles of outstanding beauty - I love it.

I reach cross-roads and turn right. This is an excellent road - relatively new, without potholes or any mish-mash mending. Rounding a bend I am hit by an amazing panorama. I am cutting through the centre of a large plain, edged by deep green mountains and topped by fluffy white clouds that

contrast perfectly with the yellowy green of the flat grassland
and the beautiful blue sky. Tufting up every now and again
are midgreen bushes and small trees, giving the whole place
a polka dot appearance. Meandering through this lot is a
picture book stream with small offshoot ponds to either side,
formed when the river had flooded into hollows and dips.
Drinking from the closest pond to the edge of the road, not
fifteen metres away, is a herd of the largest cattle I have ever
seen. Huge sandy coloured beasts with great big horns that
have to be two metres across.

I stop the bike on the hard shoulder and get off. A couple of
the animals stop drinking and casually look up at me. The
others take no notice. By this time the van is approaching
and I motion to them to stop a way away so as not to disturb
my new acquaintances. Not that they seem to be particularly
worried by traffic. Living so close to the road, they are used to
the huge lorries that often thunder past. They give me just a
momentary glance before going back to their business. I walk
off the road and slip down a steep bank to try and get a closer
look. Most had finished drinking and moved away a little to
graze. I stop; keeping quiet and motionless, to give them a
little time to get used to me. Creeping forward, the closest
is now about ten metres away. His looking up appears to be
a signal to the rest. The whole herd of a few hundred stop
what they are doing and clear off. I am devastated. I try to
follow, but they are off at great speed - over the river and away.
Within moments, they are tiny dots in the distance. Only the
odd straggler remains, perhaps too greedy or too lazy to be
concerned about the others. I had tried not to startle them
but had failed. Perhaps, in reality, that was for the best. My
intrusion may have upset their tranquillity. On reflection that
could have been disastrous. Although they look peaceful and

serene, I could have been flattened!

An hour or so later, Steve wants to take over riding the bike. Cooped up and hot, he is fed up in the van. That is OK by me. My bum is getting sore by now and I could do with a rest. That turns out to be a bad decision. Going onto Phuket Island (Ko Phuket) Steve gets flash and roars off. He thinks he knows where he is going. Obviously he does not. We lose him. Prat! We keep going towards Phuket town, hoping he will turn up. He doesn't. By now we are on the approach to Patong Beach, at the far end of which is our final destination - the Holiday Inn. Steve is a fucking dick-head. I am really pissed off by now. Where is he? Has he fallen off? Is he injured? Has the bike broken down? Recent history suggests this is the most likely. But, by being thoughtless and stupid and not sticking with us, he has disappeared. How the hell can we find him? He could be anywhere. Shit. Shit. Shit. The arrogant little bastard has got no brains sometimes. He knows it must be me that rides into the hotel.

Chris and I get out of the van. We are on the only road to the main resort area and reckon that, if he is coming, he must come past this point. The others go searching in the van. Perhaps he is in front and waiting at the hotel? Doubtful, but you never know.

It is now dusk - around five thirty. Chris and I are miles from anywhere and alone. We are hungry, thirsty, tired, and dirty, with no van, no bike, and no idea when either will return. We are thoroughly pissed off. Yet again, we say what an arrogant wanker Steve is and kick an empty Coke can about in frustrated fun.

About an hour later the van turns up, followed by Steve. It seems Steve took a wrong turn as we passed some road works a while back. We turned right and he didn't. It took about twenty miles for him to realise he'd fucked up. Prat! Anyway, he gets in the van and, as he relates his story again, I pull a new, clean t-shirt out of a bag and change out of the now smelly one that I have been wearing all day. I get on the bike for the final few minutes to the hotel.

And, I'm glad I did.

HOLIDAY INN

Seeing a sign for the Holiday Inn, I turn left, off the beach road, onto a partly made up, partly potholes filled with water, side street. About a hundred metres on the left is a floodlit stone sign, showing the name of the hotel, set in a flower bed about three metres in diameter slightly raised from the road. I pull round it onto the neatly tarmacked 'D' that forms the hotel approach. To one side is the obligatory shrine to Buddha that blesses every building in Thailand. This one is particularly grand, as would befit such a prestigious hotel. Four metres tall, a square, white stone plinth topped with a beautifully gilded pergola, under which sits Buddha himself. At his feet are a few small yellow flowers, gifts from passing devotees.

I ride a few metres further to the brightly lit canopy that protects arriving guests from the weather as they enter the hotel. Stretched across the left hand side is a white cloth banner, around four metres long with large red letters sewn on - "WELCOME FAT BOY IN PARADISE TO PHUKET".

What a wonderful surprise. How that has lifted my spirits after the dismal recent hours. I can't contain myself, I am so chuffed. Bumping up the curb, I park centrally under the banner, lock the bike up and march up to the reception area to ask who was responsible for my marvellous welcome.

I turn round, and, low-and-behold, another great surprise. Walking towards me is Patrick Fiat, my Holiday Inn host from Bali. He is accompanied by a taller, slimmer, bespectacled Aryan-looking chap, neatly dressed in a short-sleeved brown and white check shirt and brown slacks. "I can't believe it, what are you doing here?" "Just checking up on you", says Patrick, smiling broadly. "This is Thomas Reiter, the manager here in Phuket. I've told him all about you and that he ought to be careful!" Cheeky sod!

Steve joins me for much shaking of hands and laughing and gratitude at the warmth of our welcome. "I've planned the evening off," said Thomas in German accented English. "Tonight's on me. I will show you the town."

And so he does but unfortunately without Patrick. He has to

leave for Bali with his family, who have joined him on his brief trip to Phuket. He has stayed longer than he should in the hope he could see me once again. How kind.

A great night was had by all. A lovely meal at Thomas' favourite seafood restaurant; a scan round the disreputable clubs to show us the lie of the land, so to speak; lots of drink and loads of laughs. He was a great host. Around midnight Thomas has to leave, but not before pointing us in the direction of the best club and an indication of what we should pay for the services on offer. After a few days on the road, some of us were desperate. A friendly, beautiful, scantily clad young Thai girl would be just the ticket to perk us up. Come morning, I may have been a few quid worse off, but I was a very happy chappy.

THURSDAY 30 JUNE

PHUKET BIG BIKE

I may be happy, but I actually feel like shit. At 7 am my Thai friend left. I am knackered. I had to go back to bed for a couple of hours. Still hung over, I hope some breakfast will make me feel better. I stagger down to the restaurant and find the others in a similar state to me. E.D. and Nong, of course, are lively and fresh as daisies. Needless to say they hadn't joined in our night of drunken debauchery.

For the crew, today is a day off. I need to get the bike checked out and see if I can organise a local ride out for the film. Rumour has it a chap called Alan at a shop called Patong Big Bike can help. I have to find him.

With the help of Thomas Reiter this is no problem. The shop is close to the main junction at the top end of Patong Beach, on the road to Phuket town.

I knew the bike wasn't quite right. On the way to Big Bike, I have a ride around; it was dark when we arrived last night and I want to get a feel for the place. I feel a shudder every now and then. Something is misfiring. Still the damn ignition problem, I am convinced. I am used to all this by now so know that I have to be sensible. I wasn't planning on straying too far from base, so the worst case would be an inconvenient walk back to the hotel. Definitely worth taking the chance to explore little!

Patong Beach is beautiful but getting spoiled. It used to be the perfect romantic location, with loving couples walking barefoot in the sand at midnight, gentle waves tickling their toes as they hold hands and kiss in the moonlight under the umbrella of a palm tree. I suppose it is still a bit like that, but those places are becoming considerably harder to find. It is far easier to get sucked into (or at) a girlie bar playing loud rock music or showing the latest pirate video. Some of the hotels are beyond belief; especially the full size replica of a luxury liner that looks like it was stranded when the tide went out. Phuket, as an island, is a beautiful place. Whatever the developers do, they cannot take that away. It is just a shame they are so reckless. Good planning could make it (or keep it) one of the best places on earth.

To the left of my hotel is the 'Golden Mile' - mixture of old and new, with its glistening new shops and arcades selling gold, leather and designer clothes. Ramshackle tumble-down stalls in between selling trinkets and crap: dodgy tapes, counterfeit watches, cheap T-shirts, shit souvenirs. There are too many restaurants to count and almost all specialising in seafood. It actually makes my mouth water to write this part. The local crabs, lobsters and prawns are delicious, griddled beautifully in a spicy hot red sauce with chillies and coconut. Highly recommended, I can tell you.

Across the newly paved, and very smooth, road, is the beach. Lined with sheltering trees, most, but not all, are palm; the sand is soft and clean. The serenity, however, is broken by never ending noisy jet-bikes and speedboats pulling daft Para gliders. It is both daft and dangerous, because the beach is also lined with power cables on tall telegraph poles. The prevailing wind sends the inexperienced towards these cables. Apparently a few tourists are lost this way each year. I decline my offer of a go. Sheltered under the trees, vendors happily ply their wares - coconuts and exotic fresh fruit, chicken skewered on wooden sticks, Coca Cola, cold beer, all the usual. A few mangy looking dogs poke their noses about for scraps.

With Thomas' instructions I easily find Patong Big Bike. It is not quite what I expect. My information was that this was the centre of the Harley world in southern Thailand, a glitzy operation servicing the needs and desires of the rich and powerful. I naïvely forgot that without the few isolated western holiday hotels, Phuket would still be still a simple island community off the coast of a rural Asian country.

Patong Big Bike is a ten metre square, open fronted shed with a pitched corrugated iron roof, crammed with small, scruffy looking Japanese whiz-bang machines typical of any sea-side hire shop. A hand painted sign, nailed to the front informs us that this establishment is for big bikes only - 250 cc - 750 cc, sport and off-road - hence the name. Inside, the oil-stained concrete floor has bits of dismantled bike in neat piles next to the ones being repaired. In the far left hand corner is a counter, around which, above which, and on which, is a clutter of bike spares - gaskets, chains, bulbs, switches and just about everything else you could think of. A real Aladdin's cave of 'I can fix it' bits. Deep in the midst of all this, sat on a stool, deep in concentration over a pile of administrative paper, punching figures into an oil-stained old calculator was a large middle aged fair haired chap dressed in a scrubby brown polo shirt and grey slacks that look about the same age as he is.

This is Alan, a biker of the old school, a rocker from the sixties who had moved from Kent many years ago to find his paradise in the sun. It would have been handy if I had met him sooner, because he turns out to be Mr. Knowledgeable. I explain the problems that I have been having with the bike from the beginning. He knew straight away what I was talking about and confirms all the symptoms. Bottom line was the rectifier. He tells me that a suspect one could last forever in Britain, but will play up immediately in the hot monsoon climate. This is not an easy problem to solve however. There are no rectifiers in Phuket to suit my machine. He would have to make a phone call to a friend in Bangkok.

Meanwhile, I need to organise a ride-out here in Phuket. Does Alan know all the Harley boys in the area and could he get them here tomorrow. The answer was yes, he did know all the big bikers, but no he couldn't get them all here. All is a bit if an exaggeration. Contrary to my information, there are only a couple of Harleys and both are away right now. He could, however, call on a few friends. Those without big bikes could borrow the Harley Sportsters he has in stock. What a great guy. Once again, a total stranger is falling over himself to help. I am very grateful. No problem, he says, be back at noon tomorrow. By then he would also have more info on the rectifier. And whatever happens he will keep me going. I think he is as excited as me at the prospect of a dozen bikes humming round the countryside.

I return to the Holiday Inn feeling very pleased with my morning's work.

MY FIRST BUNGEE JUMP

I have to admit, making my first ever Bungee jump will be an interesting experience - particularly so because I am absolutely petrified of heights. I cannot even climb a ladder to clean an upstairs window or look over the edge of a cliff without coming over a bit funny.

Reading a complimentary copy of the "Phuket" magazine in the hotel foyer, I noticed an advert for "Tarzan's Jungle Bungee Jump." A stunning colour photograph showed a man in mid-air, suspended over a beautiful vista of jungle and water. I decided there and then that if I was ever to jump, here was the place to do it. Not for me a dodgy old crane above a travelling fairground in Milton Keynes. Not for me to pay for an anonymous production line jump over an anonymous lump of local authority grass.

Nope. If I am going to do it at all, this enormous thing in my life, if I am going to be scared shitless, I want to be scared shitless in style. I want it to be recorded for ever. I want to see what I went through. I want to make my jump special.

The others couldn't believe it when I told them. They, like most other people, including me, thought bungee jumpers were kamikaze lunatics. Knowing my phobia about heights, they also doubted I'd go through with it.

We shall see…

By now I have psyched myself into it. There is no turning back. I want to go now. Not this afternoon, not tomorrow, not next week, now. So they climb in the van, I jump on the bike and we go. Tarzan's Jungle Bungee Jump is almost exactly five kilometres from the Holiday Inn at Patong Beach, and fortunately very well signposted. I cannot not get there quick enough. Up the long winding road that snakes its way over the mountain behind Patong, I ride, taking care to avoid the maniac bus and truck drivers that have no regard for which side of the road they're supposed to be on. When I get to the Kathu Road junction, I turn right towards Phuket Town. I pass a few roadside stalls selling coconuts and coke and things and then see a large sign with an arrow, pointing down a humpety, bumpety, dusty track. To be honest, the entrance makes me wonder how kosher the whole thing is, but on reaching the place itself, a couple of hundred metres down this track, I have to say I am quite impressed.

I found out later that the site was reclaimed from land degraded by tin mining. An area of water, too big to be a pond but too small to be called a lake, is surrounded by lush tropical jungle. Beautifully kept with manicured lawns and neatly trimmed bushes, the whole place is designed to blend in with the environment. Thatched, traditional-style, wooden buildings help keep up the jungle feel. Even the specially designed tower is painted green to make it as inconspicuous as possible. Tricky, I know, to make an enormous crane inconspicuous, but at least they made the effort.

Always after a deal, I park the bike and go looking for Ian Jamieson, an Australian who, I read, runs the place. I find him sitting in his restaurant, dressed the same as in his advert in a white t-shirt and khaki trousers. A fit, white hunter kind of guy, from his look he strikes me as a very in control person. I tell him who I am and that we are filming a ride on a Harley to Bangkok from Bali. If I could do my first bungee jump here we could film it and publicise his business. It transpires Ian is an ex-stuntman and film producer. Heavily into Harleys in Australia, he is more than willing to co-operate. It couldn't be better. He is a real pro. Confident and re-assuring, you get the idea from him that leaping into nothingness one hundred and fifty foot up is an entirely sensible thing to do and no more dangerous than sitting in church on a Sunday morning.

In Gaza!!!

With his permission we go back to the entrance to film my
arriving, this time riding right up to the reception centre,
rather than leaving the bike in the car park. As I step off, Ian
approaches and welcomes me; I follow him to the desk where
I have to sign the insurance and indemnity forms.

The magnitude of what I am about to do is now slowly sinking
in. The gung-ho attitude was alright back at the hotel, but
now is the time to stand up and be counted. Shit or bust time.
No going back now. This is it.

I look up at the tower and begin to realise how high fifty
metres is. That is bloody high. One false move and I'll end
up splattered like a jelly fish all over this lake. I'll have to be
taken home in a bucket. Sod that. Much like a condemned
man being led to the gallows, Ian's assistant grabs my hand
and leads me to the preparation area. The idea is not to dwell
on the situation. Quick efficient progress is the rule. Except
that in my case I have to repeat every operation three times
so that the film and sound are right. Ian reeks confidence and
fortunately that is catching. So much so, I have to say, that my
fear has all but disappeared.

The preparation is very thorough. I am weighed and
measured to ensure the equipment is adjusted perfectly. I
am even asked how far I would like to fall. Would I like to
stay dry, stopping short of the water? Would I like to just
touch the water with outstretched arms or go right under, my
head submerged? My head submerged - you must be joking.
Only a total arsehole would want that. My head could be
totally flattened as I hit the water at a thousand miles an hour.
Plonker! What a stupid question. I'll stay dry, thank you very
much.

310

I am sat down and my lower legs are bound together so tight I am sure my toes are turning purple. I seem to have safety harnesses attached to every part of my body. At every stage, Ian's assistant is explaining what he is doing and why. Finally, bound up like an oven turkey, I am lifted out of my chair and encouraged to hop over to the platform. The final five metres is like being in a school sack race without the sack. I grab the rail and drag myself in.

With a jolt the platform starts to move. Heading skyward almost silently, the only noise is a gentle creaking as the cage in which we are carried flexes slightly as it takes the strain. All the while Ian speaks reassuring words of encouragement, going over and over the procedure so that I fully understand exactly what I have to do. Surprisingly, I am not scared, so confident am I in Ian's capability. I think, perhaps, I am so committed; there is no point in being nervous. This event is being filmed; there is no way I could permit myself to back out. If I fail, the whole world would see it. I can't slink back to the hotel and pretend it never happened; I can't go back home and keep my cowardice quiet. I couldn't possibly act like a big tough Harley rider for the rest of this journey; the crew would think me a"wanker". So, the only way off this platform is via a leap into space. That's it. Decided!

As I rise, the view is spectacular – a wonderful three hundred and sixty degree panorama of deep green lush jungle. Below me, getting ever smaller, is the lake. The still, blue water contrasts beautifully with the trees and foliage that hug its amoebic edge. To the right is the open-sided restaurant, empty at this time of day, except for Ian's eleven year old son who has just turned up to watch us and is sitting at a table drinking a coke. There is a young local girl working outside. Between the restaurant and the reception centre below, the crew are preparing to film my imminent demise. Or that's the way it feels.

As I rise to the heavens, the whole situation takes on a surreal quality. I begin to think how ridiculous it all is. How could I have been so dumb to put myself here. Nobody in their right mind jumps off a platform one hundred and fifty feet in the air. In fact it is worse than that. According to Ian I must dive off. If I jump, I will plummet like a stone and the rope will stretch too much and I will either bash my head in on the concrete wall that water becomes when hit from this height or successfully enter the water and then be agonisingly held under and drown. Ian didn't exactly say that this would happen, he just said the rope would stretch too much - I worked out the rest for myself.

After a few minutes another sharp jolt brings the cage, Ian and me to an abrupt halt. We pause for a few seconds to allow everything to settle and Ian once again painstakingly goes through my instructions. I grip the rail tightly and try to relax a bit and fully appreciate the view. I want to enjoy this as much as possible. I want to savour the moment. Ian asks if I am OK, telling me how many jumps he has done - hundreds - and how exhilarating bungee jumping is. He reinforces his confidence building by telling me about the sense of achievement I will feel when it's all over. How proud I will be of myself. As the countdown begins, the magnitude of what I am about to do once again hits me. I feel like I am being collected at dawn from death row. I have had my last plea for a reprieve refused. This is it. The pastor's hand is on my shoulder. Feet tightly bound, I am hopping toward my destiny. Any minute now the trap door will open and I will plunge into oblivion.

312

This Aussie Albert Pierrepoint knows exactly what will happen and I have to trust him. I have to trust that this total stranger does in fact know how to adjust the tension on the rope so I will stop short of the water. I have to trust that he has bound my feet securely and correctly so the rope and I go in the same direction. My worst fear is that the rope will stop and I won't. I have to trust that as I descend my legs won't be snapped off. I do not fancy floating in the water with two ragged stumps attached to my bum.

I look at the view again to take my mind off disaster thoughts. Kamikaze man I am not. Enjoy it. You can only do your first bungee jump once. Enjoy it.

I feel detached from reality. Ian's voice echoes in my brain as I blindly follow his instructions. "Walk to the jump area" - Shuffle would be more accurate - my legs are totally encased from the knee down and bound together giving me even less movement than an early sixties bimbo in a Diana Dors skirt. I am now at the gap in the cage, the bar has been raised and I am now only five seconds from IT. "One," I wiggle a little closer to the edge. "Hanging Ten" as a surfer would say. "Two," I stare forward, chin slightly up, staring blankly at the mountains in front of me. "Three," I raise my arms in a pose similar to the statue of Christ on top of the hill in Rio de Janeiro. "Four". I feel very elegant, very pompous, and very detached; serene almost. There is no turning back now, so if I am going to do it, do it in style, I say. "Five" - I leap forward and up. Trying to do exactly as Ian had instructed. Arms out and you fly........straight downwards.

My mind is actually totally blank from this moment. Involuntarily, I scream. Take it from me, there is no alternative. There is no wilder experience. Nobody has invented a dafter thing to do. The first drop is OK; the elastic rope takes the strain in a very controlled manner. I feel comfortable and impressed with myself. How easy was that? Whew! I am glad that's all over, I thought. Time for a beer and look at me lads! If only. What nobody told me, (and bear in mind I was the first of the day, so had not seen anyone else jump) was that the rope does not act like a shock absorber at all, but more like a yo-yo. On reaching the bottom, I am catapulted back up where I came from, almost reaching the cage again on the rebound. I couldn't believe it. It is like being in a Road Runner cartoon, and I am the coyote. I feel as if my legs are being pulled out of their sockets. All the puff is taken out of me. I feel totally out of control, there is nothing I can do except bounce up and down for what feels like an hour and a half but is, in fact, just a minute or two. As the bounces diminish, the idea is to grab a long bamboo pole that is being offered by a guy stood on a small jetty that protrudes into the

314

lake. Once caught you are pulled onto the deck. Such is the
rapidity of the oscillations, it takes a few goes to achieve it,
but, believe me, catching that pole is like winning the lottery.
All your problems are over. Thank God. As I am being pulled
in someone cradles my shoulders and gently lowers me to
the deck. I just lay on my back unable to move, my arms
still splayed out like a crucifix. I am totally out of it. I feel
as if I have smoked a bucket of dope soaked in whisky. I am
like a rag doll; my legs are lifted so I can be unwrapped and
untangled. I am helped up. I stand transfixed. I keep looking
up to see where I had just come from and looking down to see
where I went.

As I wibbly, wobbly walk along the jetty towards the
restaurant, Steve comes up and congratulates me. He says he
didn't think I would go through with it and how impressed

he is that I did. I slump into a chair, prostrate almost, legs splayed out and arms dangling down. I ask Chris for a cigarette to calm my nerves. Ridiculous really, because I don't smoke! I just need something to help me chill out.

Ian joins us and sits down. "Well done," "Perfect" etc. etc. "Did you get that, lads?" he said, enquiring about the film. "You know what would look terrific? - shooting from the platform, that could give a perspective from Mike's point of view". "Great idea, they all agree. Ian's right, what we have got is a bit one-dimensional."

So here I am, relaxing, totally wasted after a mind-blowing experience, and the question is "Can you do it again?" Bastards!

So I do!

But that's it. My bungee jumping days are over. I had to do it once in my life. I did it in the jungle. I did it on film.......twice. But, that's it. Game, set and match. All over! Next…

DEAD BIKE AGAIN

After lots of shaking hands once again and general bonhomie we walk back down the gravel path to the bike. I sit on the saddle, put the key in, turn the switch, press the starter and ......nothing. Dead as a bloody Do-Do. Fucking thing. Shit. After being a bungee hero. I now feel a total prat. We have to bump start it once again. I have been truly brought back down to earth.

On the way back to the hotel I call in at Big Bike. Alan puts the battery on charge and suggests I call back later.

FRIDAY 1 JULY

It's amazing what you can get away with, with a film crew in tow. Lunch time and we are on our way to Big Bike - me in front, the van and crew following on behind. Gently cruising along the seafront, I notice a restaurant. It's called the Paradise Bar. That's handy - could be The Fat Boy in Paradise Bar. I wonder if they will swop lunch for a mention in our film. Lots of bullshit later, me, the crew, E.D., Nong, the driver and the Thai film board man who has now joined us (for the privilege of whom I have to pay wages and all expenses), are all eating and drinking for free, with the proprietor, a jolly Australian, surprisingly named Bruce, grateful for the publicity. A good start to the day!

PHUKET RIDE-OUT

We arrive at Alan's place around two o'clock. The plan was to start at half past, which gives me thirty minutes of booster charge for my battery. That is healthy enough; my real problem is the charging circuit, so if I am careful and keep my headlight use to a minimum, hopefully, I should be alright. Alan's friend can't get a new rectifier here for three days, which we haven't got, so the plan is to bodge it best we can for now and collect the new part ourselves in Bangkok.

In the end we have six riders for our ride-out - me, Steve, Alan, a Thai who likes to be called Eagle or Vulture or something; an accountant, rugby playing sort of chap from France in a nice clean white shirt, jeans and braces; and a real groovy looking woman in her thirties, Alan's wife, I think. She is a bit Suzy Quattro. A real cool biker bird with a black waistcoat covered in badges, Harley cap, Ray-Bans and boots. Eagle or Vulture or whatever is cool too; at least in the way he looks. He must be bloody boiling, though. Mid-afternoon in the tropics, it is at least ninety degrees and he arrives, and stays all day in, leather jeans and cowboy boots; a full leather biker jacket, zipped across; a denim jacket with the sleeves ripped off and a few badges sewn on; a red bandanna with white spots, tying back his long black hair; counterfeit Ray-Bans. His signature trait is his mean smile. Riding his Sportster he wouldn't have looked out of place in an L. A. gang movie. He would be perfect for the role. He was the silent type too, it didn't seem very keen on telling me who he was or what he did or anything.

A motley crew, I know. But they have made the effort, for which I am extremely grateful. I know that I have said it before, but the people I have met on this trip have been truly outstanding. The friendship and generosity shown to a stranger is something you could never find the like of nowadays in Britain.

Phuket Beach Road

The ride is very enjoyable but uneventful. Crazy really because, whilst I have always longed for some peace and normality on this journey, when it comes, it is a bit of an anti-climax because, as Steve keeps telling me, we need disasters to make an interesting movie. We travel along a coast road with a beautiful vista across a bay of dark, jungle covered mountains. Promontories of green, sliced into pieces as the water level rose many thousands or maybe millions of years ago, leaving dots of small islands trailing off into the sea. As we climb, we cut through the jungle, each side of the narrow tarmacked winding lane an impenetrable mass. As the afternoon progresses, the sky clouds over. It is still very

319

warm and very humid. The gentle wind is just perfect as we twist and turn though the hills. Breaks in the foliage give tantalising little glimpses of the never ending vista of slowly darkening mountains that disappear into the distance. This is always my favourite part. No hurry to be anywhere, great scenery, great weather, T-shirt and no crash helmet. This is the dog's bollocks. If only the entire journey had been like this. (Steve says if all the trip had been like this we would have the most boring film in the world!)

Eventually we stop at the top of a long hill. It is a tourist spot by the look of it, because there is a car park with a few stalls selling fresh coconut (my absolute favourite now) and various other bits and bobs. At the highest point of Karon Viewing Point is a covered area and a place for taking holiday shots against a lovely background, approached by some neatly made stone steps. To the left is one of those sign posts that show how far everywhere is - London that way, Tokyo, New York, all that sort of stuff. No one here mind, because it is off-season, except us and a couple of Thai tourists in a black Toyota. We line up for some group shots astride our bikes, the line we form pointing off towards the most interesting panorama at this location. It is crap really, because some prat had planted a row of the ugliest telegraph poles you have ever seen right across this beautiful view. Yet another example of how easy it is to fuck up paradise. Anyway, that is it. It is now about four thirty and time for Alan and his friends to go back and do some work. I thank them for their help and wish them a warm farewell as they ride off.

We go back to the hotel for a shower and change before our last night out on the piss before leaving Phuket. I'll be sorry to leave here - great new friends, great food, great sex, great weather - what more is there?

320

SATURDAY 2 JULY

ENJOYABLE RIDE

After fond farewells to the friendly folk at the Holiday Inn, it's back on the road again. It is time to leave Phuket Island and head north. So far, this has been just about the only non-eventful day of the entire journey; or rather non-disaster day. For once I have had a totally enjoyable ride through some wonderful scenery, on decent roads, with very little rain and no breakdowns.

Thankfully, I am on my own, away from the constant bickering of the crew and the pompous nagging of the eye-twitching dragon that thinks she is in charge even though I am paying her wages. Nong, bless her, sails over it all. She is the only one who never moans.

Through the plains, over the hills, past quiet little villages where it seems nothing could disturb their peace and tranquillity. Little shacks on stilts nestling next to gently meandering streams, fishing nets strung out on impossibly long sticks. They are like huge net parachutes that catch just about everything that comes their way. I wonder how there could be anything left for the poor sods fishing further downstream. Groups of little old ladies with great big black coolie hats, shuffle along in the dust at the side of the road - miles from anywhere and seemingly with nowhere to go. I see kids on rickety old bicycles - more often than not with one on the saddle, one on the crossbar and one on the rack over the back wheel.

As I progress into the skinny bit of Thailand between Burma and the Gulf of Siam, the scenery turns to prairie grassland, its plainness broken only by the short scrubby bushes and small trees that dot the landscape. Every so often there is a backdrop of outcrops of naked grey rock that springs out, pushed haphazardly through the surface by some enormous underground force eons ago.

To the left is Burma or Myanmar as it is now called, only a few miles away but untouchable behind a three hundred mile fence of dark mountains that stretches along the horizon. Still a secret, unknown place, visited by few westerners and controlled by a less than friendly regime.

We stay the night in the non-descript Chansom, a medium quality hotel in Chumphur. Not a place to dally.

SUNDAY 3 JULY

HUA HIN

The only point of major interest we decide to visit after leaving Chumphon (sometimes Chumporn) is Hua Hin. This is the country's oldest beach resort and much less of a loud, rock and roll, shag-a-hooker-for-ten-quid type of a place, than many of Thailand's other tourist places.

There are noticeably fewer visitors and it has a bowls-playing Eastbourne atmosphere to it. Like everywhere the seafront is a mish-mash of unplanned incongruity, neat little houses, fifties-looking shops, and stalls selling coconuts. Overall, it is a peaceful, quiet place, favoured by the Thai's themselves as a welcome escape from Bangkok.

The Royal Family has a retreat here, built by King Rama VII in the thirties and, as a consequence, there are lots of period hotels and buildings dotted around town.

This is obviously the favourite place of E.D., because she breaks into one of her rare bouts of happiness when recalling her childhood visits. She insists we visit her favourite restaurant for lunch and then move on to the area's most famous monument - the hilltop temple on the coast near Prachuap.

This suggestion is met with a serious number of groans from

the crew. 'We don't want to see another temple. We're all templed out', is the chorus. 'No, No!' E.D. insists 'This one is special, believe.' Her twitching intensifies as she becomes visibly excited. There is no point in arguing. She has decided - we are here to obey!

It certainly is a big temple; a very big white temple, in fact, with a Buddha in it, and lots of monkeys scurrying around. I notice a solitary orange clad monk gently going about his business. That was the most interesting part!

Strangely, I can also see a couple of dozen young Thais crawling along a wooden jetty. They are totally prostrate, others stand chanting as their comrades scrape along on their bellies towards the centre of the lake close to the temple. This goes on for twenty minutes - a continuous stream of young devotees showing reverence to their surroundings. I am transfixed. What is this all about - a coming of age ceremony perhaps? Or is it a spiritual elevation to demonstrate faith? Penance, maybe? I have to ask. Find one who can speak enough English to explain it to me.

I do find one. "Please can you tell me the significance of this ritual", I ask respectfully. His reply stuns me. Religious devotion - not exactly - it was a college Rag Week stunt!

BANGKOK

True to form on this project, nothing goes quite to plan; nothing is how we expect it to be. Arriving in Bangkok around seven thirty in the evening, once again I am happy and surprised to find the Holiday Inn have laid on a special welcome for us. The hotel approach is very grand; an imposing driveway that rises from the street into a large covered glass entrance manned by an army of uniformed doormen, porters and other assorted can-I-do-anything-for-you-Sirs. As they had been warned about my imminent arrival, it was fairly obvious to them who I am, preceded as I am by a pick-up loaded with two cameramen, soundman and a director waving instructions and holding a handy cam.

As I stop an elegant young lady in a traditional silver blue silk dress appears to welcome us. With a bow and an elegant throw of her hand, she asks me to follow her. As I look around, I see on the wall opposite a large cotton banner saying "Fat Boy in Bangkok welcomes Fat Boy in Paradise". A wonderful gesture, this time apparently organised by the kitchen staff of the hotel. My escort explains that the Fat Boy in Bangkok is the Head Chef who is heavily into Harleys. My escort reverently leads me through the foyer to reception, this road grimy individual being studied by a number of startled guests who can't quite fathom why such a scruffy Herbert is being followed by a film crew and an ever increasing number of highly attentive hotel staff.

I go through the motions of officially checking in and am lead, once again by my charming escort, to my room on the fourteenth floor. On the way up I find that Noy - her nickname -, who speaks excellent English incidentally, has a degree in marketing and public relations. Such is the employment situation in Thailand at the moment; she says that this is the best job she can get - as a welcome hostess in a hotel. What a waste of a fine education!

A fleeting visit to dump some stuff and it's back down for some more filming. Steve wants to redo the entrance scene from different angles and so on. Mahmood, the General Manager, who, although on his day off, has heard about our arrival and has kindly come down to meet us personally. We exchange friendly greetings and agree to see him and the mysterious Fat Boy Chef tomorrow morning at 10 o'clock for a photo session.

Time is getting short now, for Steve and I have an appointment at the Hard Rock Café in Siam Square at nine to meet the manager, James, and arrange a party there on Friday. The crew pack up the gear as Steve and I rush off to our rooms for a hasty shower and change.

Our trip to the Hard Rock is very successful, James having been previously contacted by Jo-Jo in Kuala Lumpur. We return to the Holiday Inn in a very good mood and true to habit, make straight for the bar.

Fat Boy Bangkok, Mahmood, the banner and me

We are shortly joined by the Manager, who, as it happens, has had more than a passing interest in strange journeys himself. Mahmood is one of those annoying bastards who has been blessed by sporting good looks, intelligence, a rich influential family and the ability to make the most of all of it. Although the name Mahmood Masood doesn't immediately infer a white Anglo-Saxon background, he looks and sounds totally

British. More Oxford than Romford, I have to say, so it comes as a complete surprise to discover he is an Afghan. I have read how Germanic-based peoples originally migrated from the Afghanistan / Pakistan area, but this was the first time I had met anyone from the area and who is informed enough to discuss it. A very interesting guy! During the period he was studying hotel management, Mahmood still found time, in his early years, to be a television presenter, soap actor, news reader and traveller.

As fellow adventure addicts, we talk for ages about our experiences, me en route from Bali, he about a trip he made in the mid-seventies in a shagged out old Toyota. Living in London, he and a friend, blessed with some time, but no money, decided to drive back home to Kabul. This was pre-Ayatollah Khomeini, Saddam Hussein and all that, so the trip was a little more feasible than it is today. They were all packed and ready to go when disaster strikes. Mahmood's friend and travelling companion is struck down by appendicitis and rushed to hospital. No going anywhere for a few weeks! Major decision time - to cancel or proceed as planned, but alone. After all the aggravation of obtaining the visas and making necessary arrangements to postpone the trip would be an anti-climax too much to bear. So off he went. Alone! Brave or stupid, I'm not sure; certainly determined. The Euro bit was easy. Not totally straightforward, of course, there were still border controls and forms to fill in, but more or less that part was hassle free. From Turkey onward the trip heated up in more ways than one. As I found in Indonesia, rules and regulations in some countries are modified as necessary by individual uniformed individuals whose main purpose in life is to extract a few quid from a vulnerable traveller. Again, much like me, time and budget constraints sadly limited too many cultural experiences; the objective being to successfully get from A to B, or in Mahmood's case B to A. He was going from Bayswater to Afghanistan.

Goodness, the things that happened to him! He was arrested, imprisoned, robbed of his passport, his car impounded by rule-bending officials and taken hundreds of miles away in the hope he would never find it. They wanted to sell it to their relations. It was only the fact that he was young, unwilling to give in and resourceful that he survived. Mind you, I guess his connections helped too. Mahmood is a great story teller. I enjoy his company immensely.

Mr. T gives me monumental relief

SUNDAY 3 JULY

MR. T AND FIVE TONS OF SOLID GOLD

The day begins with a crucial errand—a visit to Mr. T's Harley repair shop, tucked away in the maze of Silom's backstreets. The shop might be unassuming, but it delivers a monumental relief. The long-sought rectifier, a gleaming chrome reproduction, not only solves my persistent electrical woes but Mr. T does so with style and expertise. The satisfaction of finally resolving this nagging issue felt like a significant victory after so many setbacks on your journey.

With the bike back to peak performance, the next stop is Wat Traimit, home to the awe-inspiring Golden Buddha. The sheer scale and opulence of this statue—five and a half tons of almost pure gold—are staggering. The story of its rediscovery adds a layer of mystique to the experience. Hidden under a protective shell of mud and cement for centuries, its true value lay concealed until an accidental crack in 1945 unveiled its golden core. It's a fascinating reminder of how treasures, both literal and metaphorical, can be hidden in plain sight, waiting for the right moment to be revealed.

The juxtaposition of Mr. T's modest shop and the grandeur of the Golden Buddha is striking. Together, they encapsulate the spirit of Bangkok—a city where the everyday and the extraordinary coexist in perfect harmony. From solving a mechanical issue in a tucked-away workshop to standing before a centuries-old testament to devotion and craftsmanship, this day captures the essence of travel: the interplay of the practical and the profound.

RIVER TRIP

During the temple visit, I casually mention that I'd love to take a river trip. Years ago, on a previous visit to Bangkok, I rented one of those strange, narrow long-tailed boats that zoom up the Chao Phraya River and slip into the canals. It was magical then, and I can't shake the thought of doing it again.

"You can grab one at the water-bus stops," I explain to E.D., "like in Venice, only these aren't tourist traps. They're everyday transport here."

Before I've even finished, E.D. springs into action. She waves at us with her usual efficiency, motioning everyone into the van while I climb onto my bike. As always, I prefer the freedom of riding, weaving through Bangkok's chaos, though I have to stick close in case I'm needed—or the bike decides to quit again.

The ride through Bangkok is, as expected, hot, loud, and smog-filled. Traffic jams test my patience, and I find myself longing for the cool breeze of the river. After fifteen minutes of stop-start agony, we pull into a hidden car park, a football-pitch-sized expanse controlled by one of those grey ticket machines. There's no guidance for motorcycles, so I wedge the bike between the van and a concrete post, hoping it'll be safe under our driver's watchful eye.

E.D. is already ahead, urging us to hurry. "We have to catch the boat," she calls back, not bothering to explain further. With her trademark robotic efficiency, she darts through a side street and onto the main road. I try to follow, but keeping up with her is near impossible.

The road opens into a vibrant street market, both sides crammed with vendors selling everything imaginable. The narrow two-meter gap is packed with locals browsing for their weekly shopping. Keeping up with E.D. becomes a lost cause, and I end up with Paul, while the others are swallowed by the crowd.

"Bollocks to this," I mutter. "Let's enjoy the market."

I buy some durian - the smelliest fruit in the world

The place is alive with vibrant colours, smells, and sounds. Stalls display dozens of shoes, bright rolls of cloth, and heaps of glittering trinkets. Fresh fish, still alive, lie on beds of crushed ice. Lobsters with bound claws sit in neat piles, ready for their inevitable fate in boiling water. The fruit and vegetables are alien to me, but their strange shapes and vivid hues are fascinating.

The market spills out onto a large open square, where the vendors shift from makeshift tables to proper stalls, much like a European market. At the far end, the Chao Phraya River comes into view. A jetty juts out about twenty meters into the water, flanked by a white ticket office and an open-air restaurant. It's picturesque, but the ticket office is useless for us—it caters to water buses, not long-tailed boats.

We regroup, only to learn we'll have to wait twenty minutes for a boat. E.D.'s rush, as usual, was completely unnecessary. I grab an ice cream from a nearby vendor and enjoy the rare moment of stillness.

THE LONG-TAILED BOAT

When the boat arrives, a fee is negotiated with the driver—or pilot, or helmsman, whatever he is. The boat is narrow and brightly painted, about eight meters long and a meter and a half wide. Rows of varnished wooden seats run down its length, and a long, exposed prop shaft sticks out from the rear. The engine roars as the driver manoeuvres the propeller like a rudder. Steve positions me at the back, the crew up front to film me solo, giving the illusion I'm the lone adventurer.

As the boat picks up speed, the front half lifts out of the water, skipping across the waves. The canopy offers some shelter from splashing water, but a rogue swell or poorly judged wave can soak you in seconds. The journey is every bit as thrilling as I remember. Passing the temples and the Royal Palace silhouetted against the skyline is breathtaking. Their vibrant colours and intricate architecture stand in stark contrast to the bustling city around them, framed by manicured gardens that offer a hint of serenity.

The real magic begins when we leave the main river and enter the labyrinth of canals. This is where life happens. Riverside homes range from rickety wooden shacks on mouldy stilts to gleaming villas with private jetties. Women sit on steps leading into the water, washing clothes and vegetables. Families laugh and splash as they bathe together. A man rings a bell on a small canoe, advertising food cooked on a tiny primus stove. Everywhere, people wave and smile. Despite the contrasts, there's a warmth and simplicity here that I love. It's a glimpse into a world untouched by the chaos of modern Bangkok, and for a moment, I feel completely at peace. Thailand truly is the land of smiles.

This morning was more than just a boat ride; it's a glimpse into a world where modernity and tradition coexist in vivid harmony. Whether it's the clatter of wooden bridges, the gleam of a gilded palace, or the cheerful wave of a riverside family, the river trip captures the essence of Bangkok in a way that few other experiences can.

TUESDAY 5 JULY

TO PATTAYA

At the crack of ten, we finally load up the van and set off for Pattaya, a coastal resort that's as infamous as it is popular. This trip is mostly logistical, so we decide to leave the pick-up behind. If we need to film some bikes once we're there, hiring one won't be a problem. To lighten the load, we also leave some of our gear at the Holiday Inn since we're only planning a couple of days in Pattaya.

Leaving Bangkok is pure hell. It's mid-morning on a Tuesday, and the traffic is a solid, honking mess. For me, stuck on the bike, it's doubly frustrating. I could weave through the chaos easily, but I have to stick close to the van in case I break down—or in case something exciting happens that needs filming. The added complication of bikes being banned from the expressway means we're forced to slog through the endless tangle of Bangkok's suburbs. It's two hours of choking smog, relentless heat, and nerve-testing traffic lights before we hit the arterial road to the coast.

Once we're on the highway, the ride finally smoothes out. The well-maintained dual carriageway is a welcome relief after the madness of the city streets. An hour later, the scenery blurs by, and we're making good time when E.D. decides it's lunch o'clock. Apparently, our driver, Oat, is hungry, and E.D. insists we stop at a restaurant she knows in Chon Buri, about halfway to Pattaya.

E.D.'s determination can be grating, but I've learned that arguing over minor things isn't worth the effort. Besides, I'm starving, and a chance to try new food always perks me up.

We pull up to a nameless, open-fronted restaurant in the town centre. The entrance is flanked by a cooking area on one side and a fruit stall on the other. Inside, it's as basic as they come—bare tables with glass condiment sets and flimsy serviettes that are practically useless. There's no menu, just two options: chicken or fish, with noodles or rice.

I choose fish with noodles and, of course, ask for some extra hot chillies to spice it up. My love for spicy food is always a source of amusement for the others. Steve and the crew recoil at the mere mention of heat, sticking to beer for their "lunch." Only Paul is brave enough to try the local fare, while the others seem more intent on staying hydrated—with alcohol.

The food, as expected, is delicious. The fish is tender, the noodles perfectly cooked, and the chillies add just the right kick. The portions are modest, so I ask to try the chicken afterward. It doesn't disappoint—it's juicy, flavorful, and exactly what I needed after the morning's ride.

Steve spots potential for some creative filming. Overhead, there's a large ceiling fan similar to one we'd seen in Krabi, and he's inspired to create an editing illusion—cutting between the spinning fan and the turning wheel of my bike. He sets me up at a separate table to look like a solitary traveller, poring over a map amid the remnants of my meal.

We shoot the sequence several times from different angles. By the time we're done, I'm ready to stretch my legs and explore.

STICKY RICE IN BAMBOO

Outside the restaurant, a fruit stall catches my eye. Among the usual coconuts and mangoes, I spot something unusual: bamboo tubes filled with a strange brown sludge. I ask E.D. to find out what it is.

"It's sticky rice," she explains. "Rice and molasses, baked in the bamboo."

Curiosity gets the better of me, and I hand over twenty baht for a tube. The vendor expertly splits it open with a cleaver, revealing a sticky, gooey concoction. She lends me a spoon, and I scoop out a mouthful. Steve's camera zooms in, probably expecting a grimace, but he's in for a surprise.

It's delicious. The sticky rice is like a cross between toffee and rice pudding, chewy yet moist, and the sweetness is perfectly balanced. None of the others are adventurous enough to try it, but they're missing out. If you're ever in Thailand, this is a must-try.

With lunch and filming wrapped up, Steve captures a final sequence of me preparing to leave. He films me donning my fingerless gloves, unlocking the bike, and starting the engine. I back it into the street, rev it up, and ride off down Chon Buri's bustling high street. Out of the camera's view, I pull over to wait for the van to catch up.

The road ahead leads to Pattaya, but for now, I'm savouring the small triumph of a simple, satisfying stop. Sometimes, it's the little moments that make the journey worthwhile.

An hour after leaving Bangkok, we roll into Pattaya, a town

with a reputation that precedes it. Depending on your perspective, Pattaya is either a buzzing paradise or a moral black hole. It's a place of dualities—part seaside escape, part playground of indulgence.

Thirty years ago (this occurred in 1994 remember), it was a sleepy fishing village, a stretch of pristine beaches and a serene bay. Then came the Vietnam War and waves of American servicemen on R&R—rest and relaxation. The locals quickly capitalized, turning the village into a hub for bars, entertainment, and other "services." By the late sixties and seventies, Pattaya was infamous, transforming into what many called the wildest place on earth.

In recent years, the Thai government has tried to rebrand Pattaya as a family-friendly destination, investing heavily in upgraded facilities and marketing campaigns. But, let's be honest, the core remains the same. Behind the polished façade, the old Pattaya is alive and well. The go-go bars are still packed, and while things are less obvious on the streets, nothing has really changed.

ROYAL GARDEN RESORT

By four o'clock, we're checking into the Royal Garden Resort, greeted warmly by Philippe Guenat, the General Manager. Philippe is a character—cheerful and instantly likable, with a striking resemblance to René from 'Allo 'Allo. His sidekick for the day is Nan, a pretty PR assistant who has shaved a few years off her age, insisting she's twenty-five. Nan is charming, efficient, and seems to have a knack for knowing exactly where things are—an invaluable skill in Pattaya.

Philippe has kindly planned a welcome party for us at the new Benihana restaurant next to the hotel in a shiny new shopping plaza. We agree to meet him later, but first, I have other plans. After a quick shower and change, I'm determined to track down some local Harley riders. My London contact, Richard Rhodes, has given me names and addresses, and I decide to start with Frank, leader of the Siam Knights biker group and owner of the Harley Bar.

SEARCH FOR THE HARLEY BAR

Armed with directions from Nan, I set off from the Royal Garden, taking the suggested route: left, left, left around the one-way system, then onto Beach Road and up to the traffic lights. From there, it's a right turn onto Jomtien Road, first left up Soi 17, and half a mile ahead I should find the Harley Bar tucked near a small block of shops.

It sounds straightforward, but five minutes later, I'm hopelessly lost. Instead of a bar, I'm riding through what looks like a middle-class housing estate. Neatly kept bungalows and villas with manicured gardens surround me—not exactly the setting I'd imagined for a biker hangout.

Round and round I go, the area eerily quiet. No roaring bikes, no neon signs, not even a stray sound to guide me. After ten minutes of aimless circling, I spot a stocky, middle-aged man in a polo shirt and shorts stepping out of his gate. He's my best bet.

"Excuse me," I call out. "Do you know where the Harley Bar is?"

"Yes," he answers in a thick German accent. "Take the next right, then the second right, and you'll be there."

Following his instructions, I turn down the second right and finally spot a cluster of three parked cars at the end of an otherwise empty street. In this quiet neighbourhood, it's a hopeful sign. As I approach, I notice a modest building with a faint hum of music and, through the open front, a flash of chrome gleaming under dim lights.

I've found it, The Harley Bar, and with it, hopefully, a chance to connect with Frank and the Siam Knights.

The Harley Bar, part of the Eden Restaurant, is a surprising and laid-back spot tucked away from the hustle and bustle of Pattaya. Entering through an archway, I find myself in a large open courtyard about the size of a tennis court. There are sturdy wooden tables arranged neatly, the kind you'd expect to find in a Bavarian beer garden. To the right is the indoor restaurant building, and behind it lies a pristine blue swimming pool, glimmering invitingly under the afternoon sun. The whole place exudes a relaxed charm.

In front of the pool, on a slightly raised platform beside an open bar, are three Harleys. Another bike, a stunning black Softail Custom adorned with a bright yellow Harley-Davidson logo in Thai on its tank, is parked right in front of the bar. It catches my eye immediately. Nearby, I spot a tall, blond man, well-built, standing about six feet four. He's wearing shorts and a Harley-Davidson T-shirt—exactly the kind of person I'm looking for. I approach him.

"Hi, I'm Mike. You wouldn't happen to be Frank, would you?"

The man introduces himself as Theo and tells me Frank is inside the restaurant, working on his bike. He offers to take me to him, so I follow.

MEETING FRANK

We walk up a couple of steps and through a pair of open double doors into a large, dark room. The contrast from the bright sunshine outside is stark, and it takes a moment for my eyes to adjust. The room has a heavy, German tavern vibe, with dark wood dominating the decor and small windows letting in only slivers of light. At the far end, I see a middle-aged man, tanned and fit-looking, bent over a Softail Springer. He's wearing cut-off shorts and a T-shirt, working intently on the bike.

"This is Frank," Theo says.

I introduce myself. Frank looks up, shakes my hand, and hospitably offers me a beer. I glance around the table nearest him, which is strewn with tools, wires, and tape—a proper makeshift workshop. Frank is polite but not exactly chatty. It's clear he's a man of few words, and making conversation feels a bit like pulling teeth.

342

I explain the purpose of my visit: I'm trying to connect with local Harley owners, film a ride-out, and perhaps organize a small event. Frank listens, but his enthusiasm is lukewarm. He explains that his bike, recently repainted in a gorgeous cobalt blue with lilac highlights, is still stripped down. Most of the reassembly is complete, but the electrical wiring is a mess. He promises to try his best to get it finished in time.

As for the other Harley riders? - It's slim pickings. Theo's bike is ready, but most of the Siam Knights—the local biker group Frank leads—are out of town. One's in Finland, another in Switzerland, and others scattered around.

The Siam Knights have turned into the Siam Knight, singular.

While we talk, Frank keeps working on his bike, trying to install a pair of Kuriakin wing mirrors with integrated indicators. Wires are everywhere as he patiently works to get them connected. Despite the setback, I can't help but admire the bike. Freshly painted, dripping in chrome—it's absolutely stunning. There's just something about Harleys that grabs me every time. No matter how many I see, I'm always mesmerized. Each bike reflects its owner's personality, making no two Harleys the same. It's this unique character that keeps me hooked.

After about fifteen minutes of strained conversation and watching Frank tinker with his bike, it's clear our chat has run its course. I thank him for the beer and tell him I hope to see him in a couple of days. With his typical brevity, Frank repeats that he'll try his best.

As I ride back to the hotel, I can't help but feel a little deflated. The prospect of a lively Harley ride-out in Pattaya is looking less and less likely.

RIDE MY HARLEY UP THE ESCALATOR

The Benihana Adventure...

Driving a 400-kilo Harley-Davidson up an escalator? That would be ridiculous, right? Yet, there I was, straddling my bike, gearing up to do exactly that. It all began with Philippe, the jovial manager of the Royal Garden Resort, who had a knack for bold promotional stunts. He wanted me to park my Harley inside the brand-new Benihana Japanese restaurant on the first floor of the adjacent shopping mall. The problem? No service lift. The only way up was via the escalator.

As dusk fell, the crew and I moved into position. The Harley gleamed under the plaza lights, drawing a crowd of curious onlookers. Two uniformed guards stood ready by the glass doors, prepped to swing them open at just the right moment. Timing was critical—too slow, and I'd look like a novice; too fast, and I'd crash through the doors. Neither was an option I could stomach. My heart was pounding, but I was determined to pull this off without looking like a complete idiot.

"Ready, action, go!" Steve shouted. I revved the engine, sending a throaty roar reverberating through the plaza. With a jolt, the Harley lunged forward, bouncing up the makeshift brick ramp onto the pavement. The guards swung the doors open, and I sped through, aiming for the polished marble floor of the mall.

That's when I realized the floor was as slippery as ice. The bike skidded, sliding left, right, and everywhere in between. My heart leapt into my throat as I fought to stay upright. Finally, I came to a shaky stop, narrowly avoiding a complete wipeout. "Let's try that again," I muttered, shaking my head. This time, I vowed to take it slower and keep my cool.

The second attempt was flawless. I hit the ramp with just enough power, glided through the doors, and maintained a steady line past the fountain and scattering onlookers. By the third take, Steve had upped the ante, placing Paul on the back of the bike to capture a rider's perspective; double the weight, double the risk. But it went off without a hitch. The plaza echoed with cheers from the crowd.

WATER TUNNEL DETOUR

Philippe, thrilled by the spectacle, had another wild idea: ride through the fountain's water tunnel. This wasn't just wet; it was seriously narrow, slippery, and perched a meter off the ground. The plaza manager was furious, but Philippe, ever the showman – and the boss - insisted.

To everyone's relief, the compromise was pushing the bike up and riding it slowly through the tunnel. Carefully, I navigated the tight space, avoiding the jet streams of water that would have drenched me and ruined the filming. The scene was shot from every possible angle—front, back, side, even from above.

Then came the real challenge; to ride a Harley up the escalator was Philippe's pièce de résistance. The plaza manager looked ready to faint, and even Steve tried to talk me out of it. But pride—and the growing crowd—demanded I go through with it.

We tested the escalator. It was flimsy, with no emergency stop button—a red flag, but too late to back out now. The plan was simple: edge the bike onto the flattened bottom step, and let the escalator carry me up while I balanced on the steel sides. Simple, in theory...!

As the escalator started, the belt slipped almost immediately, straining under the Harley's weight. The engineer panicked and stopped the machine, leaving me stranded halfway up. Walking the bike backward down the escalator was nerve-wracking. My legs wobbled, my palms were sweaty, and the crowd held their breath.

SHOW-STOPPING DINNER

After resetting the other escalator, the key was turned, and I started the climb again. This time, the belt held, and I focused every ounce of strength on keeping the bike steady. The ascent felt like an eternity. At the top, I let out a sigh of relief and rolled onto the second floor, greeted by applause and cheers.

Inside Benihana, I was treated to a show-stopping dinner. The chefs juggled knives and drummed on pans, turning the meal into a theatrical delight. Philippe's speech was full of laughs, and I even tried my hand at juggling—unsuccessfully, of course.

But all the fun couldn't distract me from the next hurdle: riding down the escalator. If going up was nerve-wracking, descending was sheer terror. Sitting low in the saddle, leaning back as far as possible, I felt like I was taming a bucking bronco. Every muscle in my body strained to keep the Harley steady. When I finally reached the bottom, I was drenched in sweat but alive—and that was all that mattered.

Looking back, riding a Harley up and down an escalator was one of the most absurd—and exhilarating—things I've ever done. It was my bungee jump on wheels. I'm glad I did it, but there's no way in hell I'm doing it again.

MISSION CALIGULA

Even after the whirlwind of activities earlier in the day— riding to Pattaya, meeting Frank, filming at the shopping plaza, navigating the escalators, and the grand dinner at Benihana—it was still only 9 PM. And in Pattaya, that meant the night had barely begun. This town doesn't really get going until 10.

My next mission was one arranged by Richard Rhodes, my London contact. He had asked me to deliver a couple of video karaoke discs to a man named Satit, the manager of the Caligula Go-Go Bar, one of the town's top spots. But more importantly, I needed Satit's help to secure something nearly impossible: permission to film inside a girlie bar. Pattaya's go-go bars, with their infamous reputation, they are extremely protective of their privacy, especially when it comes to being filmed. Cameras are often met with hostility, and there's a real risk of smashed equipment—or worse.

Caligula is located in the heart of South Pattaya, right in the thick of the action. Walking in, I was immediately struck by how upscale and polished it was. Forget the grimy, shadowy dives you might imagine. This was a clean, glitzy, and very well-organized establishment. Fifty young women, nearly naked, were dancing under the shimmering lights on a central stage. Around them, patrons sipped their beers, relaxed, and watched the show without any hint of the heavy hustling or aggression you might expect in a similar venue elsewhere.

The vibe was strikingly different from London's infamous Soho. In my experience, those places were often dirty, intimidating, and staffed by individuals you'd cross the street to avoid. Caligula was the polar opposite: vibrant, welcoming, and oddly... safe.

I ordered a beer and sat near the edge of the room, waiting for Satit to arrive. The music throbbed, and the energy of the place buzzed around me.

About 15 minutes later, a tall man, for a Thai—probably around 5'10"—approached me. His presence was commanding, his demeanour calm but unmistakably no-nonsense. This was Satit, and you got the sense that crossing him would be a grave mistake.

He greeted me warmly, and after some small talk, I handed over the laser karaoke discs I'd been entrusted with. This simple gesture helped set the tone for what I hoped would be a productive conversation.

"I hear you're looking to film," he said, his voice measured and direct.

"Yes," I replied. "I'd like to capture the energy of your place—not for any exposé or anything negative. This is about showing people a good time, where they can relax and enjoy themselves without fear of being ripped off or hassled. That's what my audience is looking for."

Satit listened carefully, nodding as I explained. He told me about past experiences with foreign TV crews, most of whom had exploited the opportunity to paint Pattaya in a poor light. His reluctance was understandable, but my introduction through a mutual contact and my straightforward approach seemed to ease his doubts.

After a bit more conversation, he agreed to let me film—under certain conditions. Firstly – the time: filming had to be done between 9 and 10 PM, before the place got too busy; secondly, a credit: his name and club had to be mentioned in the film.

He even spelled out his name for me—repeatedly—ensuring I wouldn't forget it. It was amusing, really. For someone so intimidating in stature, there was an endearing excitement in how he spoke about being featured on TV.

I assured him that the footage would show his establishment in the best possible light. This wasn't an investigative documentary or a moralistic critique. It was a rock-and-roll travel film for a like-minded audience—bikers, adventurers, and those who appreciated a good time.

Around 11 PM, I thanked him for his trust and assured him I'd be back tomorrow to begin filming. As I left, Satit followed me out to admire my bike, his eyes lighting up as he took in the chrome and leather. We exchanged a few more pleasantries, and he wished me luck as I rode off into the night.

Securing permission to film at Caligula felt like a major win—not just for the film, but for my journey through Pattaya. It was proof that, with the right approach and a bit of goodwill, even the most guarded doors could be opened.

CRUISING

Leaving Caligula Go-Go, I couldn't resist the urge to cruise around town on my Harley. The night was perfect—still, warm, and balmy at around 80 degrees. There wasn't a hint of wind. It was one of those rare moments when I could truly embrace the freedom of being on the road. No crash helmets required here, just jeans, a T-shirt, and the wind in my hair. For someone who usually has to bundle up against the cold and follow every road regulation back home in England, this felt like pure freedom.

I felt like the coolest guy on the planet—posing on a wild bike in a wild town. This was a moment to flaunt it, and Pattaya was the perfect stage.

I cruised past the hotel and onto Pattaya's 2nd Road, weaving through traffic lights and honking baht buses. The energy of the town was infectious. I passed by the beer bars opposite the Alcazar Theatre, a landmark known for its dazzling transvestite cabaret shows. Tiller "girls," elaborate sets, and costumes that could rival the West End—only here, the "girls" were actually "ladyboys." - or as the Thais say, katoys. I chuckled at the thought of some unsuspecting tourist discovering the truth late at night. Note to self: always check the hands, feet, Adam's apple, and voice!

As I rode on, I passed clusters of beer bars—small, square, roadside establishments owned by foreigners trying to live out their tropical dream. The cacophony of sound spilling from the bars, each blasting its own music, was a chaotic symphony of Pattaya's nightlife. Girls of all ages staffed the bars, from fresh-faced jungle recruits to hardened veterans of the trade. For as little as ten pounds, everything in this town seemed to be for sale. It left me pondering the superficiality of it all. Was there any genuine emotion left here, or was Pattaya a well-oiled machine of commercialized hedonism?

I made my way to the roundabout at the top of the road, deciding to take the beach circuit. Beach Road was alive with activity. Mopeds zipped past, often driven by locals in shorts and flip-flops, with women perched side-saddle on the back holding bags of shopping. Baht buses, those modified pick-up trucks, honked incessantly to attract passengers.

The scene was electric. Even in July, Pattaya buzzed with life, though it wasn't as crowded as peak season. It was just the right level of busy—a happening place without the crush of high-season madness. The clubs and bars were thriving, and the atmosphere was alive with music and neon lights.

As I approached Jomtien Road, something extraordinary caught my eye: an Indian motorcycle. Its cream paintwork gleamed under the streetlights, and its massive, rounded mudguards screamed 1940s Americana. The rider, a middle-aged man with a ponytail, dressed in a baggy white designer shirt and matching shorts, looked like a character straight out of a movie.I couldn't resist pulling up beside him. "Nice bike!" I called out, and he turned with a grin. He seemed as intrigued by my Harley as I was by his bike.

"Follow me—Manhattan Bar," he said, gesturing forward.

A couple of minutes later, we arrived at a large restaurant with tables set outside. As we parked, the mystery of the Indian motorcycle was solved—it wasn't an Indian at all. It was a Honda. I was stunned. From a distance, it was a convincing replica. While it wasn't something I'd personally want, I had to admit, it was an impressive piece of work for just $5,000.

The man introduced himself as John, a Frenchman and a partner in the Manhattan. The restaurant was a cut above most places in Pattaya, with an unmistakable French flair. Inside, it was polished and welcoming, offering good food, billiards, and a cosy ambiance that reminded me of French country cafés. Even here, though, Pattaya's unique touch was present—the waitresses discreetly offered "extras" for a small fee. The Manhattan seemed to be a hub for French-speaking ex-pats. Over the next couple of hours, I enjoyed some casual conversation, practicing my terrible French while listening to their equally terrible English. It was a relaxed and entertaining way to wind down from the day's chaos.

By the time I left, it was past 1 AM. Exhausted but content, I climbed back onto my bike and headed for the hotel. The streets of Pattaya had shown me their vibrant, eclectic, and sometimes surreal charm. And as I rode into the night, I couldn't help but feel a little bit lucky to be living this wild adventure.

WEDNESDAY 6 JULY

I NEARLY DEAD

Today was meant to be a day off for the crew, a bit of relaxation for everyone. But for me, it turned into a near-death experience—one that I would feel in every sore muscle and bruised inch of my body for days.

The morning was lazy, with nothing planned. But by early afternoon, Nan, our ever-enthusiastic PR guide, had organized a little sightseeing adventure around Pattaya. At 2 PM sharp, we all piled into the hotel's minibus, ready for a mix of temples and tourism.

THE TEMPLE CHALLANGE

The first stop was a beautiful Buddhist temple perched on the highest hill overlooking Pattaya. To get there, we drove along a picturesque winding lane. As the temple loomed above, Nan revealed a surprise: we'd have to climb 120 steep stone steps to reach it. She turned it into a challenge, goading us into a race to the top with the promise of a cold can of beer for the winner.

I gave it my all, huffing and puffing my way up while counting the steps as I went—because that was part of the deal. I came in second but still earned a beer for my efforts. Nan, being the cheeky sort, abandoned the race after just five steps, claiming she'd done it countless times before and only wanted to test our fitness.

The temple itself? - Honestly, a bit underwhelming. After weeks in Southeast Asia, temples were starting to blur together. Gold, stone, intricate carvings—seen it all. Beautiful, sure, but this one didn't stand out. A quick look around, and we were back in the van.

THE CRASH

Nan suggested go-karting next, her enthusiasm cranked to full throttle. I wasn't overly excited, but her relentless cheerleading wore me down. Off we went to Pattaya Speedway, a proper race track with a chicane, a pond, and all the bells and whistles. I didn't expect much but was genuinely impressed.

We had three choices of karts: beginner, intermediate, and full-throttle Formula One-style machines. Naturally, we went for the big boys. After donning overalls and helmets, we were lined up on the grid with four other racers. A pace kart led the way, NASCAR-style, before the race officially began.

As soon as the pace kart pulled away, I floored it. The adrenaline rush was immediate. These things were fast, proper little rockets on wheels. My years of racing Minis and stock cars in my youth kicked in, and I started overtaking the others one by one.

There was just one guy ahead of me. Lap after lap, I tried to overtake him, staying inches from his back wheel. My competitive streak kicked in hard. I was determined to take him on the next left-hand chicane.

As we approached the bend, I saw my chance and went for

the inside line. But the guy must have sensed me. He swerved, shutting the door, leaving me with nowhere to go. At sixty miles an hour, I clipped his back tyre and the track barrier simultaneously.

The next few seconds felt like slow motion. My kart launched into the air, flipped upside down, and slammed into the ground. My head and shoulder hit the tarmac with a sickening thud, and I slid across the track. I came to a stop on the verge, dazed and in pain. Out of the corner of my eye, I saw another driver lose control, his kart veering off into the pond.

I lay in a crumpled heap, assessing the damage. My leg throbbed, and my shoulder felt like it had been smashed with a sledgehammer. But nothing was broken—thank God for the crash helmet. Without it, I wouldn't be here to tell the tale.

The track's rescue team arrived, towing my mangled kart back to the pits. I limped behind them, still a bit dazed. A first-aid guy cleaned my wounds with iodine, which stung like hell, and I nursed my bruised ego with a beer.

The kart looked like a wreck. The rear axle was bent at a right angle, and I dreaded the repair bill. Before we started, we'd signed a waiver agreeing to pay for any damage. I envisioned a hefty price tag.

Nan went to negotiate. She returned five minutes later, smiling. "Give him 200 baht," she said.

I blinked. "That's it?! Less than eight dollars?"

I didn't question it. I handed over the cash, grateful to escape so lightly. The track manager barely looked at me. I was just another overconfident tourist with delusions of being Nigel Mansell, leaving battered and bruised.

Back at the hotel, I collapsed onto my bed, exhausted and aching. I'd come within inches of serious injury, but the thrill of the race still coursed through me. It was a reminder of how close to the edge this trip often brought me—and how alive it

SIX SEXY GIRLS, PLEASE

At 9 PM, Steve and I were back at the Caligula Go-Go, ready for what promised to be one of the more unusual parts of this journey—finding six models for the glamour section of our film. Pattaya is famous for its "anything goes" reputation, but we needed to keep things tasteful. Skimpy swimsuits, not X-rated content, were the goal. The images had to be suitable for mainstream television and magazines, so there was a clear line we couldn't cross.

Still, even in Pattaya, anything can happen.

When going out at night in Pattaya, it is easier to use the baht bus. These modified pickups are cheap, plentiful, and convenient. More importantly, they allow me to avoid the temptation of riding my Harley after a few too many beers. I love cruising the bike around town, but drinking and driving is a no-go. From the Royal Garden Resort to Soi Diamond was just a short walk anyway.

By 9:10, we were seated with Satit, Caligula's manager, at one of the comfy stools circling the stage. He'd promised to help us recruit the six girls we needed for tomorrow's photo shoot. As always, the club was bathed in flattering coloured and ultraviolet lighting. On stage, about twenty girls danced, their toned bodies moving rhythmically under the soft glow.

At first glance, every girl looked flawless. But under this lighting, everyone looks flawless. The ultraviolet hides any imperfections, smoothing out scars and blemishes. While most customers aren't paying attention to the girls' faces, we had to. For our shoot, facial structure was critical.

Satit was incredibly helpful, explaining to the girls what we were looking for. Their reactions were amusing— hands covering their faces, bursts of giggling. Despite the stereotypes, Thai girls are shy by nature. Outside the club environment, they're reserved, polite, and even demure. Inside, it's a performance, but the shy core remains.

Part of the job

These aren't brash Western-style workers. To them, being with a customer is part of the job—whether it's for an hour, a week, or longer. During that time, they'll go out of their way to please. Many men wake up after a night of passion to find their socks washed, clothes folded, and everything tidied up.

For most of these women, this isn't about romance—it's

survival. Coming from impoverished rural areas, this work offers them the highest wages they'll ever earn. It's a job, nothing more. Unfortunately, some men fall for the fantasy, marry these women, and lose everything when the "contract" ends.

As the local saying goes:

"You can take the girl out of the bar, but you can't take the bar out of the girl."

We eventually found six girls willing to model for us. If our budget had allowed, I'd have picked twelve or more, but after the financial mess in Indonesia, we had to be careful. The plan was straightforward: two girls at 10 AM; two at noon; and two at 2 PM.

We'd rent a jeep for transport, with Chris (our photographer) in the front alongside Steve. The girls would ride in the back, while I led the convoy on the Harley.

To simplify things, we decided to pick all six up from the club. Satit made a point of hammering the meeting times into them. Still, I wasn't entirely confident. These girls are notoriously bad at getting up early, given the nature of their work.

I'd been advised to plan for no-shows. Pick eight girls if you want six. Fingers crossed!

Tomorrow was going to be an interesting day.

THURSDAY 7 JULY

It's 10:00 AM sharp, and I'm standing outside the Caligula Go-Go, exactly as planned. The problem is, I'm completely alone. No girls, no sign of Satit, and no clue what's going on. Steve and Chris are supposed to follow in a rented Toyota Jeep, but even they're not here yet.

The jeep, by the way, is a disaster waiting to happen. It's one of those vehicles that's clearly had a rough life—torn seats, busted switches, and windscreen wipers that look decorative rather than functional. Still, for $15, it's what we could afford.

WAITING FOR THE GIRLS

By 10:10, the cleaners arrive to unlock the club. In a mix of hope and desperation, I ask them if they've seen Satit. They haven't.

At 10:15, Steve turns up, leaving Chris with the jeep to guard the equipment. Parking on Soi Diamond is a nightmare, so it's easier to leave the vehicle on the main road. Still no sign of the girls, though. I'm fuming.

By 10:30, I'm officially pissed off. We've already lost 30 minutes, and this is time we simply don't have. Each girl is supposed to have an hour for her shoot, including travel, set-up, and photos. It's all crumbling before my eyes.

Steve decides to move the jeep closer while I head off on the bike to scout for suitable photo locations.

Finding a beautiful, exotic spot in Pattaya sounds easy, right? Wrong. This city has grown haphazardly, with little regard for aesthetics. Everywhere I turn, potential views are ruined by ugly buildings, construction sites, or the ever-present cranes that seem to loom over every corner of paradise.

You want a lush background with palm trees and a clean horizon? Forget it. The best I can find are scrappy patches of beach overshadowed by high-rises or cheap condominiums.

Frustrated, I return to Caligula. It's now 11:15, and finally, two girls have arrived. Progress, at last. But just as I'm breathing a sigh of relief, Steve delivers the worst news of the day.

IN JEEP SHIT

Because parking on Soi Diamond is so tight, security asked Steve to park the jeep in an underground car park nearby. What he didn't check—brilliantly—was the roof clearance. The jeep is over two meters high, and the garage ceiling? - A little bit less than that.

Now, the jeep is stuck halfway down a steep, 45-degree slope, wedged tight. To make matters worse, the damn thing is out of petrol. Yes, Steve, in all his infinite wisdom, didn't check the fuel gauge either.

I take charge because, frankly, nobody else seems capable. I leave Steve to manage the girls while Chris and I jump on the bike to buy fuel. There's a Shell station about 2 km away, back past the Royal Garden Resort.

Luckily, the attendant lends us an old oil can. Unluckily, it has no cap. So, Chris has to hold it at arm's length on the bike, trying not to spill petrol all over the exhaust.

Back at Soi Diamond, we refuel the jeep, and after some nervous starter whirring, it roars to life. With much effort, spinning wheels, and a bit of manual pushing, we finally get the damn thing back on flat ground.

By now, we're two hours behind schedule, and the situation has not improved much.

Three more girls have arrived, along with Satit.

The sixth girl isn't coming. She's taken off with a more lucrative client.

The weather's turning gray, with flat, uninspiring light for photos.

We've got all five girls crammed into the jeep now, along with the crew and equipment. Finding a good location to shoot is an absolute nightmare. Every suggestion falls flat.

First stop: Royal Cliff Resort.

It's beautiful but surrounded by a high security fence that would ruin every shot.

Next: Sugar Hut Hotel, a replica Thai village with lush gardens and wooden huts. Perfect, except the manager refuses to let us in without the owner's permission. No amount of persuasion works.

By now, it's 1 PM, and still no photos have been taken. The frustration is overwhelming. I jump back on the bike and lead the convoy toward Ban Chang, hoping for some inspiration.

After several dead ends, I spot a narrow road leading to the beach. It's not spectacular, but it's clean, quiet, and secluded enough for what we need. I return to fetch the jeep, only to discover they've disappeared.

For 20 minutes, I ride back and forth in search of them, cursing under my breath. Finally, I spot the jeep heading toward me.

"Where the bloody hell have you been?!" I shout.

Cue the usual excuses:"We didn't see the turn.""We thought you'd gone ahead."

I'm livid. My patience is gone, and I'm ready to throttle someone. But what's the point? We're all exhausted, stressed, and fed up with each other. I bite my tongue and lead them back to the beach.

Finally, we unload the kit and the girls. It's not the dream shoot we'd envisioned, but it's something. At this point, I just want the day to be over.

THE PROMOMTORY

The beach itself is underwhelming, but sticking out into the bay is a small promontory, about a hundred meters long. If I can get the bike halfway along it, we'll have a stunning backdrop of water and hills curving around the coast. Getting there, however, is the tricky part.

The approach is treacherous: firstly, a grassy dune, tangled and uneven; then a stretch of fine sand - the kind that swallows anything heavy; finally, the promontory itself—partially damp and loosely packed but with a solid base beneath.

I decide to go for it. I've tackled worse on this journey, and the worst-case scenario is needing a group of people to haul the bike out.

Revving the engine, I aim to cross as quickly as possible to keep the wheels from sinking. Tackling the dune diagonally, I manage to skim across the grassy section without much trouble—until I abruptly stop dead.

The rear wheel is spinning in place, caught behind a hidden piece of driftwood buried under the sand. It's dug itself into a trench, buried up to the swinging arm. There's no way I can budge it alone.

Steve and Chris, trailing behind with the equipment, arrive just in time to help. Using more driftwood, we build a makeshift ramp under the wheel, lifting, pushing, and shoving until I'm free. The next section is no less nerve-wracking. The bike fishtails like a drunken speedway rider, but I manage to keep it upright and reach the promontory without further incident.

Once I'm there, Chris finds a flat piece of wood to place under the side stand. Even parked, the bike sinks several inches into the soft sand. But there's no time to worry about that now— we've got photos to take.

THE SHOOT

For the next hour, we shoot one of the girls draped over the bike. She's wearing a string bikini that's barely there—two postage stamps for a top and a thong for the bottom - Classic Harley calendar material.

We try to keep things discreet, but our activities attract attention. A man approaches, and I walk over to meet him, unsure if he's curious or about to complain.

Turns out he's Lance Clinton, a Harley enthusiast from Louisiana. He's here visiting family and couldn't resist investigating the sight of a Harley and a scantily clad woman on the beach. We chat for a bit—he's proud of his own bike, a yellow Low Rider custom he'd bought back home in El Paso. As always with Harley folks, we bond instantly.

The return journey is a slightly smoother affair, thanks to Steve running behind the bike and pushing whenever I start to lose momentum. There are a few dicey moments, but we make it back to the jeep without disaster.

We head back toward Pattaya, turning off toward Jomtien in search of a decent spot with palm trees. We find a patch near the main beach road, next to a bus turnaround area. It's far from ideal, but it'll have to do.

Our model here is Ling, tall and slim in a red bikini and

matching headband. She looks great, but the flip-flops don't work. I lend her my cowboy boots, and she transforms. Sexy girls in cowboy boots—what's not to love?

The next stop is at the eastern end of Jomtien Beach, where we position the bike at the base of a boating slipway. The view is decent: the bay curving into the distance, green hills, and hazy skyscrapers on the horizon.

This time, our model is Po, a striking girl with a statuesque figure. She's wearing a black one-piece swimsuit, baseball boots, a red headscarf, and sunglasses. Po is a natural in front of the camera, confident and cheerful, making the shoot a breeze.

A hundred meters along the beach, we find the best spot of the day: a patch of palm trees with a marooned wooden fishing boat. Pointing the camera the other way offers a stunning view of Pattaya Bay.

By now, we're down to four girls. Ling had to leave, but we still have Po, Na, Lu-An, and Nark. Lu-An, in particular, is an absolute stunner—petite, with long, flowing hair, a tight figure, and a sultry vibe. Wearing only a thong, my leather biker's waistcoat, and sunglasses, she looks every bit the superstar. If she were in Europe or the U.S., she'd be making a fortune as a model. Nark is a live wire. Dressed in a blue bikini, she loves posing on the bike and has an infectious energy. At one point, I notice a tattoo on her left bum cheek and take a closer look. It's a well-executed bird design, but the words above it leave me stunned: "Fuck for Money." She laughs hysterically at my reaction, and I can't help but laugh along. Only in Thailand!

The shoot here is fantastic. The lighting improves, the location is perfect, and the girls are in great spirits. We shoot them individually, in pairs, and as a group.

Despite the chaotic start and endless obstacles, we end up with some brilliant photos. As I watch the girls laughing and joking with each other, I can't help but smile.

It's been one hell of a day, but that's just par for the course on this journey. Every setback becomes part of the adventure, and somehow, it all comes together in the end.

ESCAPE FROM THE BEACH

With the light fading and our photo shoot wrapped up, it was time to leave. But as I gazed at the steep, sandy wall between me and solid ground, I began to question whether riding onto the beach had been a good idea. Gravity had been my ally on the way down. Going back up was another story.

The slope was a near-vertical two-meter wall of soft sand—an obstacle that didn't look remotely promising. To make matters worse, the access ramps at either end of the beach were only reachable through water, so retracing my path was the only option.

Plan A is to build a ramp.

Chris and Steve set off to scavenge materials. Ten minutes later, they returned with the best they could find: a meter-long plank about six inches wide. It looked pitifully inadequate. Still, we laid it on the slope's shallowest section and stood back, surveying the absurdity of the situation.

"Decidedly dodgy," I muttered. But we had no better options.

I backed the bike as close to the waterline as I dared, giving myself the longest possible run-up. Steve stood ready to push if needed, and I revved the engine, ready to make the attempt.

The bike surged forward, but the rear wheel slithered all over the place, kicking up sand and losing traction. I approached the ramp out of control, the bike veering to the side, nowhere near the plank. The wheel spun uselessly, digging a trench instead of propelling me forward.

I stopped before disaster struck. "This isn't going to work," I said grimly, stepping off to reassess the situation. We needed a bigger ramp.

Plan B is to find a bigger plank.

Steve and Chris returned from a second scavenger hunt with a sturdier plank—twice as wide and thick as the first. We overlapped the two, creating a ramp long enough to reach the top. It was still precarious, but it would have to do.

I smoothed the sand leading up to the ramp, ensuring no hidden branches or rocks lay in wait. This time, I took a more measured approach, easing the throttle to avoid spinning the rear wheel.

The bike climbed halfway up before trouble struck again. The rear wheel slipped off the narrow plank, embedding itself deep in the sand. I fought to keep the bike upright as Steve and Chris rushed to steady me. Slowly, we guided the bike back down, inch by inch, until I was back on level ground.

It was clear I needed more speed and precision to make it to the top.

Third time lucky, we hope!

With one final adjustment to the ramp and the path smoothed once more, I prepared for a do-or-die attempt. This time, I hit the first plank with just the right amount of speed, accelerating as the front wheel climbed. My feet trotted alongside the bike to help maintain balance.

The engine roared as the bike powered up the slope. At the top, the front wheel bounced off the edge, and I gave it one last burst of throttle to avoid the exhaust catching. The rear wheel hit the plank's end, sending it flying like a projectile into the air. Luckily, no one was in its path.

Finally, I was back on solid ground. The girls cheered, rushing up the slope to congratulate me. My heart was pounding, but relief flooded through me as I parked the bike safely on the pavement.

After loading the gear into the jeep and thanking the girls for their patience, I handed each of them a thousand-baht note. Po, the statuesque beauty from the slipway shoot, asked if she could ride back to town on the bike.

"Of course," I replied, unable to resist her charming smile.

She climbed onto the pillion, wrapping her arms tightly around my waist as we cruised toward Pattaya. Her delight was obvious, and I couldn't help but enjoy the moment too. The day's challenges faded into the background as we rode along the beach under the dimming sky.

Though her signals left little ambiguity about what she might be offering, I kept things strictly professional. Today, it was all about the adventure—and what an adventure it had been.

PHILIPPE'S PARTY

After my little interlude, all I had time for was a quick shower and change before the next item on my schedule.

Philippe, our host at the Royal Garden had recently bought a new house in one of the better areas of Pattaya and has arranged a house warming party, partly to celebrate his new acquisition and partly to show his "movie star" guests off to his friends. Anyway, it was a good excuse for a piss-up. The only problem was Steve and I had already arranged to film an interview with Toi, the owner of one of Pattaya's oldest and most famous Go-Go bars, the Caligula. This was quite a coup for us. Toi is a very rich and very influential person in Pattaya and not given to interviews, particularly on film. We were afforded this privilege because of an introduction through a mutual friend in England, Richard Rhodes. Because of all the adverse publicity usually given to Thailand, and Pattaya in particular, most residents hate everything and anyone that has anything to do with the British media. So many distorted exposés have been done on Pattaya's so-called dens of iniquity that undoubtedly, had we not had the benefit of an introduction, and the protection of the Harley fraternity, filming would have been very difficult indeed. In fact, it was not unknown for some cameramen to have had their equipment shoved up some very uncomfortable places should they unwisely have photographed something without permission.

Anyway, Philippe understood the position. We would stay as long as possible, perhaps even come back if we could, depending on what time the interview finished.

Steve, Chris, Sean, Paul and I gather in the foyer of the hotel at six thirty. We are joined by Nan, Philip's P.R. assistant, who is to guide us to his house, ten minutes away in North Pattaya. Ready to go, they pile in the jeep, not due back for a few hours, and I follow on the Harley.

Turning left off the main road and left again a hundred metres later we find ourselves in a new housing estate. Lots of interlocking little streets with nice middle class retreats and neatly tended gardens filled with exotic and succulent plants and small palm trees that had not yet reached full maturity. The area reminds me of a retirement estate in Florida. Executive houses not quite big enough for a family, but luxuriously appointed and well situated. Many of the drives had Mercedes and BMWs parked in them - hugely expensive in Thailand - indicating this was indeed an exclusive area. Definitely a ghetto for ex-pats and the rich of Bangkok, who want a bolt-hole near the seaside.

It was quite a maze of a place. Without assistance, I don't reckon we would have ever found Philippe's place in the dark.

As we arrive, Philippe rushes out to greet us, insisting I park the Harley in pride of place under a spotlight on his drive. I feel a bit like the Queen at the Royal Variety Performance, Philippe's friends and guests dutifully lining up to be introduced to the adventurer from England who has conquered innumerable difficulties in his travels on a motorbike from the far flung reaches of Indonesia. After a drink and much shaking of hands Philippe invites me to join him on the balcony of his bungalow. A crowd gathers below as we stand in our slightly elevated position and attracting everybody's attention with some loud handclaps, Philippe begins his Renée-esque welcoming speech.

"Hello, hello everybody. I would laak to welcome you 'ere tonaht. We 'ave a very special guest from England oo 'as riden his motorbahk all ze way from Bali, over sex sousand kilomet. I would laak to ask im to tell you zom of 'is experiences."

I am now confronted by over thirty expectant faces, all waiting for some amusing anecdotes of my traumatic journey.

Well, so much has happened to me over the preceding

month that I have to say, I am not short of a story or two: the problems in Jakarta, the ride out in Bali, Bromo, Borobudur, breaking down in the jungle. I thought I was being eloquent and interesting. Sean tells me to shut up. Perhaps he is right; I could have talked all night. I take his advice, however, and shut up. I might have gone on a bit longer than I should, but it couldn't have been too desperate, because a number of guests collar me later to finish the story over a glass of beer.

Speech complete, it is time for the food. A beautiful spread of salad and fruits accompanied a barbecue of steaks and chicken. It is all beautifully prepared and presented, as you would expect from the General Manager of one of the premier hotel resorts in Pattaya. Philippe's friends were almost exclusively from the upper end of the ex-pat business community. Top executives from international companies represented in Thailand. I share a table on the veranda with the managing director of Pirelli and his wife (whose names unfortunately I have forgotten), until being invited to accompany Philippe on a tour of his house. He is rightly very proud of his new acquisition. After spending so long living in the hotels in which he worked, he now has somewhere private to escape to, albeit all too infrequently, only managing a day or two a week at present.

Steve, Chris and Paul stick together, circulating amongst strangers not being their forte. Sean is monopolising Nan, with whom he has got on rather well over the preceding day or so.

Unfortunately time presses on. I have mentioned before how much I regret our schedule being so tight. The enjoyable bits always seem to be interrupted by work. Steve is keen not to miss our appointment. The interview with Toi, owner of the

Caligula Go-Go Bar, is quite a coup. Very few people are allowed to film in such establishments, so this was a privilege that couldn't be wasted.

Dutifully, I say good-bye to as many people as possible. I appreciate Philippe's efforts enormously and seek him out to give special thanks. This may be the last time I see him, as tomorrow, at six a.m., he is off to Phuket for two weeks holiday.

As we load the jeep with the camera equipment, (having filmed some elements of the proceedings for posterity), Steve is talking to Sean. Apparently he is on a promise with Nan and wants to follow in another vehicle with her. He promises to meet us at the Caligula at nine o'clock.

With many wishes of good luck, I start the bike and pull out of the drive onto the road. I park in front of the jeep as Steve,

Chris and Paul get ready to follow. Sean and Nan walk off round the corner and get into her car.

I wait until I hear her car start and see the headlights come on. Waving to Philippe and his friends assembled by the roadside, Steve and I pull away and disappear into the darkness. I look behind and see Sean and Nan. Weaving through the estate I do make a few mistakes, turning left, when I should have turned right, but fortunately we do eventually find ourselves back on the main road. Assuming we are in convoy, I am therefore somewhat puzzled to discover that we seem to have lost Sean and Nan. We wait a few minutes, but as no one turns up, conclude that they must be in front - Nan knowing the correct way out of the maze when we did not.

WHERE'S SEAN?

The night was buzzing as I rode into Soi Diamond, the epicentre of Pattaya's nightlife. The uniformed guard at the entrance handed me a ticket and raised the barrier, granting access to this infamous U-shaped stretch of beer bars and go-go clubs. The scene was a sensory overload: flashing neon lights, pounding music, and the relentless chatter of hustlers touting everything imaginable.

I parked my bike outside the Caligula Go-Go Bar, where the doorman kindly shifted a few mopeds to make room. "Don't worry, sir," he assured me, "I'll keep an eye on it for you." Inside, the air was thick with bass beats and the hum of conversation. Twenty scantily clad dancers moved to the rhythm on a brightly lit stage, each wearing a small number clipped to her bikini bottoms—a surreal sight for anyone unaccustomed to Pattaya's unique charms.

Steve, Paul, and Chris soon arrived, lugging camera gear from the jeep parked on Beach Road South. We settled onto one of the cushioned bench seats that lined the walls and ordered beers. As we waited, I noticed the tension growing. We were still short one critical member: Sean, our soundman.

It was nearly 9:30, and Sean was nowhere to be found. Toi, the local celebrity we planned to interview, hadn't arrived yet either, so we weren't in immediate trouble, but the clock was ticking. I was getting impatient; Steve was angry; Paul was full of excuses for Sean, and Chris seemed perfectly content soaking in the scenery.

By 9:45, it was clear Sean wasn't showing up. We had to get started. Fortunately, the camera's onboard microphone would suffice for these initial shots, which were more about capturing the club's atmosphere than recording sound.

After checking in with Satit, the manager, we got the go-ahead to film. To boost the energy onstage, Satit grabbed the DJ's microphone and asked the dancers to turn up the enthusiasm. The girls barely reacted, continuing their half-hearted movements, clearly uninterested in breaking a sweat for our cameras. Frustrated, Satit took the microphone again, this time with more urgency, and the dancers reluctantly perked up.

Paul, however, didn't need any encouragement. Energized by a few beers, he leapt into action, weaving around the stage with the camera on his shoulder. His top light cast dramatic shadows as he captured every angle—close-ups of the girls, sweeping shots of the stage, and even crowd reactions. At one point, he climbed onto the stage itself, mingling with the dancers, much to the confusion of the audience.

A Japanese businessman seated nearby visibly panicked when

he realized he might be caught on camera. He quickly ducked out of sight, probably imagining the disaster that could unfold if his boss—or wife—saw him on film.

Paul was in his element, but it didn't take long for his enthusiasm to spiral out of control. Stumbling slightly, he became a liability. Steve decided to intervene, gently taking the camera from him to prevent any accidents. Paul flopped back onto the bench, laughing to himself as Steve took over filming duties. Meanwhile, Chris was off in his own world, snapping stills of the club's vibrant chaos.

I tried to stay out of the fray, nursing a beer with Satit and occasionally posing as a weary traveller enjoying some downtime. By 10:30, we had the footage we needed. Steve handed the camera off to Chris and joined Paul on the bench, while I stepped outside for a breath of fresh air.

As I leaned against the wall outside, the question still lingered: Where the hell was Sean? His absence was uncharacteristic, and I couldn't help but worry. But for now, the night wasn't waiting for anyone, and there was still work to do.

FRACAS

Just as I was starting to decompress from the chaos of the day, a commotion broke out behind me. Turning around, I was stunned to see Paul lunging at Steve, his hands clamped around Steve's throat. For a brief moment, it felt like all the pent-up frustrations of the past few weeks had erupted in one violent, alcohol-fuelled burst.

The fight was over almost as quickly as it began, but the damage was done. Steve shoved Paul off with a furious glare, and the club fell silent as everyone turned to stare. I was mortified. This wasn't some back-alley brawl; we were in Caligula, a place that had already taken a risk by letting us film. British film crews were not exactly welcomed with open arms in Pattaya, thanks to a long history of sensationalist reporting that painted the town in the worst possible light. I had worked tirelessly to gain the trust of Caligula's management, and now my crew was undoing all that goodwill in an instant.

I immediately pulled Paul aside, and he was visibly shaken. His embarrassment was palpable, and he began apologizing profusely to Steve. The argument had stemmed from Sean's no-show, which had pushed Steve over the edge. Sean's absence wasn't just unprofessional; it was a betrayal. Over the past five weeks, we had bent over backward to accommodate him, giving him ample downtime and treating him more like a friend than a subordinate. This wasn't some corporate job—it was a once-in-a-lifetime adventure. For Sean to throw it away for the sake of whatever dalliance he was pursuing with Nan was both baffling and infuriating.

Steve was still fuming, but he accepted Paul's apology. The two shook hands reluctantly, though it was clear the incident would leave a lingering tension.

Meanwhile, I turned to Satit, struggling to find the right words. "I am so sorry," I began, my tone pleading. "This isn't us. It's been a stressful trip, and—"

He waved me off with a knowing smile. "Too much beer," he said with a shrug. "No problem." His nonchalance did little to ease my own embarrassment, but I was grateful for his understanding. Clearly, he had seen worse.

ENTER TOP GUN RON

As the dust settled, an open-top car pulled up outside the club. Behind the wheel was an impeccably dressed Thai woman in her forties, exuding wealth and confidence. Beside her sat a young American with a buzz cut, whose sheer presence demanded attention. As they stepped out of the car and approached, the man introduced himself as Ron, and I instantly recognized the type.

Ron was every bit the archetypal Top Gun pilot, down to his brash demeanour and all-American grin. He regaled us with stories of his six hundred hours of combat missions during the Gulf War, describing death-defying flights over Iraq with the kind of casual bravado you'd expect from someone who had cheated death more times than he could count.

Despite his larger-than-life personality, Ron was fascinating. His tales were gripping, and his fiancée—graceful and poised—stood by, clearly amused by his storytelling.

As the evening wore on, tensions eased. Paul kept to himself, nursing his beer and likely reflecting on his outburst. Steve, while still simmering, focused on reviewing the footage we had captured earlier. For my part, I found myself chatting with Ron, grateful for the distraction.

Despite the rocky start, the night ended without further incident. Still, the events had left their mark. Sean's absence, Paul's outburst, and the stress of the shoot were all reminders of just how fragile our dynamic had become. The finish line was in sight, but it was clear we'd have to work harder than ever to keep everything—and everyone—together.

I EAT A BIG BROWN BUG

It all began innocently enough as I stood outside the Caligula chatting with Ron, a former Navy pilot whose sole conversational topic seemed to be his exploits in the Gulf War. He was entertaining, though, and I listened intently as he described the raw realities of combat—far from the sanitized version we got back home. I was particularly struck by his admiration for British pilots, whose skill and cheerfulness under fire had clearly left a mark on him.

As we talked, Satit reappeared and settled onto a stool by the door, where a street vendor was selling roasted locusts. These weren't the dainty insects you might imagine but massive, dark brown creatures the size of a cigarette packet, complete with wings, legs, and plump, shiny bodies. A local delicacy, apparently.

"Energy," said Satit with a grin as he handed over a hundred baht for a bagful.

Ron was visibly horrified.

"It's a roach. It's a big-ass roach," he drawled in his Texan accent. "Back in Texas, we step on these things, not eat them." To drive home the point, he grabbed one from the bag and ground it under his boot.

"That's my food!" protested Satit, laughing. "That's my energy!"

Despite Ron's protests, I knew I had to try one. This was one of those moments—part of the adventure, something to tell stories about later.

"Show me how," I said to Satit.

He happily obliged, holding up one of the roasted monstrosities. "First, you lift the wings," he explained, demonstrating the process. "Then you twist and pull the body."

I followed his lead, delicately separating the bulbous body from the rest of the insect.

"Oh no!" wailed Ron. "He's eating a bug! He's eating a fucking bug!"

With Paul filming, I examined my prize. There was no turning back now. Slowly, I popped it into my mouth and began to chew. The taste was strange, to say the least—salty and chewy, somewhere between a prawn, a snail, and soft toffee.

"What does it taste like?" Paul asked, camera rolling.

After a moment of consideration, I declared, "It tastes like a ladybird; a big, salty ladybird."

That was it - one yummy bug for the experience, and never again, another bizarre memory to add to my growing collection.

With the bug-eating adventure recorded, we retreated back into the club to spend more time with Toi. Any hope of conducting a proper interview had long since evaporated, but no matter—the insect-eating episode would more than suffice for the day's footage.

Sensing the night might take an unpredictable turn, I decided to err on the side of caution and return my bike to the hotel for safekeeping. It was a good call.

When the club closed at 1 a.m., Toi invited us upstairs to her karaoke bar for a nightcap. "Nightcap" turned out to mean a bottle of Chivas Regal, a bottle of brandy, and an assortment of other drinks.

Toi loved to sing. And sing she did—for over two hours, non-stop. Her enthusiasm was admirable, though her talent left much to be desired. Thankfully, by that point, we were all sufficiently drunk to find it endearing rather than excruciating.

By 3 a.m., we staggered back to the Royal Garden, thoroughly soused and buzzing from yet another unforgettable night in Pattaya.

Tomorrow, it was time to head back to Bangkok. Another chapter of this wild journey would soon come to a close, but not without leaving a few more stories in its wake.

 # FRIDAY 8 JULY

ARRESTED

My day began with an unexpected twist—I got arrested. Well, not in the traditional sense of handcuffs and cells, but it was close enough.

I was toodling through Bangkok on my way back to the Holiday Inn when I stopped at a traffic light. Near the junction was a small police cabin, and out of its window, a uniformed officer spotted me. He motioned to his colleague at the lights, who promptly stepped into the road, halted traffic, and waved me onto the pavement beside the cabin.

"Please step inside," he gestured, leading me into the tiny, sweltering room.

I was informed, in halting English, that I had stopped on the "wrong line." Whatever that meant! Before I could protest, they started hinting that this was a serious offense—serious enough, they suggested, to warrant my immediate appearance at the police station.

Their grins grew wider as the implications became clear. It wasn't long before they dropped their real demand: a bottle of Johnny Walker Black Label to "avoid court proceedings." Translation: a $25 bribe.

There wasn't much choice. After handing over the money, I left fuming, muttering all sorts of unprintable things under my breath. Bangkok's streets: one moment exhilarating, the next infuriating.

THE HARD ROCK IN BANGKOK

The day ended on a much higher note with our third Hard Rock party of the trip. After a private affair in Jakarta and a major event in Kuala Lumpur, I was curious to see what Bangkok had to offer.

The Hard Rock Café, like its counterparts worldwide, charges similar prices everywhere. While reasonable in America, in Bangkok it's a top-tier venue, catering primarily to wealthy Thais and tourists. And tonight, wealthy Thais were out in force.

At nine sharp, we left the Holiday Inn Crowne Plaza in the van, navigating Bangkok's chaotic night-time traffic en route to Siam Square. I rode my bike behind, grumbling about having to wear a helmet. Safety aside, it would've been magical to feel the warm night breeze in my hair.

When we arrived, the sight took my breath away. Dozens of Harleys packed the parking spaces outside the café, their owners mingling nearby. A massive banner stretched across the front of the building, reading: "Fat Boy in Bangkok Welcomes Fat Boy in Paradise." It was the same banner the Holiday Inn chef had prepared, and seeing it again warmed my heart. The Hard Rock event was a biker´s dream. Two groups were represented: the Farang Angels (a mix of expats from around the globe) and the Bangkok Immortals (a group of Harley-loving Thais).

Upon arrival, I was greeted like royalty. Cameras flashed, handshakes were exchanged, and the camaraderie was palpable.

Inside, we were shown to long tables reserved just for us. I found myself seated with an eclectic mix of individuals.

One standout was an American member of the Farang Angels, a stocky guy with a red bandanna and an unmistakable toupee. He owned a jewellery business and had made a fortune from it. As a gesture of goodwill, he handed me a heavy silver ring bearing the Farang Angels crest—a beautiful piece he had designed and crafted himself.

Across from me sat two young Thais, 'A' (Pimol Srivikom) and 'Nin' (Chayanin Delohakam). Both were highly educated, fluent in English, and deeply international in outlook. A was preparing to open Bangkok's first official Harley dealership, while Nin, heir to the Singha Brewery fortune, extended an open invitation for me to stay with him whenever I returned to Bangkok.

After a fantastic evening of food, drinks, and rock and roll, I ventured outside to admire the bikes. And what a sight they were!

While there were plenty of stock Softails and Road Kings, they were overshadowed by a dozen jaw-dropping custom Harleys. These weren't just bikes—they were works of art, each a $100,000 masterpiece. Most were owned by twenty-something kids from wealthy families, whose stunning girlfriends hovered nearby, completing the picture of extravagance.

The paintwork, airbrushing, and chrome on these machines were like nothing I'd ever seen. When they roared off into the night, their thunderous pipes left the pavement quaking.

The night wrapped up with more handshakes, waves, and promises to keep in touch. As I mounted my bike, I felt a few drops of rain—a forewarning of Bangkok's infamous monsoons. Luckily, it stayed dry, and I made it back to the hotel unscathed, buzzing from yet another unforgettable day.

Tomorrow, it would be time to reflect and prepare for the next adventure. For now, though, I let the city's electric energy seep into my bones, carrying me off to a restless sleep filled with dreams of roaring engines and shimmering chrome.

SATURDAY 9 JULY

The day began in the early hours. At 6:30 a.m., we were scheduled to leave Bangkok for a ride-out to Pattaya. This event, centred on the legendary Jammer shop, was intended as the dramatic climax for our film.

I had been meticulous in ensuring that E.D. and our van driver, Oat, knew exactly where we needed to be. Several people at the Hard Rock party last night had been kind enough to provide detailed instructions. Still, I couldn't shake the uneasy feeling that things might go awry.

The weather wasn't promising—light droplets of rain splashed on my arms and glasses. Though minor, the damp streets hinted at the potential for a full-on downpour. With the sky overcast and the roads slick from the earlier rain, it was anyone's guess whether we were catching the tail end of the storm or bracing for its beginning.

Driving through Bangkok early on a Saturday morning turned out to be a relief compared to the usual chaos. The city was busy but calm, with none of the usual honking, squeezing, or elbowing for space. Even the throngs of whizzing mopeds, typically ridden by helmetless maniacs with flip-flops and a side-saddling girlfriend, seemed to have vanished for the moment.

That said, the streets were slick with a treacherous mix of rainwater and diesel. It was a morning that demanded extra vigilance.

We followed a circuitous route through Bangkok. Turning right, then left, I began to wonder if Oat really knew where he was going; that suspicion was confirmed when we pulled into an empty shopping mall car park and stopped.

"Are we here?" I asked with a smile, already knowing the answer.

Oat simply looked around, hands on hips, a sheepish smile creeping across his face. After a moment of awkward silence, we were back on the road. Eventually, after a few wrong turns and some roadside inquiries, a helpful man on a moped pointed us in the right direction.

Five minutes later, we pulled up at Jammer, where a long line of gleaming Harleys stood like a congregation of chrome gods.

JAMMER

Jammer is an unofficial Harley dealership and home to the Bangkok Immortals, the largest biker group in Thailand. The Immortals are divided into two camps. The group I had met at the Hard Rock the previous night represented the "fashion freaks"—young, wealthy bikers who viewed Harleys as stylish accessories to complement their glamorous lifestyles.

The group gathered this morning, however, were the purists— the true enthusiasts. These were bikers who loved Harleys for their essence, their sound, and the freedom they symbolized. Many had been riding long before it became fashionable, and their camaraderie extended beyond bikes to charitable work. Today's ride to Pattaya was a charity event.

Jammer chat

The shop itself was delightfully scruffy, a treasure trove of Harley paraphernalia and parts. Chrome accessories, boots, T-shirts, and leather jackets were piled and stacked haphazardly. Out back, I spotted a Harley shipping crate— identical to the one used to transport my bike from England— destined for the dump. The Jammer boys were thrilled when I offered to take it off their hands.

By 7:30 a.m., about twenty Harleys were lined up, engines rumbling. Another group waited ten kilometres away at a petrol station. The challenge now was coordinating the bikes and our pickup truck carrying the camera crew. Bangkok's relentless traffic was bound to make things difficult.

I swung my leg over my bike, fired up the engine, and felt the familiar vibration as the Fat Boy came to life. The Immortals roared out of Jammer, their thunderous exhausts announcing our departure. This ride promised to be memorable—a celebration of Harley culture, camaraderie, and the open road.

Next stop: Pattaya.

We don our helmets, fire our bikes and are away. A strange Thai law states that helmets must be worn at all times, but only on two hundred or so Bangkok roads. Throughout the rest of Bangkok and Thailand they are optional. How anyone is supposed to know which roads I do not know. The matter is to be complicated further by a new law expanding the number of roads in Bangkok city and to a number of provincial districts throughout the country. Why they can't have everywhere or nowhere, I don't know. It is most confusing. I decided to wear my helmet until I get to Pattaya. Fifty or more bikes en mass travelling at high speed makes travelling with no protection crazy.

Within just five minutes that philosophy is justified. Turning a corner at a busy intersection a lady biker is hit by a passing car. No serious damage, but ten minutes of Harley straightening and some road-rash dampened her spirits I dare say.

This episode slowed us down, so our stop at the petrol station was very brief. Those who needed to, filled up. I drank a bottle of water, greeted some of the new guys and was told the next stop was an Esso garage on the Pattaya road, around twenty miles away. We now have a Mercedes to escort us: an old, mid-seventies Mercedes, a white 230E that had seen better days and was now used as the rescue vehicle with spares and drinks and bits and bobs.

Weaving in and out of the early morning traffic was great. A long snake of Harleys is an impressive sight. New Springers, Low Riders and Dressers mixed with some great bikes from the past. An old Shovel-head police bike, for example, brought in originally to act as part of the King's escort, and a chopper with ape hangers ridden by a guy looking so wild he'd frighten your children.

So strange to my Western eye, we pass enormous fifty storey glass and chrome skyscrapers with two Billy goats grazing close by. In front of majestic buildings are small ramshackle stalls of wood and canvas selling rice and bits of flattened chicken on a stick. Peddle-driven trishaws line up with 600 SEC Mercedes at traffic lights. Yuppies with slick suits and mobile phones cross the road with bare-footed old men in sarongs and coolie hats.

Keeping up with this mob is difficult. They know where they are going and I don't. I get trapped in the wrong lane of a five lane highway as they zip in, out and away. Fortunately I have ridden to Pattaya before so I know the general route, but with many signs only in Thai script, and miles and miles of seemingly identical shop houses, it is easy to get confused. As time goes by fewer and fewer bikes are in view. Glimpses a few hundred yards ahead reassure me occasionally, but deep inside I know the writing is on the wall. I just hope the pick-up doesn't get lost. As long as they film the ride I don't care about me, I'll get there somehow. I pass Central City, a huge modern complex on the outskirts of Bangkok, where once again glass and concrete monsters are snuggled in between simple shop-houses. One thing I've noticed in these transitional developments is the standard of wiring both for telephones and electricity. At work in England, the Health and Safety people freak out if a single 13 amp wire is not run in conduit. Here it seems the whole city's power system relies on huge tangles of wires wrapped around lampposts, nailed onto the side of buildings ready to fall down or hanging in loops from totally unprotected transformers and substations. Maintenance must be a nightmare. No coding, make it up as you go along. Inside buildings there are no connecting blocks, spur units or fused outlets - wires are simply twisted together. They are rarely protected with insulating tape, more often Sellotape or nothing. Multisockets, with an endless number of appliances connected at the same time. I think of it as Thailand's way of keeping down the population. There are no natural disasters, no earthquakes, no hurricanes, no major wars, no starvation, and no purges. Thailand has electricians, their resistance movement fighting Ohm's Law, waiting for the day when the switch is thrown, frazzling every household in the land.

The highway to Pattaya is relatively straight forward. I know I must make one major turn though I am not sure where. The last bike disappeared from view ages ago. I wonder if I can find the Esso meeting point, and if they will wait for me there. An uneasy feeling creeps over me. A few miles back I rode through a very confusing spaghetti junction and I knew then something was wrong. The highway soon transforms into a suburban main street that I do not recognise. I stop at some traffic lights next to a brand new BMW. Whenever lost on this trip I found the most sensible thing to do was to ask directions from the driver of an expensive car. They generally spoke English. Successful businessmen in Asia all speak English, and are always helpful. I ask the driver if he had seen any other Harleys and was this the way to Pattaya. As we are speaking a young guy on a moped drew alongside and although speaking no English made it perfectly clear that I had taken the wrong road. I should have turned left at spaghetti junction. I already knew that really, of course, but was grateful for his confirmation. I had to U-turn and get back there as soon as possible if I was to catch up with the rest. I thanked him and as soon as the lights were green, proceeded cautiously, looking for a place to turn round. I was still on a dual carriageway and there was no gap. The moped man caught up with me and gestures I follow him to a flyover where I could cross over. No problem. We were the Marcel Marceau twins; we were having a complete conversation with no words. Confident I now know where to go I speed off. I have to catch up and I am perhaps ten or twelve miles off course. It feels good actually, speeding in and out of the traffic. The sun is shining, the road is good, I am on my way, and I am flying. I soon reach the infamous junction. Life is never simple here and to turn right I have to feed off left onto another dual carriage. I cannot see any way of turning round. The road is long and straight and I want to go the opposite way. I have to make a decision. Either travel along this road for as long as it takes, maybe miles, until I can filter off and cross over or do something illegal and cross as soon as the barrier breaks. I decide to be illegal and bump across the centre reservation. Two minutes later I see a line of garages. BP, Caltec and thank goodness, ESSO. On the hard shoulder is the pick-up. "Where the hell have you been?" was the obvious question. "Got lost!" We are together again, the final contingent of bikes, the pick-up, the van and me.

The Pattaya highway is a straight, flat, two lane dual carriage and we fly down there. Speeding up, slowing down, cruising in pairs, threes or a pack of ten, was terrific. Head down for a burst of speed to catch the group in front then laid back for a softer run. Feet on the forward pegs sat deep in the saddle, an easy cruise in the sun surrounded by the Immortals is what life is all about. I love it.

On previous occasions to Pattaya I had always taken Route 3, the main road through a series of industrial towns like Chon Buri. These boys turned off onto Route 36, a new road and absolutely beautiful. It passed through endless palm groves and green hills; past farmers selling pineapples, durian, rambutans and bananas on small roadside stalls. It begins to rain, and once again tiny needles of rain painfully hit my face and arms. I slow down, but as soon as it started it stops. One minute of downpour. How strange. My t-shirt sleeves and the front of my shins are wet but that is all. The hot sun and wind would soon sort that out. I stay for some time at around forty miles an hour, the perfect speed to enjoy the scenery.

In front I notice two bikes parked on the hard shoulder and a hundred yards or so further on most of the others have pulled over. I stop when I reached the major group. Apparently one of the older bikes has developed an electrical problem (how unusual!) and they are trying to fix it. To be honest, I appreciate the rest, so take off my helmet and sit down on the grass verge. Why I hadn't travelled on this road before I don't know. It has much less traffic, less hassle, prettier, quicker, and newer.

BANALAMUNG ORPHANAGE

At twelve thirty we enter the Banlamung Boys Orphanage. A long tree lined drive winds its way past the long dormitories that houses the boys. Built on stilts in the traditional way, the wood and brick structures blend in harmoniously within their attractive setting amidst the trees and greenery. Boys are hanging out of the first floor windows, marvelling at the procession of glamorous machines. In the gardens, rows of boys in white T-shirts and orange shorts, some holding hands to comfort the smaller ones, who look terrified by the noise and commotion. The Bangkok Immortals have supported the home for many years, raising money, organising parties and generally doing what they can to ease some of the boys' problems. Today the treat is a concert by Thailand's top rock star Lek Carabao and his Indian Band. Based in Pattaya, he is truly revered by millions in Asia and beyond. A kind of Bob Dylan, protest song, good cause type of performer he is constantly in trouble with the establishment, stirring up comment on situations the government would rather ignore. In a pretend democracy like Thailand, this really annoys the establishment. His popularity pisses them off even more. A really quiet, shy, guy, tall, thin with long black hair and a Victorian style moustache of the kind you buy in a magic shop. I wish I had the opportunity to know him more. His English was crap, much like my Thai, and speaking through an interpreter who was in awe of him was really difficult.

Good luck to him.

The whole orphanage is a lovely place. Desperately underfunded, of course, and needing all the help it can get, it has nevertheless been carefully designed and beautifully situated within a wood next to a deserted section of beach on the Gulf of Thailand.

As we arrive the boys are sat in the shade of the trees enjoying a picnic. To be honest, they seem a bit overwhelmed by it all. What are a great number of thunderously loud motorcycles destroying the tranquillity of their afternoon doing here?. A Thai television crew is here, we are here, and Lek Carabao is here. I began to wonder who is enjoying it more. Them or us! I hope they like it because it is all done with the very best intentions.

At the end of the lane, is the pavilion, location of the main event, the front of which is being transformed into a massive Harley park, with lines of tasty Hogs. Squads of riders, all with regulation jeans, cowboy boots, Harley T-shirts and bandannas pause for a minute and then dismount to polish their gleaming chrome. In such company we have to keep our scoots perfect at all times.

I wander around, marvelling at some of the great bikes, chatting to their owners, telling them of my adventures and finding out what they do. I met Surasak Sopanna, "Dang" to his friends, president of the Bangkok Immortals and a biker for forty years. He knew his Harleys all right; every nut and bolt. A partner in Jammer, the Bangkok shop, his real job, so to speak was as a financier to large building projects. A very successful guy, he loved riding and the Harley spirit. Really genuine, I enjoyed speaking to him.

I wander up the stairs into the pavilion. On the balcony, Lek is holding a cup under the tap of a silver urn so large no one would ever run short of coffee. Inside the main part of the large wooden building, a couple of hundred plastic chairs are set out in front of the stage. Three of Lek's roadies are setting out the drums and amplification. One is dissecting a jack plug to find out why it doesn't work. A member of the band asks when they will be ready for a sound check.

I walk back to the balcony and see a long stream of boys walking from the dormitory area. They filter through the parked bikes to take shade under the trees. Organisers in white T-shirts and baseball caps get them to form neat, orderly lines in what appears to be their classes, the boys in each individual line being roughly the same age and height. Arms folded, standing quietly, they wait for the next instruction.

I am invited to sit, crossed-legged on the floor, in the privileged position of centre front with the President of the Bangkok Immortals to watch the magic show that precedes Lek Carabou's concert. As always, kids are mesmerised by magic, simple tricks are greeted by rapturous applause and excited laughter.

While all this is going on a few more Harleys arrive. I go
and see who they are. I am amazed. For all Frank and Theo's
pessimism when I spoke to them at the Harley Bar they have
certainly come up trumps. Just about every Harley in Pattaya
is here. There are Swiss, English and American bikers with
some serious machines with great paint jobs and acres of
chrome.

Graham, partner in the Wild Chicken Bar in South Pattaya
is from Perivale, near London. A builder pissed off with the
recession, he, like so many others came to Thailand on holiday
and found it so good, he just never went home. Woody, like
Graham, a Low Rider owner, is a real long term Pattayan.
Although originally from the States, Woody has done
everything and been everywhere; he is fluent in Nepalese,
and organises Himalayan treks when he needs a rest from
Thailand. As owner of one of the oldest Go-Go bars in town,
the Tahitian Queen, I can understand that. Now over twenty
years in business, that and its sister bar, the TQII has over one
hundred girls. Imagine keeping that lot organised. Thank
goodness he has good managers!

I asked Graham what life is like in Pattaya. This is what
he said, 'How could my lifestyle in England ever match up
to what I have here? Thailand has beautiful weather and
beautiful women. I have a great bar and a great bike. Over
the years The Wild Chicken has become the centre for Harley
boys, where they have breakfast, organise their day, plan their
night. Breakfast comes around lunch time, just in time for
the BBC news on satellite television. A few business matters
are quickly resolved and then it's on the 1981 Low Rider,
Shovel head, (resplendent with black paint, loads of chrome
and a special cobra skin seat), and round to see Woody; at his
Tahitian Queen Go-Go bar, where we have a few beers, a few

laughs and a blow-job. What do you think? Would you go back?'

Whereas Graham is a pony-tailed greaser and Woody is a Dennis Hopper degenerate, Ian is more Chamber of Trade. He is still a lover of Harleys, but a little less rebellious. Ian is fifty, fit, tanned, and walks with a limp. Not because of any war wound but because he owns a red and yellow, 1974 Sportster with a kick-start. Anyone who has owned any bike with a large engine and no electric-start will know exactly what I mean. And have scars to prove it. Designers of bikes in those days insisted on putting horrible, sharp, sticking out bits precisely in the line of leg travel. For the first few kicks in the morning the mind is fresh, enthusiastic, aware of the protuberances and careful. After the twentieth kick you are tired, angry, frustrated........and careless. All sorts of things can then happen; resulting in a variety of cuts and bruises and subsequently - kick-starter's limp.

John has the same problem with his beautiful black 1957 side shift Panhead. An absolutely stunning bike restored locally by Colin Marshall, an ex-Isle of Man racer now running the Castrol Motorcycle Team in Thailand.

One more that is particularly worthy of a mention is Ron Amero's 1972 FLH(AMC). Although now personalised with a Road King paint job this was originally imported as a Kings Honour Guard police bike, so it is a particularly rare machine with an interesting history.

TOGETHER FOR THE FIRST TIME

Never before has anyone managed to get all the Thai Harley groups in the same place at the same time. I have the Bangkok Immortals, the Farang Angels, the Siam Knights and all the other boys that didn't want to be club members together for the first time, and I want to film them in a unique ride-out. As you can imagine, to organise these boys is tricky. I speak to as many as I can and try to explain the plan, but get the feeling most of it is going in one ear and out of the other. The only solution is to get the pick-up with the film crew ready to shoot, and block the exit. As they attempt to leave I can again explain the situation and corral them into one semi-controllable unit.

Marion, wife of the manager of the Thai Garden Hotel in Pattaya, wants to fulfil her dream and ride on a Harley. She jumps on my pillion and I and the pick-up head for the main gate. We position ourselves as awkwardly as possible; making sure anyone wishing to leave would have to drive over or through us. One by one they throb up the winding path that leads back to the main road. One by one I explain, yet again, what is going on. I want to keep everyone as tight as possible; a squadron in close formation thundering their way to the

401

Thai Garden, the Bangkok Immortals overnight resting place. Finally I gathered over sixty bikes. The sound was deafening, exhaust noise laws being either less stringent, or perhaps more flagrantly ignored, than in the UK.

As we leave the orphanage, all traffic is stopped in both directions of the main Sukhumvit dual carriage that runs from Bangkok to Pattaya and beyond. The crew yell to the front riders to keep close to the truck, so they can keep the action tight and exciting. To be surrounded by so many Harleys is incredible. Marion could not have chosen a better occasion for her first ride. Her eleven year old daughter is following close behind on the back of Ian's Sportster. Poor old dad has to drive the car back.

The local traffic looks totally bemused, being passed on both sides by more chrome than had ever been seen in Pattaya before. The atmosphere is electric. To be leader of this pack, albeit only briefly, is orgasmic. Thais, Brits, Americans, Germans, Swiss, Danes, Aussies, financiers, property magnates, military men, restaurateurs, Go-Go bar owners. A more diverse mixture of people would be difficult to imagine, yet all brothers under the Harley banner. A great climax to my Harley voyage of discovery and a voyage not over quite yet. So much has happened; so much in such a short time. I've broken down in the Sumatran jungle, I've been to the Crown Prince of Malaysia's Palace, I've Bungee jumped for the first time, I've eaten huge insects and I've still got two and a half days to go. What else can possibly happen?

AROUND THE POOL

Philippe at the Royal Garden Resort has taken a lot of trouble to organise his Harley Reception. My problem is that the Bangkok Immortals are staying with his number one competitor at the Thai Garden Resort. I leave the crew to return to Philippe's hotel and organise their end of it. I feel time could best be spent with the Immortals, chatting them up, making sure they come to Philippe's event. I know they are exhausted after an early start, the long hot run to Pattaya and the party at the orphanage. For them to help me repay Philip for his hospitality requires a lot of tolerance on their part. Needless to say, I need not of worried. Once again the Harley spirit came to the fore.

At five thirty, in they came, one by one, in a never ending stream. It is a fabulous sight. We position them at one metre intervals, front wheels to the water all around the perimeter of the huge Royal Garden swimming pool. I thank Frank and Theo from the Siam Knights, Dean of the Ferang Angels, Dang from the Immortals and Woody and Graham and the boys for coming. They and their friends are making the final

Harley Party really special. We drink, eat and generally make merry. Night falls early and very quick in the tropics. By seven it is dark, the coloured swimming pool lights making amazing reflections in the sea of chrome.

Hotel guests have postponed their engagements to witness this incredible spectacle, endless numbers of them asking who I was, why we are here, why have we got a film crew etc.... I admit I am enjoying my short lived fame, but answering the same questions with the same answers does become tedious after a while.

At seven thirty the bar is shut. Philippe had intended to allow free drinks to seven o'clock, but the event was so exciting and so successful he kindly extended the facility for an extra half an hour.

To watch the bikes leave was possibly better than watching them arrive. This time, we had the noise accompanied by a flood of headlights, blinding as well as deafening onlookers as they parade past the pool and onto the winding path that leads to the Pattaya Beach Road.

After a few minutes the hotel is eerily silent. Tranquillity returning to a place normally respected for upmarket elegance rather than leather clad decadence.

Thanks to all who participated - it was great, truly rock and roll!

SUNDAY 10 JULY

CREW GONE

Today is the day I have been looking forward to. Today is the day the crew go home. Or at least, stop being paid by me. Steve is off to meet his girlfriend Yvette in Bangkok. She has flown in after visiting her parents in Australia and together they are off to Southern Thailand for a holiday. Chris is staying with me for a few days in Pattaya. Sean and Paul are going back to London. And so they did - without as much as a good-bye.

That says it all to me!

The departure of the crew marks a bittersweet turning point. After weeks of shared adventures, challenges, and moments of creative synergy, their unceremonious exit feels like a letdown. It underscores the complexity of working relationships under intense conditions—what begins as camaraderie can sometimes end in disconnection.

Yet, this moment also brings relief and a sense of liberation. The end of this chapter signals the beginning of a more personal and reflective part of the journey

MONDAY 11 JULY

E.D. LEAVES ME IN THE SHIT

Well, the final day has arrived. Perhaps tomorrow I can relax. After all the trials and tribulations, today is the day the bike goes back to England.

I hope.

With everything I have had to put up with over the past five weeks, I will not be happy until the bike is back safe and sound in Milton Keynes. I just do not trust anyone out here. Without the requisite back-hander nothing happens. In my experience nothing in business or officialdom here can be taken at face value. Everybody seems to interpret the rules to their own advantage.

I am leaving my Harley with a reputable firm of international shippers, booked in England by Steve Bradley who, I have to say, up to now, has been a real diamond. I trust him and he trusts them, so I trust everything will be all right.

We are back in Bangkok. The appointment with Excel Transport International is for ten o'clock, so E.D. decides we should leave prompt at nine thirty to ensure that we get there on time through the terrible Bangkok rush hour traffic.

406

The pallet that the guys at Jammer had given me is already there, delivered by our pickup before it had to be returned. All that remains is the bike. I want to see it safely packed in the crate and secured ready for shipment.

Thankfully E.D. is cheerful for once. Throughout the Thai section of our journey she has worked efficiently, everything she said would happen, did happen. She tended to do it without humour though, which we all found very tedious. This trip was supposed to be fun and although in Thailand we had experienced relatively few problems, laughter has been scarce to say the least. Sean had let us down badly in Pattaya which had pissed Steve off more than words can say. Sean had sacrificed his professionalism for one illicit shag and that was unforgivable. According to Steve, Paul's talent as a cameraman was, at times, questionable, and that resulted in arguments and eventually a fight between them. Life was always tense. Five weeks on the road had taken its toll on our nerves. E.D. didn't help. An Englishman's nature is to laugh in the face of adversity. E.D. is a moody cow, who had to be forever treated with kid gloves.

Steve said we should respect her ability even if we don't like her. Fair enough. Thank goodness Nong was so nice. She was a ray of sunshine in a cloud of despair. Always smiling no matter how put on by E.D., her boss, for many years.

E.D. and I walk over to the bike, parked as usual just outside the Holiday Inn entrance. With some sadness I look up at the banner "Fat Boy in Bangkok welcomes Fat Boy in Paradise." I am about to embark on my final journey - the last few miles of my great adventure. How I wish I could keep my bike here just a little longer. Enjoy riding through this wonderful country without my crew to worry about or a schedule to keep. Still, that cannot be. I need E.D. to ensure my prized possession leaves safely. I need her help to fill in the documents, her customs connections, her expertise. Alone, with no experience, I cannot be sure that I would ever see my bike again. If I arrive home in the UK only to find it has been impounded for some reason, what could I do then?

Sat on the pillion, I turn round to ask if she is OK. She says 'Yes, thank you' and I pull off down the ramp and turn right into the street beyond. Although wet and puddley, it is thankfully not raining. The morning is damp but warm. Crash helmets are compulsory in Bangkok, but E.D. is unconcerned, wearing only a T-shirt and shorts.

We turn left onto Silom, a one-way street, and as soon as possible right and right again onto Surawong Road, one way in the opposite direction. Even on a bike we get stuck in traffic, dozens of mopeds filling every space in this very crowded street. Up to the top past Patpong, one the world's most notorious streets, full of go-go bars and sex clubs, and right at the lights onto Rama IV Road, named after a famous Thai king.

Surprisingly Rama IV is almost deserted. We go from mega congestion in Surawong to the odd bike and taxi stretched over this wide boulevard. We go under the expressway and meander around a bit until we hit Sumkumvit. Excel Transport is on Sumkumvit, at the junction with Prakanong, wherever the hell that is. Given that Sumkumvit goes all the way from here to Cambodia, I could have done with a few more clues.

Still E.D. knows the general direction and after a few misses and a few more stops to ask passers-by, we eventually get where we are going.

Hidden up an alleyway, marked by a tiny sign that I would never have seen on my own, is a tired looking three storey office block. A glass and steel affair much like the pastel painted English schools built in the early sixties. The ground floor was an open warehouse, packed with cardboard boxes off to destinations around the world.

I follow E.D. through a door at the side and up one flight of stairs into an open plan office full of girls beavering away at their clerical duties. E.D. speaks to one who stands up and points to a glass fronted side office where a middle aged man in a bright white shirt and dark tie sits making a phone call behind his wooden desk. We are waved in and sit down, while, as he finishes his call, a pile of papers are presented to us to read.

Speaking in Thai, the final arrangements for shipping the bike are concluded. My one stipulation being that the receipt I receive for the bike would be in English. That presents no problem, Mr Paungthong Pansiri, Director of Cargo Operations, was being as helpful as Steve Bradley had promised.

He insists I pack the bike myself, to ensure I know exactly what is being sent and the condition it was in when I left. Obviously that suits me fine; I still have my lingering doubts as to whether everything would be OK.

Taking us downstairs I am introduced to the young man in charge of packing, who would help me load the pallet to a satisfactory standard. I follow my instructor's advice, draining the fuel, disconnecting the battery and so on before going off to check all the spares had arrived safely in our van a short time before. Unfortunately some things were missing. Fairly insignificant things - a spare brake handle, cables etc., but nevertheless enough to ask E.D. if she could ring the hire company to see if they knew where they were.

She went ballistic! Shouting, marching up and down, waving her arms about....what's all this about? One minute she was calm and smiling, the next screaming and raving. I ask her to calm down. It's not that important. I would rather her stay happy than freak over a few missing bits. With that she turned and marched off. 'You're all the same', she shouted, 'You don't trust me. I wish I never come on this trip. I knew you would be difficult!'

I ran after her, saying I was sorry if I had offended. 'I need your help here' I pleaded, 'I can't speak Thai and they can't speak English.'

'That's your problem,' she said, as she ran across the road to flag down a taxi.

I am utterly dumbstruck. The young man that was helping me looked to the sky and shook his head. 'No problem,' he said, 'You OK, she crazy' 'Thank you', I reply as my chin hits the ground.

Anyway, cut a long story short, the bike did get crated; I did get my documents in English and I did get safely back to the hotel.

However, I was livid. I couldn't wait to search out Steve and tell him the story. As it happens, he knew already. E.D. is sorry she was so hasty, is all he says, and shrugs his shoulders. Bollocks. She is working for me. If she wants to get paid she finishes the job, she does not leave me in the shit. That was unprofessional and very stupid. She left me to fend for myself at the most important moment in the whole journey. I trusted her to help me make sure my bike gets home safely. She has a tantrum and pisses off. That is totally unacceptable; totally unacceptable. Throughout the whole episode here in Thailand, she has been happy one moment and moody the next; very unpredictable. It's been like I have been working for her rather than the other way round. I rant for a few minutes, trying to get the anger and frustration out of my system.

I can't wait to get back to Pattaya. I have just about had enough with moody people. Sean and Paul had gone, Steve was off to the airport to meet his girlfriend and disappear to a remote island for a couple of weeks. Chris and I were planning to have some fun for a few days before he clears off back to reality. I am going to hang around for a further month, hopefully surrounded by a beautiful Thai girl as I endeavour to document my experiences.

 # MONDAY 11 JULY

CHILL OUT

All my aggravation is over now. Starting today I am on holiday. A month in Pattaya to chill out; a month to sit by the pool and gather my thoughts; and a month to forget the shit I fancy will confront me when I get home. Spending so long away from my company in England does worry me. I had not concerned myself too much with the day to day running of the Incredible Sign and T-shirt Factory for six months prior to leaving. Add to that the two months or so I will have been away and that is a long time. I have a feeling that will have a high price. I have always put that from my mind. In everyone's life there comes a time when something has to be done. I felt so frustrated, so confined. Trapped in a prison of my own making, from which I had to escape. By circumstance, rather than by design, I had built a moderately successful business over a number of years producing signs and exhibitions for a number of well-known companies. Like so many others we were obviously affected by the recession, but struggled on regardless and survived by the skin of our teeth. Always wobbling on the tightrope but never quite falling off.

Then, one morning in January, I come to work and find the computers and cutting machinery missing from the workshop. The others arrive, bar one, and are as puzzled as me. Perhaps

an urgent job came in and Vince (my partner) has had to
go on site? We couldn't understand why he had not called
anyone.

How naïve I was! My partner had absconded, after five years
together. The person I had trusted implicitly for all that
time had simply turned up at the dead of night, taken the
equipment and done a bunk. I was devastated. I was left with
all the problems, all the debts, all the staff to pay, all the jobs
and no kit to do it with. What do I tell the customers? What
do I tell the suppliers? What do I tell the bank?

Thanks to terrific support from the staff, Carl and Marcus and
Paul in particular, and very understanding and sympathetic
clients and suppliers we muddled through. In fact we went
from strength to strength and 1993 was ultimately a very
successful year, considering the upheaval.

Nevertheless, the stress was enormous. The legacy of debt
Vince had left me and the situation he had put me in, made
me question whether it was all worthwhile. The recession,
endless pointless government regulations, health and safety,
income tax, corporation tax, business rates and so on and so
on and so on were too much to bear. I had to do something
else. I hated sign making. I hated working twelve or fifteen
hours a day for nothing. I was going nowhere. I was just
working to pay off debts and wages and suppliers with no light
at the end of the tunnel. I could not see myself making signs
for the rest of my life. It was all so pointless.

It was the start of another cold, grey English winter and I
was depressed; very depressed. Something had to be done.
I knew there was a big world out there, full of sunshine and
interesting places and I was stuck in Milton Keynes making
bloody signs. I made the decision to gamble everything on

this trip. I begged, borrowed and worked tirelessly to make it happen, and it did happen. If I don't sell this book and the film I am in the shit. My nob is on the line. Nevertheless it had to be done and that was that.

All that begs the question - was it worth it?

I've asked myself that question more times than I can count. Especially during the tougher moments of this trip—stranded in the Sumatran jungle, clashing with the crew, or watching my bike being crated up in Bangkok. Every setback, every moment of doubt, seemed to weigh heavily against the success of this gamble. Sitting here now in Pattaya, sipping a cold drink by the pool, the answer becomes clearer -

Yes, it was worth it.

Not because everything went smoothly—it didn't. Not because I found some magical escape from life's pressures—those are waiting for me back in Milton Keynes. It is because this trip was never about an easy ride or guaranteed success. It was about breaking free, challenging myself, and finding out whom I really am when the safety nets are gone.

I've seen incredible places, met unforgettable people, and tested my limits in ways I never thought possible. I've laughed, cried, cursed, and celebrated—all in a whirlwind five weeks that have redefined what I'm capable of. Every mile on that Harley, every obstacle overcome, every connection made—it all adds up to something far greater than what is written in this book.

So yes, it was worth it. I'll always have the memories, the lessons, and the proof that I had the guts to take the leap. That, in itself, is a triumph.

POSTSCRIPT ONE

I never realised what a profound effect this experience would have on me.

I knew I would be exhausted; a recuperation period of four weeks was planned from the outset. The intention being to spend some time relaxing in Pattaya, soaking up the sunshine, writing the journal of my journey while it was still fresh in my mind and I was still in an oriental environment.

That was the plan. But then again nothing had ever gone to plan.....

I did stay in Pattaya. Arriving by Harley had given me an instant introduction into Pattaya society; at least the society of Pattaya's ex-pats. Away from the rip-offs of tourist life, I will be forever grateful to Spencer, Wes, Colin, Frank, John, Graham, Woody and so many others for their welcome and friendship.

Spencer became a good friend. I spent virtually every evening with him and many a time did we get totally pissed and out of hand. Wes, his ex-US navy father, a huge Burl Ives kind of guy with a bushy Father Christmas beard and Harley-Davidson cap permanently stuck on the top of his balding head, owned a Go-Go bar in South Pattaya Beach. Every evening around

415

five thirty I went to the 'Hogs Breath Saloon' for my dinner. It certainly was a novel experience, sat at the bar, eating sausage and mash, half a dozen almost naked girls cavorting before me. Being a regular, and a friend of the family, certainly had its advantages. I got to know the girls very well and often played jokes on them or lent a sympathetic ear to their troubles and worries. In return they played little jokes on me, like trying to find interesting ways of putting me off my dinner!

I have to admit though, the shallowness of this environment, the false sexuality, the fair weather friendships, did become tiresome after a while. I saw so many unfortunate middle-aged men who had come to Thailand to seek love and affection, but had found their relationships were only as deep as their pockets. Men totally smitten with their beautiful dusky maidens, showering them with gifts, sending money to their families in the country after hearing and believing obviously made-up tales of woe and misery. Behind their backs, I saw these girls ridiculing their benefactors, openly saying their legs would shut at the same time as his wallet. Sometimes these couples had been together years - a factor that made these situations even sadder. Whenever their men returned to Europe or America for a few weeks, their 'loving' partners would sell themselves to someone else, often entertaining their new suitors in the flat provided by sucker number one.

A few weeks of endless sunshine, permanent inebriation and limitless sex does get to you after a while. I know that is hard to believe but it is true. I never got fed up with the weather. Too much beer and not enough exercise were making me fat, so that had to stop. I resolved never to drink alcohol before six o'clock, keeping to orange juice, fresh coconut milk or

416

water before then. I stopped getting taxis and began to walk as much as possible. My hotel was about a mile or more from the Hogs Breath so I felt that was a start. I love beautiful girls, but mechanical sex is a waste of time. I longed for the comfort of a proper relationship.

In retrospect I believe this insecurity and inability to have a good time was a result of the trauma I had experienced on my journey. The bond of friendship and loyalty I had hoped to forge with the crew after weeks of getting out of trouble together had not materialised. Their commitment to quality and hard work was not up to the standard I had hoped for. I felt let down. Going through the film rushes, so many times did Steve find the sound missing on crucial areas of the footage. So many times were things not filmed when they should have been. It is my entire fault of course. I should have exercised more control; been stronger in command. It was after all my money they were spending. I trusted their ability and professionalism. I was naïve. I was an idiot.

Try as I might I could not concentrate to write. Five weeks in Pattaya was more than enough to complete my book. I frittered the time away in cafés and Go-Go bars.

Colin managed the hotel 'Weekender.' Colin was a totally crazy Australian with a mouth that was permanently engaged in overdrive. Had he omitted the word 'fuck' from his vocabulary he would have been virtually mute. As it was, you could never shut him up. He was hilarious; a man with an avalanche of stories and anecdotes, most of which I could repeat word for word after a few days, he repeated them so much. Although not as plush as the Royal Garden I opted to stay with Colin at the Weekender for the duration of my stay. This was quite a major decision, I might add, as Philippe, the

General Manager, had offered to let me stay there free in five-star luxury. Colin could only give me a 60% discount, but I reckoned the £10 a night was worth it for the entertainment value. I could never quite work out Colin's past. In his forties, he had seemingly worked for the Australian railways for twenty years at quite a senior level. Family troubles had forced him to abscond first of all to the Philippines and then to Thailand. His blarney had eventually got him this job in Pattaya. He had in six short months, turned a loss making hotel into a profitable one by firing half the staff and eliminating most of the fiddling done by the half that remained.

But, and this is a big but, he was yet to be paid. The deal was he would phase in a sizeable percentage of the profits he generated. I had no doubts as to his managerial qualities but I do think his business acumen is suspect. He had no written agreement and was employed by a Chinese businesswoman known for her ruthlessness. It will be interesting to find out if Colin is still in Pattaya when I return.

Anyway, why should I worry? Colin was a great host and companion when he and I and John, a journalist on the English language Pattaya Mail newspaper, went out on the razzle.

Coming back to England, after two months that had lasted a lifetime, was a great shock. I had neglected my business for almost a year and the results of that neglect were catastrophic. My team had done their best. They had delivered on time and kept the clients happy. Unfortunately the company had lost a fortune and was on the point of collapse. The next few months were horrible. My journey of a lifetime had drained every ounce of my energy and now I had to cope with this. I

418

only survived because of the loyalty and dedication, with very little reward I might add, of my friends and staff.

Believe it or not, I could not bear even to look at the photographs of my trip for almost a year after my return. I was frustrated at my lack of motivation to get the project completed. My dreams of producing an enjoyable film and book turned into a nightmare. Concentration and enthusiasm were impossible. Perhaps I was in my mid-life crisis, I don't know. Whatever, I could not face the prospect of reliving my experiences. Eventually, I had to do it. What a waste to have spent all that time, all that energy, all that money, to no avail.

They say there is no pleasure in adventure if you know what will happen the next day. I'm not sure there is pleasure in adventure. There certainly is a great sense of achievement.

For all that happened - yes, I would do it again, tomorrow.

UPDATED IN 1995

Well, I purposely waited over a year before writing this next bit. I wanted time to consider that question properly. As you know, the whole journey was full of experiences: the Indonesian bureaucratic nightmare, the problems entering Malaysia, the run to the border. Temper those with the hospitality of everyone I have met; their kindness, their generosity. It is true we did not have the most compatible of crews. Never has so much happened to me in such a short time. I have had a true adventure. Many times I was desperately frustrated, many times angry, and many times sad. But never have I regretted my decision. I have done something nobody else has ever done. I have ridden a Harley-Davidson from Bali to Bangkok. I consider myself to be very privileged that I have experienced the fraternity of Harley. Sat

419

in their ivory towers in Milwaukee, I wonder if they realise what they have created. I know the Harley hierarchy visit the big events and tour the world. But it is only on the road, alone, in the shit in the middle of the night, in the middle of nowhere do you really find out what it is all about. Someone always came to rescue me - Dave in Jakarta, Smitty in Bali, Mohammed in Pasir Gudang, Mao in Kuala Lumpur, so many in Thailand. All total strangers offering the hand of friendship. Would a Honda have that power - I think not!

So, no, I don't regret anything. I would do it all again tomorrow. Differently, of course! Hindsight is a powerful thing. Time is a great healer. I will forget the shit, but I will remember the people, the Harley people to whom I am so grateful. They made this journey special.

UPDATED AGAIN IN 2024

It is now 2024 and thirty years have passed since my adventure.

Reading through my experiences, I am amazed how much has changed and, indeed, how much has not changed in the countries I visited. Having recently visited Thailand, for example, I know that, sadly, it has certainly gone downhill from a paradise point-of-view. Unrestricted building has destroyed much of the beauty in Phuket; Pattaya is just dirty and degenerate and a lot bigger; the Land of Smiles is certainly a lot less smiley to my mind.

The biggest difference is the proliferation of travel and adventure documentaries similar to mine produced by both terrestrial, satellite stations and especially YouTube. I am proud that I was one of the first and that I did it as a freelancer, without the financial or logistical support of a television company.

Billy Connolly, Ewan McGregor, Charley Boorman and the rest all came after me and I am still one of the few people to have ridden a Harley-Davidson across the equator. I certainly believe that I am the only one to have ridden a FAT BOY across the equator!

It has taken a long time for me to finish this book and I don't really know why. Still, all I can is, I hope it was worth the wait and that you have enjoyed reading it.

THANKS AND ACKNOWLEDGEMENTS

To all the people that made this adventure possible:

The staff at the Incredible Sign and T-shirt Factory, Carl Allen, Rob Cave, Paul Kitchen, Marcus Richardson; Ian Highley at Le Park TV who helped me put the DVD together despite everything. Harley-Davidson UK. The wonderful friends who had faith in a project that never managed to fulfil its promise, especially: Lesley Goundry, Mark Hughes, A.M. Williams, S.K.M. Williams, Michael K. Beynon, Jonty Arkell, M.T.M. U.K., Milton Keynes, Paul McSweeney, Julie McSweeney, Gablegate Limited, Chris Ireland at Desperate Dan's in Leighton Buzzard, The Foundry, Harley-Davidson, Bang Bang Sugiarto, Nazaruddin Sharuddin, Encik Yahya A. Jalil, Steve Bradley, Jim Beam whisky, Holiday Inn, Marriot Resort, Pattaya. Special thanks to Rob Cave who helped create and finance the bike in the first place.

Plus..all the great people that I met on my adventure!

Michael Orr

Printed in Great Britain
by Amazon

61667805R00238